Music of the Golden Age,
1900–1950 and Beyond

MUSIC OF THE GOLDEN AGE, 1900–1950 AND BEYOND

A Guide to Popular Composers and Lyricists

ARTHUR L. IGER

GREENWOOD PRESS
Westport, Connecticut • London

Library of Congress Cataloging-in-Publication Data

Iger, Arthur L., 1926–
  Music of the golden age, 1900–1950 and beyond : a guide to popular
composers and lyricists / Arthur L. Iger.
      p.   cm.
  Includes bibliographical references (p.   ) and indexes.
  ISBN 0–313–30691–5 (alk. paper)
  1. Popular music—United States—History and criticism.
  2. Composers—United States.   3. Lyricists—United States.
  I. Title.
  ML3477.I44   1998
  781.64'0973'0904—dc21   98–12203
                                 MN

British Library Cataloguing in Publication Data is available.

Library of Congress Catalog Card Number: 98–12203
ISBN: 0–313–30691–5

First published in 1998

Greenwood Press, 88 Post Road West, Westport, CT 06881
An imprint of Greenwood Publishing Group, Inc.

Printed in the United States of America

The paper used in this book complies with the
Permanent Paper Standard issued by the National
Information Standards Organization (Z39.48–1984).

10 9 8 7 6 5 4 3 2

First and foremost, this book is dedicated to my wife, Mimi, who inspired, encouraged and demonstrated infinite patience—before, during and after the book was written!

And to my children Willow and Bob, Carolyn and Eli, and my five ''favorite'' grandchildren: Jenny, Kate, Jordan, Amanda, and Jessica.

Finally, to the memory of two great friends, with whom I enjoyed so many happy hours of jazz, swing, and music of the Golden Age: Gordon Goodman and Sheldon Wax.

Contents

Acknowledgments

Thanks to the fine professionals at Greenwood Publishing—to Pamela St. Clair, who was supportive and encouraging through the year or two that we worked together; to Bridget Austiguy-Preschel, Meg Fergusson, and others at (and affiliated with) Greenwood for editing, revising, and re-editing, as well as their attention to the many details necessary to publish this book.

Special thanks to Dr. Robert Schuessler, friend and colleague at the New York Institute of Technology, who formatted and structured the book, and advised and excised the irrelevant, for which I am most grateful.

And last but not least, to two dear friends and fellow afficionadoes—Howard Groveman and Norman Stoll—for their suggestions, criticisms, ideas, and musical knowledge. Thanks!

Introduction

Rather than define *Music of the Golden Age* as a period of time—particular years gone by—we define it more as a style or a genre: music with melody; literate lyrics; music for dancing; songs of rhyme, rhythm, and romance. This book is largely made up of chronological listings of song hits of the Big Band Era and those years of Hollywood escapist musicals. The most prominent composers and lyricists we present created their ballads, blues, swing, and jazz tunes in the 1920s and on through the 1940s. However, the style and mood of the music we refer to as "Golden Age" was written before and after those defined decades. In the early 1900s, songwriting superstars Irving Berlin, Jerome Kern, Oscar Hammerstein, and a few others were beginning to write in that style. In the 1960s, 1970s, 1980s, and up to the present, the likes of Stephen Sondheim, Marilyn and Alan Bergman, Cy Coleman, and Jimmy Webb write much that falls under the Golden Age category.

This text is designed for the sheer enjoyment and shared enlightenment of both fans and students of Golden Age music. It is divided into five chapters, each utilizing alphabetical coverage of songwriters. It begins with Pioneers in Chapter 1, covering about fifty composers and lyricists of the pre-World War I period, who paved the way, so to speak, for the writers and composers who followed. Chapter 2, the main Golden Age section of the book, includes more than 160 songwriters of prominence and productivity—alphabetically, along with chronological listings of their hits and important songs. Reference is usually made to the stage musical or Hollywood film (distinguished by italic bold) in which the song was introduced. Brief biographical sketches of the songwriters precede the listings. Anecdotes (sometimes trivial, but nonetheless, interesting) also are added.

Chapter 3, Contemporaries, consists of songwriters of the past four decades, including the 1990s. These are composers and lyricists who have written, and continue to write, in the Golden Age vein. I have excluded, because of a lack of expertise and involvement, writers of country, rock, new age, world, rap, techno, folk, and other forms which have gained and maintained popularity and success but whose style and work fit other musical molds. However, along with outstanding contemporaries such as Antonio Carlos Jobim, Johnny Mandel, and Norman Gimbel, we could not exclude Paul Simon or the Beatles, whose music and lyrics are sung by Golden Age performers. Less than forty contemporaries comprise this chapter.

Chapter 4 acknowledges that the three preceding chapters covered only significant collaborators—lyricists and composers who partnered with the major songwriters on more than just a few hits. I use this chapter to cover a number of writers of single hits.

Chapter 5 is essentially made up of two listings: Celebrities in and out of the music business who wrote hit songs, and women of song, who are included with the firm belief that these talented people have, for too long, gone unrecognized for their tremendous contributions and accomplishments within the world of music and elsewhere.

Finally, a note or two of qualifiers and tips for those who use this text as a reference. I have made every effort to locate all the composers and lyricists in this category I am calling, Golden Age. Certainly a few may have been omitted, and genuine apologies are offered. The resumes of these creators of song were intensively sought after, in three years of searching sources. Some, as in the case of Porter Steele, composer of *High Society*, did not seem to exist. But the search continues; omissions will be published in a future edition, should readers and publisher approve. Innocent and unavoidable errors are sincerely regretted.

METHODOLOGY, RECOLLECTION, AND RESEARCH

The original foundation for this book is a six-decade collection of records, tapes, and CDs, totaling more than 5,000 popular songs. Concurrent to collecting, an obsessive habit of annotating resulted in thousands of words about the songs, the songwriters, the musical shows and the films from which the songs came. Additionally, attendance at concerts, performances, night clubs, and many, many conversations with fellow musicians and collectors were all taken in and turned into written notes on the world of popular music.

Inveterate radio listening for sixty years became another important source of information. Most especially, in New York, I am grateful to the late William B. Williams (whose real name was Billy Breitbart) of Babylon, Long Island and Syracuse University—a fine acquaintance—and his cohorts at the AM station then using the call letters, WNEW. Jim Lowe and Jonathan Schwarts were disc jockeys, now commonly referred to as radio personalities, who worked at the same station. While not directly quoted, they were assuredly my on-air musical teachers.

A rather formidable card file has been maintained for the included songs, noting composer/lyricist; date of publication; show/film source and any other pertinent data, such as a Grammy, an Oscar, or other honor for the songwriter. A thirty-year membership in a Friday jam session called *Jazz at Noon* in New York City gave me an introduction to many famous and not-so-famous jazz musicians, who also provided rich texture for the card file and this book.

In translating the collection of notes for *Music of the Golden Age*, I have used some abbreviations to save time and space. The symbol (wm) stands for words and music, and (instr.) stands for instrumental; the designation follows the name of the songwriter. From the earliest days of the music business, credits were frequently given as ''words and music by Sam Jones and Joe Smith,'' which revealed that each writer was responsible for both the words and the music. Of course, several great songwriters did write both words and music. Irving Berlin and Cole Porter were most outstanding in this regard. Johnny Mercer, Stephen Sondheim, and the Beatles—Paul McCartney and John Lennon, in particular—wrote words to their own music and vice versa. Another abbreviation used is the slash mark (/), which separates the composer, listed first, and the lyricist. Thus, Rodgers/Hart would follow *Blue Moon*. Interestingly enough, many songwriting partnerships have routinely stated the lyricist first. An example everyone knows: Lerner and Loewe.

The entries are all cross-referenced: an asterisk indicates composers and/or lyricists who have complete entries in Chapter 2. If a name appears as an entry elsewhere in the book, the chapter is noted immediately following their name. To distinguish song titles from films and Broadway productions, songs appear in italic type, while films and Broadway shows are in bold italic.

For ease of reader access, reference sources are all cited together on the final pages of this text. A considerable amount of cross-checking was done to try to assure accuracy in dates, names, spelling, and bibliographical material.

Chapter 1 _____

Pioneers: Songwriters of Yesterday

LONG AGO AND FAR AWAY

Long Ago and Far Away is the title of a great Jerome Kern/Ira Gershwin song; it is appropriated here to list just a few pre-1900 ballads and such that are still performed and have certainly withstood the test of time:

1788 The lyrics of the New Year's Eve theme song, *Auld Lang Syne*, were added to a 1711 composition (unknown composer) by the Scottish poet Robert Burns (1759–1796). Burns was also the songwriter (lyrics only) on *The Campbells Are Coming* (1745), *Flow Gently Sweet Afton* (1789), and *Comin' Thro' the Rye* (1796). *Comin' Thro'* is often performed by contemporary jazz musicians.

1853 *Good Night, Ladies* is often played at the end of an orchestra's performance at dances and other celebrations. The composer is unknown, but the lyrics were written by the great minstrel man, Edward P. Christy (1815–1862). The song is usually performed by tired musicians with "sore chops" (tired lips and/or fingers).

1854 As a tribute to his wife, Stephen Foster (1826–1864) wrote *(I Dream of) Jeannie with the Light Brown Hair*. Foster is acknowledged as the first songwriter of American Negro songs, inspired by his friendships with the slaves his father kept. He also wrote *Oh! Susannah* (1848), *De Camptown Races* (1850), *Old Folks at Home* (1851), *Massa's in de Cold, Cold Ground* (1852), *My Old Kentucky Home* (1856), *Old Black Joe* (1860), and *Beautiful Dreamer* (1864)—the year he died, an alchoholic and a pauper.

1869 *Little Brown Jug* is a swinging standard that was made popular more than seventy years later in the Big Band Era. It was credited to Joseph Winner, a Philadelphian who used the nom de plume, R. A. Eastburn. Winner was the brother of Septimus Winner, writer of the Civil War novelty tune, *Oh Where Has My Little Dog Gone?*, also used by swing arrangers and bands much later.

1876 *I'll Take You Home Again, Kathleen* was the work of Thomas Paine Westendorf (wm).

1879 *In the Evening by the Moonlight*, a romantic ballad, was the work of James A. Bland (wm), an African American born in New York City and an honors student at Howard University. Bland also wrote *Carry Me Back to Old Virginny* (1878), and *Oh, Dem Golden Slippers* and *Hand Me Down My Walking Cane* (1879). Bland was also a banjoist with Billy Kersand's minstrels.

1884 *(Oh My Darling) Clementine* was written by Percy Montrose (wm).

1896 *When the Saints Go Marching In* is a classic jazz tune written by James M. Black and Katherine Purvis. It was popularized by Louis Armstrong in his 1930 recording. Also in 1896, stage star Maude Nugent (1874–1958) wrote the words and music to *Sweet Rosie O'Grady*.

1899 Musicians and others do not take this one too seriously—and many a parody has been made of—*Hearts and Flowers*, composed by Theodore Moses Tobani, with lyrics by Mary D. Burke.

THE PIONEERS

At the beginning of the twentieth century, popular music was created for vaudeville, early stage musicals, and operettas (light opera). African-American minstrel shows, and the white imitators of that style, generated music and lyrics, which also influenced popular music and the production of sheet music. As racist as the term and the topic may sound to us now, "coon songs" were written by the hundreds and became a means of commercial success on the metaphorical Tin Pan Alley. A fusion of blues and ragtime became known as "jass," or jazz—and a truly great American art form was created in New Orleans and weaned in Chicago, Kansas City, and New York. Jazz musicians played Kern. Stage musicals and recording companies thrived on dance music, "race" records, and the singing of ballads.

There are several theories about which one of these styles was more influential than the others. Suffice it to say, popular music, or what I am calling the Golden Age, was created out of all of those categories of song. Despite so many of its composers and lyricists being immigrants from Germany, Italy, Ireland, and a number of Eastern European countries, it all became American popular music. Its style, its genre was an intriguingly appetizing ingredient in the cultural melting pot. This chapter emphasizes turn of the century hit songs, which may be classified as ballads, love songs, dance tunes, and compositions from which the music of the Golden Age was born. It also should be noted that a number of the composers and lyricists of the early 1900s wrote on into the Golden Age.

Four songwriters are cited as being most influential in the creation of Golden Age songs: George M. Cohan, from vaudeville and the gaudy stage musical;

Victor Herbert, from the world of light opera; Scott Joplin, a creator of ragtime; and Jelly Roll Morton, who claimed to have invented jazz. We have omitted these four songwriters from this chapter and placed them among the superstars in Chapter 2.

NAT D. AYER, Composer (1887–1952) and SEYMOUR BROWN, Lyricist (1885–1947)

Little is known of Ayer and Brown other than the fact that they were Tin Pan Alley songwriters in the early part of the century. Ayer wrote for Flo Zeigfeld until about 1913 and then relocated to England, where he composed for the musical theatre. Brown, an actor and librettist from Philadelphia, was the lyricist on *Rebecca of Sunnybrook Farm*, composed by Albert Gumble (1883–1946).

Chronology

1911   *Oh You Beautiful Doll*. Ayer/Brown.

1929   *If You Were the Only Girl in The World (and I Was the Only Boy)*. Ayer/Clifford Grey.

ERNEST BALL, Composer (1878–1927) and J. KEIRN BRENNAN, Lyricist (1873–1948)

Cleveland born, Ball was a charter member of the American Society of Composers, Authors, and Publishers (ASCAP). To earn money for his musical education, he gave music lessons when he was only thirteen. By age fifteen, he composed a march. For twenty years, beginning in 1907, Ball was a staff composer on Tin Pan Alley. While in New York, he met a New York State legislator and flamboyant character by the name of James J. Walker (Chapter 5). Together, they wrote *Will You Love Me in December*. Jimmy Walker, later mayor of New York City, earned $10,000 on that song and collected royalties for years. Brennan was a native of San Francisco and, like Ball, was a vaudevillian. He also became, of all things, a cowboy. A recording artist, Brennan wrote a poem named *Empty Saddles*, for which music was written by another cowboy/performer named Billy Hill*. Brennan was also an early Hollywood songwriter.

Chronology

1905   *Will You Love Me in December as You Do in May?* Ball/Jimmy Walker.

1912   *When Irish Eyes Are Smiling*. Ball/Chauncey Olcott and George Graff. Olcott wrote *My Wild Irish Rose* (wm) in 1899.

1914   *A Little Bit of Heaven, Sure They Call It Ireland*. Ball/Brennan.

1918   *Dear Little Boy of Mine*. Ball/Brennan.

1919   *Let the Rest of the World Go By*. Ball/Brennan.

FELIX BERNARD, Composer (1897–1944)

A native of Brooklyn, New York, Bernard received a civil engineering degree from Rensselaer Polytech Institute, in Troy, New York. His father, a professional violinist, provided Bernard with a solid musical education. Bernard went on tour as a pianist, played in several orchestras and led his own band.

Chronology

1919   *Dardanella*. Bernard/Fred Fisher.

1934   *Winter Wonderland*. Bernard/Richard B. Smith. A Christmas standard. Smith, with Jimmy Rogan and Frank Winegar, wrote the lyrics to *When a Gypsy Makes a Woman Cry* (1936), composed by Emery Deutsch.

EUBIE BLAKE, Composer (1883–1983)

James Hubert ''Eubie'' Blake was the son of slaves. He was born in Baltimore and by age fifteen was playing piano at night clubs in that city. In 1915, he formed a partnership with bandleader/songwriter Noble Sissle (1889–1975). Their hit Broadway musical, **Shuffle Along**, ran fourteen months, a very long run in 1921. Blake lived to be one hundred years old and was beloved in the world of jazz and popular music.

Chronology

1921   *I'm Just Wild About Harry*. Sissle and Blake (wm). From *Shuffle Along*.

1930   *Memories of You*. Blake/Andy Razaf*. From Lew Leslies' *Blackbirds*, on Broadway.
        A Dollar for a Dime. Blake/Razaf. A delightful number done so well by Joe Williams.

EUDAY L. BOWMAN, Composer (1887–1949)

Born in Fort Worth, Texas, Bowman was an orchestra arranger. He wrote only one hit, the jazz standard *Twelfth Street Rag*.

Chronology

1914   *Twelfth Street Rag*. Bowman/Earl Fuller.

SHELTON BROOKS, Composer/Lyricist (1886–1975)

Part Native American and part African American, Brooks was raised in Detroit and was a pianist, vaudeville comic star, and early songwriter. He was a friend of vaudeville/music hall star Sophie Tucker's maid, and brought his first hit to Tucker (real name, Sophia Abuza, 1884–1966).

Chronology

1910   *Some of these Days*. Brooks (wm). Brooks' first hit, which became Tucker's theme.

1917   *Darktown Strutters Ball*. Brooks (wm). Introduced that year by the Original Dixieland Jazz Band (Chapter 1) at their very first recording session.

1919 *Jean*. Brooks (wm). Brooks' ballad, which became moderately popular when played by the Isham Jones* Band.

ERNIE BURNETT, Composer (1884–1959) and GEORGE A. NORTON, Lyricist (1880–1923)

Born in Cincinnati, Ohio, Burnett set out to become a concert pianist and studied in Europe. When he returned to the United States at age seventeen he played piano in vaudeville. He composed in New York and Hollywood and later became a music publisher in Saranac Lake, New York. Norton was born in St. Louis and attended the Peabody Conservatory of Music. As a pianist he also toured on the vaudeville circuit.

Chronology

1912 *My Melancholy Baby*. Burnett/Norton. The original title of this all-time classic was *Melancholy*. The use of the word ''baby'' has appeared in popular songs ad infinitum.

HUGHIE CANNON, Composer/Lyricist (1877–1912)

Cannon was a song and dance performer who gave a man named Bailey a couple of bucks for a hotel room. Bailey had been turned out by his wife, but Cannon was inspired, so he wrote a song that has been kept alive for generations. Jimmy Durante and his vaudeville partner, Eddie Jackson, popularized it; Ella Fitzgerald had a hit recording of it.

Chronology

1902 *Bill Bailey Won't You Please Come Home*. Cannon (wm).

BOB CARLETON, Composer/Lyricist (1892–1962)

Robert Lewis Carleton was born in St. Louis and, while in the Navy in World War I, wrote musical shows for the Great Lakes Naval Training Station.

Chronology

1918 *Ja Da*. Carleton (wm). A jazz evergreen.

HARRY CARROLL, Composer (1892–1962) and HAROLD R. ATTERIDGE, Lyricist (1886–1938)

Carroll, born in Atlantic City, New Jersey, began his career as a pianist in movie theatres. He later became an arranger for New York music publishers. He also played piano in New York cafes. In vaudeville, Carroll played in his own musical productions. He was a co-composer of the popular **Passing Shows** at New York's Winter Garden and was one of the composers retained by Ziegfeld for the **Follies** of 1921 and 1922. Atteridge was a Phi Beta Kappa graduate of the University of Chicago and a playwright. As Richard Harold Atteridge, he wrote books and lyrics to more than forty stage productions and was a writer in the early days of radio. He also adopted stage musicals for early films.

Chronology

1913 *On the Trail of the Lonesome Pine.* Carroll/Ballard MacDonald*. This song was based on the popular novel of the same name.

1914 *By the Beautiful Sea.* Carroll/Atteridge.

1918 *I'm Always Chasing Rainbows.* Carroll/Joe McCarthy (Chapter 1). Music adapted from Chopin's Fantasie Impromptu in C-sharp minor.

HENRY CREAMER, Lyricist (1879–1930) and TURNER LAYTON, Composer (1894–1978)

Born in Richmond, Virginia, Henry Creamer was an actor, a dance instructor, a lyricist, and a producer. He grew up attending public schools in New York City. Turner Layton quit medical studies to become a singer, pianist, and vaudeville entertainer. His full name was John Turner Layton. Layton and Creamer toured Europe as vaudeville partners.

Chronology

1909 *That's a Plenty.* Bert A. Williams/Creamer. A great jazz standard. Bert Williams was a famous vaudevillian.

1918 *After You've Gone.* Layton/Creamer. Their first hit, which also became a jazz classic. The most memorable version was soloed more than twenty years later by Roy Eldridge with the Gene Krupa Band.

1921 *Dear Old Southland.* Layton/Creamer. An adaptation of the spiritual, *Deep River.* Louis Armstrong made the classic recording.

1922 *Way Down Yonder in New Orleans.* Layton/Creamer. The songwriting team introduced it in vaudeville.

1926 *If I Could Be With You.* James P. Johnson*/Creamer. Also known as *One Hour*, it became the theme song for McKinney's Cotton Pickers, the famed jazz band. Johnson (1891–1955), a great jazz pianist, composed *Charleston* in 1923 with Cecil Mack and was the first to record the first jazz piano solo in 1921.

PAUL DRESSER, Composer/Lyricist (1858–1906)

In David Ewen's book, *All the Years of American Popular Music*, John Paul Dreiser is called, ''the foremost composer of sentimental ballads in the 1880s.'' Born in Terre Haute, Indiana, he was the older brother of the famed novelist, Theodore Dreiser. Dresser (as he spelled his name) attended a seminary to study for the priesthood, but apparently preferred show business. He began his career as a vaudeville singer, monologist, and minstrel. Later he became an actor, author, and producer of plays. In 1900, Dresser became a full partner in the highly successful music publishing firm of Howley, Haviland, and Dresser. Younger brother Theodore wrote the screenplay to the film biopic of Paul, **My Gal Sal.**

Chronology

1897   *On the Banks of the Wabash (Far Away).* Dresser (wm). Theodore took credit for some of the lyrics.

1905   *My Gal Sal.* Dresser (wm).

GUS EDWARDS, Composer (1879–1945)

Born Gus Simon in Hohensaliza, Germany, Edwards was one of the most successful composers of vaudeville music. He was also famous for his production of the so-called kids vaudeville, where he helped develop the talents of such performers as Eddie Cantor, Ray Bolger, Groucho Marx, Hildegarde, and fan dancer Sally Rand. His first published work was a ''coon song.''

Chronology

1898   *All I Want Is My Black Baby Back.* Edwards/Tom Daly. Edward's first song published.

1905   *In My Merry Oldsmobile.* Edwards/Vincent P. Bryan.

1906   *Sun Bonnet Sue.* Edwards/Will J. Cobb.

1907   *School Days.* Edwards/Cobb.

1909   *By the Light of the Silvery Moon.* Edwards/Edward Madden. From *Ziegfeld Follies*.

1911   *Jimmy Valentine.* Edwards/Madden.

FRED FISHER, Composer/Lyricist (1875–1942)

Born Fred Breitenbach in Germany, where he served in the navy, he later joined the French Foreign Legion. Arriving in the United States in 1900, he soon changed his name to Fischer, then Fisher. While much of his work was composed after World War I, he is included among the pioneers because of some old standards written in the early part of the century. Fisher founded the music publishing firm of Fred Fisher Music; and he was also the father of songwriters Doris* and Marvin (1916–1993). Marvin and another son, Dan, took over the publishing business after their father's death. Fred Fisher never lost his German accent, but his songwriting was quintessentially American.

Chronology

1905   *If the Man in the Moon Were a Coon.* Fisher (wm). Fisher's first published song was a non-hit.

1910   *Come Josephine in My Flying Machine.* Fisher/Alfred Bryan.

1913   *Peg O'My Heart.* Fisher/Bryan. From *Ziegfeld's Follies*.

1915   *There's a Broken Heart for Every Light on Broadway.* Fisher (wm).

1919   *Dardanella.* Johnny S. Black and Felix Bernard/Fisher. *Dardanella* was originally titled *Turkish Tom Tom*, a piano rag composed by Johnny S. Black. But Bernard (Chapter 1), a vaudeville actor, claimed that he, not Black was the composer. He asserted that Black sold the rights for $100 and Bernard sued Fred Fisher. Now, *Dardanella* is credited to composers Black and Bernard with Fisher as lyricist (and publisher). Fisher later brought suit against Jerome Kern* for using the tune in a portion of Kern's *Ku-lu-a*. It is not known if Fisher and Kern settled, won, or lost.

1922   *Chicago (That Toddling Town)*. Fisher (wm).

1926   *I Found a Millian Dollar Baby*. Harry Warren*/Billie Rose and Fisher.

1936   *Your Feet's Too Big*. Fisher with Ada Benson (wm).

1940   *Whispering Grass*. Fisher/Doris Fisher*. A big Ink Spots hit.

LEO FRIEDMAN, Composer (1869–1927) and BETH SLATER WHITSON, Lyricist (1879–1930)

Credit Friedman, a native of Elgin, Illinois, and Whitson, who was born in Goodrich, Tennessee, for creating two of the finest old ballads.

Chronology

1909   *Meet Me Tonight in Dreamland* Friedman/Whitson.

1910   *Let Met Call You Sweetheart* Friedman/Whitson.

RICHARD H. GERARD, Composer (1876–1948) and HARRY ARMSTRONG, Lyricist (1878–1951)

Sweet Adeline was used by John Fitzgerald, Boston legend and grandfather of President John F. Kennedy, as his political theme song. It was made popular by barbershop quartets. The lyrics were written in 1896, and Armstrong, a quartet singer and professional pianist who later became a producer (having earlier been a boxer), invited Richard Gerard Husch to set it to music. Husch used the pseudonym, Gerard.

Chronology

1903   *Sweet Adeline* Gerard/Armstrong. First titled *Down Home in New England* and *You're the Flower of My Heart*.

JOHN GOLDEN, Lyricist (1874–1955) and RAYMOND HUBBELL, Composer (1879–1954)

David Jasen, writing in the book *Tin Pan Alley*, called Raymond Hubbell a hack writer. Golden, on the other hand, was referred to by Gerald Bordman, in *The American Musical Theatre*, as "one of the most beloved and successful of all Broadway producers." Golden was originally a newspaperman, became an actor, and with Hubbell, wrote for Flo Ziegfeld. A founding member of ASCAP, Golden claimed to have been elected treasurer of that worthy organization while he was out of the meeting room, in the men's room.

Chronology

1916   *Poor Butterfly*. Golden/Hubbell. From **The Big Show** on Broadway.

W. C. HANDY, Composer/Lyricist (1873–1958)

William Christopher Handy, the son and grandson of clergymen, was born in Florence, Alabama. He worked as a school teacher and as a laborer in iron mills. In 1893, the cornetist/bandleader organized and booked an orchestra at the Chicago World's Fair. Later, he became a bandmaster in Kentucky. Handy started his own music publishing firm in 1913. Honored as a prominent American, as well as a musician, he had theatres, public squares, and other landmarks named for him. Handy edited books and anthologies as well as writing songs.

Chronology

1907 *In the Cotton Fields of Dixie*. Handy and Harry M. Pace (wm).

1912 *Memphis Blues*. Handy/George A. Norton (Chapter 1).

1914 *Saint Louis Blues*. Handy (wm). A classic—and one of the most performed songs of all time.

1916 *Beale Street Blues*. Handy (wm).

CARRIE JACOBS-BOND, Composer/Lyricist (1862–1946)

Jacobs-Bond was said to have been impoverished when she wrote *I Love You Truly*. Certainly, her financial condition must have taken a turn upward, with this song performed at so many weddings.

Chronology

1912 *I Love You Truly*. Jacobs-Bond (wm).

WILLIAM JEROME, Lyricist (1865–1932) and JEAN SCHWARTZ, Composer (1878–1956)

''Billy'' Jerome was a singer/actor who was born in Cornwall-on-the-Hudson, New York. He studied law for a while, but at age eighteen, joined a minstrel show. He eventually became a music publisher of note. Schwartz was born in Hungary and came to the United States at the age of thirteen. A song plugger and accompanist, he was a songwriter partner of Jerome's for several years.

Chronology

1910 *Chinatown, My Chinatown*. Jerome/Schwartz. From *Up and Down Broadway*.

1918 *Rock A Bye Your Baby*. Jerome/Schwartz. For the musical, *Sinbad*. A huge hit for Al Jolson.

PAUL LINCKE, Composer (1866–1946)

A native of Germany, Lincke wrote *Glow Worm* for the opera *Lysistrata*—his most important work. It was then adapted for the musical *The Girl Behind the Counter*. That show was eventually adapted for Broadway and called, *The Glow Worm*, with English lyrics by Lilla Cayley Robinson. Fifty years later, Johnny

Mercer* rewrote the lyrics to this hit song. Lincke was also a basoonist and musical director.

Chronology

1902   *Glow Worm*. Lincke/Robinson.

JOSEPH MCCARTHY, SR., Lyricist (1885–1943)

Born in Somerville, Massachusetts, Joe McCarthy left school to clerk in a haberdashery and moonlight as a cafe singer. He briefly worked for a Boston music publishing house and went on to write for many Broadway reviews. His lyrics were heard in *The Ziegfeld Follies, Rio Rita, Irene*, and *Kid Boots*—all on Broadway. His son, Joseph McCarthy Jr., collaborated with Cy Coleman many years later.

Chronology

1913   *You Made Me Love You*. James V. Monaco*/McCarthy.

1918   *I'm Always Chasing Rainbows*. Harry Carroll (Chapter 1)/McCarthy.

1919   *Alice Blue Gown*. Harry Tierney/McCarthy.

1926   *Rio Rita*. Tierney/McCarthy.

WALTER MELROSE, Lyricist (1899–19?)

Melrose owned a record store in Chicago with a brother and cousin, and they later formed a publishing firm devoted to the exciting new music called jazz. Chicago was the city known as "the capitol of Dixieland" and the Melroses published the music of Jelly Roll Morton*, King Oliver, Louis Armstrong*, and the Original Dixieland Jazz band (Chapter 4). Walter Melrose wrote the words to some of the fine jazz tunes of the day.

Chronology

1901   *High Society*. Porter Steele/Melrose. A song with a special place in jazz history. Melrose wrote the lyrics two decades after the song was composed.

1923   *Tin Roof Blues*. George Brunies, Melville J. Stitzel, Leon Roppolo, Paul Joseph Mares, and Ben Pollack/Melrose. The composers were all members of the New Orleans Rhythm Kings.

1924   *Copenhagen*. Charlie Davis/Melrose. Became a hit twenty years after it was composed.

1925   *Milenberg Joys*. Jelly Roll Morton, Mares, Roppolo, and Joe "King" Oliver/Melrose.

1926   *Sugar Foot Stomp (Dippermouth Blues)*. Oliver/Melrose.

GEORGE W. MEYER, Composer (1884–1959)

Meyer composed most of his hit songs prior to World War I. It must be noted, however that he also contributed a few fine popular standards in the

Golden Age. Born in Boston, Meyer worked as a song plugger for Irving Mills on Tin Pan Alley, in New York. He composed for the Broadway theatre and became a music publisher himself.

Chronology

1909 *Lonesome.* Meyer/Edgar Leslie*. This was Meyer's first published song.

1916 *Where Did Robinson Crusoe Go with Friday on a Saturday Night?* Meyer (wm), with Sam Lewis and Joe Young*. Written for Al Jolson's Broadway musical, **Robinson Crusoe, Jr**.

1917 *For Me and My Gal.* Meyer/Edgar Leslie* and E. Ray Goetz (Irving Berlin's brother-in-law). This was probably Meyer's first really big hit.

1918 *Everything Is Peaches Down in Georgia.* Meyer/Grant Clarke (Chapter 4).

1921 *Tuck Me to Sleep in My Old 'Tucky Home.* Meyer/Sam Lewis* and Joe Young*.

1924 *Mandy, Make Up Your Mind.* Meyer and Arthur Johnston*/Clarke and Roy Turk*. Co-composed by Arthur Johnston*, it has that "Berlin flavor." This song was first heard in **Dixie to Broadway**, a New York revue. Twenty years later, Tommy Dorsey's orchestra recorded a swinging hit version.

1942 *There Are Such Things.* Meyer (wm), with Stanley Adams (Chapter 4) and Abel Baer (Chapter 4), a bandleader and pianist. This song fit Frank Sinatra like the proverbial glove.

FREDERICK ALLEN (KERRY) MILLS, Composer/Lyricist (1869–1948)

Mills, a Philadelphian, was originally a classical violinist who graduated with a degree in music from the University of Michigan, where he eventually became head of the Violin Department. He left the classical music world to become a founder of the "cakewalk," a late-nineteenth century dance. It was then that he changed his first name to Kerry. Mills teamed up with Andrew B. Sterling (1874–1955) to write the famed standard, *Meet Me in St. Louis*. Sterling was a New Yorker who wrote parodies of popular songs for vaudevillians. Mills went on to become a song publisher in New York.

Chronology

1897 *At a Georgia Camp Meeting.* Mills (wm). A protest against the racist "coon" songs of the time.

1904 *Meet Me in Saint Louis, Louis.* Mills/Andrew Sterling. Sterling also co-wrote. *When My Baby Smiles at Me.* Sterling, Ted Lewis and Bill Munro (wm).

THEODORE MORSE, Composer (1873–1924) and DOROTHY MORSE, Lyricist (1890–1953)

Theodore Morse was born in New York, studied at the Maryland Military Academy, and somehow managed to study violin and piano as well. He was a clerk with a publishing house and eventually formed his own firm. Morse also composed *Hail, Hail the Gang's All Here*, with lyrics by his wife, Dorothy. Dorothy Morse was born in Brooklyn and wrote songs under her maiden name, Dorothy or Dolly Terris, and D. A. Esrom (Morse spelled backwards).

Chronology

1917   *Hail, Hail the Gang's All Here.* T. Morse/D. Morse (as D. A. Esrom).

1921   *Three O'Clock in the Morning.* Julian Robledo/D. Morse (as Dorothy Terris). Written for **Greenwich Village Follies**.

1929   *Siboney.* Ernesto Lecuona/Dolly Morse.

ABE OLMAN, Composer (1888–1984)

Olman was born in Cincinnati and became a staff composer with a Cleveland music publishing firm before going on to New York. While in Manhattan, he managed a theatrical office and produced vaudeville pieces. He appeared in European night clubs beginning in 1913, then returned to New York where he eventually became an executive with his own publishing firm. Later, as a publishing consultant to his nephew, Howard Richman, Olman helped to develop the project that eventually created the National Academy of Popular Music and its Songwriters Hall of Fame, established in 1969 with Johnny Mercer* as its first president.

Chronology

1914   *Down Among the Sheltering Palms.* Olman/James Brockman. Brockman (1896–1967), also an Ohioan, and a singer/comedian, had another hit, *I'm Forever Blowing Bubbles* (1914). The 1952 ASCAP Directory indicates that Brockman co-composed *I'm Forever* with Jean Kenbrovin (Kendis), with lyrics by John Kellette. Jacobs and Jacobs ("Who Wrote that Song") credit Kenbrovin/Kellette only.

1917   *Oh, Johnny Oh.* Olman/Ed Rose. This Olman composition went to the top of the charts for the Andrew Sisters, but it was actually introduced by Nora Bayes (Chapter 4).

1920   *O-HI-O.* Olman/Jack Yellen*. Also known as *Down by the Ohio*.

THE ORIGINAL DIXIELAND JAZZ BAND

Four of the members of this legendary jazz organization composed a few well-known jazz tunes. The ODJB was in business from 1916 to 1925 in New Orleans, Chicago, New York, and abroad. Dominick James "Nick" LaRocca (1899–1961) was the organizer of the ODJB and co-composed three of the songs in the chronology. He managed the band's affairs and played cornet. He was from New Orleans. Anthony "Tony" Sparbaro (1879–1969)—or Spargo, as he called himself—also contributed to three of the hit songs. He was the original ODJB drummer and opened with the band at the famed Reisenweber's Restaurant in New York in 1917. Spargo played with several big bands, too. Edwin B. "Eddie" Edwards (1891–1963) was a violinist/trombonist who played with the ODJB and also led a society orchestra during World War I. With Spargo, he toured with the Katherine Dunham dance troupe. Larry Shields (1893–1953) was the clarinetist who co-composed two of the songs and Henry Ragas (1891–1919) was the original pianist.

Chronology

1917   *Tiger Rag*. Edwards and LaRocca, (instr.). Taken from a French Quadrille (dance) and also "claimed" by Jelly Roll Morton.

1918   *Clarinet Marmalade*. Edwards, LaRocca, Shields, and Spargo (instr.).

19?   *At the Jazz Band Ball*. LaRocca, Shields, and Spargo (instr.).

LEE G. ROBERTS, Composer (1884–1949) and J. WILL CALLAHAN, Lyricist (1874–1946)

Roberts, a San Franciscan, was a self-taught musician who went into the business of manufacturing pianos and selling piano rolls and catalogs for pianists. Callahan was an author who began as a young accountant and protegé of James Whitcomb Riley. The Columbus, Ohio, native left accounting due to failing eyesight; and went on to become a singer and then a lyricist.

Chronology

1917   *(There Are) Smiles*. Roberts/Callahan. Not to be confused with Charlie Chaplin's *Smile*.

J. RUSSEL ROBINSON, Composer (1892–1963)

Born in Indianapolis, Robinson was, according to ASCAP, a "composer/lyricist/radio/television/phonograph/piano roll recording artist." He was credited (with apologies to Messrs. Armstrong and Ellington) with introducing jazz abroad. A man of many talents, he was an original cast member of the famous **Children's Hour** radio broadcast.

Chronology

1918   *Palesteena*. Robinson and Con Conrad* (wm).
        Original Dixieland One Step. Robinson, Nick LaRocca (Chapter 1) and Joe Jordan (wm).

1919   *Margie*. Robinson and Conrad/Benny Davis*.

1922   *Aggravatin' Papa*. Robinson and Roy Turk (wm).

1923   *Beale Street Mama*. Robinson and Turk (wm).

1943   *A Portrait of Jennie*. Robinson (wm). Film title song in the 1940s, recorded—and made a hit—by Nat King Cole.

CHRIS SMITH, Composer (1879–1949)

Born in Charleston, South Carolina, Smith was a baker by trade. He was also a guitarist and pianist. His major hit as a composer is still a popular song.

Chronology

1913   *Ballin' the Jack*. Smith/James Henry Burris. Written for **The Passing Show**.

EGBERT VAN ALSTYNE, Composer (1882–1951)

The Chicago Musical College, directed by Florenz Ziegfeld's father, was attended by many musical geniuses from the Midwest and elsewhere. One such prodigy, an accomplished organist at age seven, was Egbert Van Alstyne of Chicago. He went on to become a pianist for a theatrical company and an entertainer/director on the vaudeville circuit with partner Harry Williams (Chapter 1).

Chronology

1905   *In the Shade of the Old Apple Tree.* Van Alstyne/Harry Williams. Made into a huge hit more than three decades later by Duke Ellington.

1915   *Memories.* Van Alstyne/Gus Kahn*.

1916   *Pretty Baby.* Van Alstyne and Tony Jackson/Kahn. Van Alstyne broke the color barrier, perhaps for the first time in American music, by collaborating with Jackson (1876–1921), an African-American pianist.

1919   *Your Eyes Have Told Me So.* Van Alstyne, Kahn, and Walter Blaufuss (wm). Blaufuss (1883–1945) was another Chicago Musical School alumnus and a pianist who composed, arranged, and conducted.

1925   *Drifting and Dreaming.* Van Alstyne/Haven Gillespie*.

ALBERT VON TILZER, Composer (1878–1956) and HARRY VON TILZER, Composer (1872–1946)

Choosing a fancier name (their mother's, before she married), the brothers Gumm became the brothers Von Tilzer. Actually, there were five males in the family, and they all went into the music business. The oldest, Harry, ran off to join the Cole Brothers Circus at age fourteen. He eventually became an actor, pianist, accompanist, and saloon singer. He arrived in New York in 1892, nearly broke. However, he soon met his mentor, Irving Berlin, and it was upward and onward in the songwriting and publishing business. Albert left the Von Tilzer's hometown of Indianapolis to become a shoe buyer in Brooklyn. Not long after, he became a vaudeville company director and later joined brother Harry's music publishing firm, as did another brother, Jack. In 1930, after writing songs for New York musicians, Albert went on to Hollywood as a film songwriter.

Chronology—Albert Von Tilzer

1908   *Take Me Out to the Ball Game.* A. Von Tilzer/Jack Norworth (Chapter 4). Written about twenty years before Albert saw his first baseball game.

1910   *Put Your Arms Around Me Honey.* A. Von Tilzer/Junie McCree.

1920   *I'll Be With You in Apple Blossom Time.* A. Von Tilzer/Neville Fleeson.
        I Used to Love You but It's All Over Now. A. Von Tilzer/Lew Brown*.

Chronology—Harry Von Tilzer

1900   *She's Only a Bird in a Gilded Cage.* H. Von Tilzer/William Jerome.

1905   *Wait 'Til the Sun Shines Nellie.* H. Von Tilzer/Andrew Sterling.

1912   *And the Green Grass Grew All Around.* H. Von Tilzer/Jerome.

1925   *Just Around the Corner.* H. Von Tilzer/Dolph Singer.

PERCY WENRICH, Composer (1880–1952)

Wenrich composed ballads, rags, intermezzos, waltzes, and more. A native of Joplin, Missouri, he studied at the Chicago Musical School and went to work for a music publisher. He arrived in New York in 1908, where he joined the well-known firm of Remick, on Tin Pan Alley.

Chronology

1909   *Put on Your Old Gray Bonnet.* Wenrich/Stanley Murphy.

1912   *Moonlight Bay.* Wenrich/Murphy.

1914   *When You Wore a Tulip.* Wenrich/Jack Mahoney.

HARRY H. WILLIAMS, Lyricist (1879–1922)

Williams was born in Fairbault, Minnesota, and joined a traveling circus as a youngster. He landed in New York in 1902, where he became an actor and later joined the staff of a small publishing house. He wrote lyrics to songs by Egbert Van Alstyne (Chapter 1).

Chronology

1905   *In the Shade of the Old Apple Tree.* Egbert Van Alstyne/Williams.

1912   *It's a Long Way to Tipperary.* Williams and Jack Judge (wm).

1917   *Rose Room.* Art Hickman/Williams. Hickman was a bandleader.

LEO WOOD, Composer/Lyricist (1882–1929)

Wood was born in San Francisco and wrote songs for vaudeville performers. He was also a writer and a performer for radio.

Chronology

1918   *Somebody Stole My Gal.* Wood (wm). Originally performed by the Memphis Five in 1921; Bix Beiderbecke made it a hit in 1927.

1921   *Wang Wang Blues.* Gus Muller, Buster Johnson, and Henry Busse/Wood. Busse was a bandleader and a trumpet soloist in the Paul Whiteman Band—and helped make this song famous.

1922   *Runnin' Wild.* Harrington Gibbs/Leo Wood and Joe Grey. Gibbs was a Savannah, Georgia, pianist and bandleader; Grey was a Salt Lake City actor and singer.

RIDA JOHNSON YOUNG, Lyricist (1869–1926)

Born in Baltimore, Maryland, Young was an actress and a playwright who became a librettist and staff lyricist for a music publishing firm. Her major work was with composer Victor Herbert* for the famed operetta, ***Naughty Marietta***.

Chronology

1910   *Ah, Sweet Mystery of Life*; *I'm Falling in Love with Someone*; and *Italian Street Song*. Herbert/Young. Lyrics for the Herbert operetta.

1910   *Mother Machree*. Theodore Morse (Chapter 1)/Young.

Chapter 2

Prominent Songwriters of the Golden Age

The four decades spanned in this chapter include some of the best popular music ever introduced. By and large, the wonderfully lyrical and often swinging songs of this era were introduced on Broadway, on film, and, in the 1930s and 1940s, by the big bands. Tin Pan Alley was beginning to fade away and the recording industry was starting to mushroom in the years following World War II (although much in the way of records was produced back in the 1920s and 1930s). It was music to dance to; music to woo to; it was music with lyrics often poetic, but sometimes downright silly. The enormously popular vocalists, from Crosby to Sinatra; the magnificent first lady of song, Ella Fitzgerald; and quite a few others were front page successes—even if only in magazines like *Billboard, Variety*, and *Downbeat*. These vocalists introduced the songs, and often made them into hits. It is important to note, however, that the icons of the singing sector (especially Sinatra and Fitzgerald) were all openly grateful to the songwriters, not only in mentioning their names when singing the songs, but also in praising their work. Many of the songwriters were bandleaders and instrumentalists as well. Some, like Mercer, Waller, and Ellington, were the best performers of their own excellent works.

This chapter covers, alphabetically, approximately 160 major composers and lyricists; their hit songs are listed chronologically. George Cohan, Victor Herbert, Scott Joplin and Jelly Roll Morton, while pioneers by era, are included here because of their great influence on composers and lyricists of the Golden Age. They all continue to enjoy fame today, as their music is still performed. Also included are three great contemporary songwriters: the late lyricist Carolyn Leigh, and composers Stephen Sondheim and Cy Coleman. Their productivity is exceeded only by the quality of their songs; and thus they, too, are placed among the most prominent Golden Agers. The choice of songwriters in this chapter is based on the number of their hits exceeding five, an arbitrary standard. Exceptions are several songwriters who wrote or co-wrote classics. These composers and lyricists are included in Chapter 2.

TOM ADAIR, Lyricist (1915–) and MATT DENNIS, Composer (1914–)

Thomas A. Adair of Newton, Kansas, wrote the words to many of Matt Dennis' songs. Adair served in the armed forces in World War II and now lives in California. Dennis, a popular saloon singer, was born in Seattle, Washington, the son of vaudeville performers. Dennis sang in well-known Big Band Era orchestras and arranged for Tommy Dorsey and others. In the 1950s, he had his own television show on NBC.

Chronology

1940   *Who's Yehoodi?* Dennis/Bill Seckler. A ridiculous novelty tune.

1941   *Let's Get Away From It All; I Brought You Violets for Your Furs; Will You Still Be Mine?*; and *Everything Happens to Me*. Dennis/Adair.

1942   *The Night We Called It a Day*. Dennis/Adair.

1943   *In the Blue of Evening*. D'Artega/Adair.

1945   *There's No You*. Hal Hopper/Adair. Beautiful ballad, went high on the charts for Frank Sinatra.

1953   *Angel Eyes*. Dennis/Earl K. Brent. Superb saloon song written for the film **Jennifer**.

HAROLD ADAMSON, Lyricist (1906–1980)

New Jersey born Adamson was educated at the University of Kansas and also attended Harvard, where he wrote for the famed Hasty Pudding shows. One of the most productive of lyricists, he worked with such eminent composers as Hoagy Carmichael*, Vernon Duke*, Burton Lane*, Jimmy McHugh*, Jule Styne*, Harry Warren*, and Vincent Youmans*. In the mid–1940s, he also worked in Hollywood with conductor/composers John Green and Xavier Cugat.

Chronology

1930   *Time on My Hands*. Vincent Youmans/Adamson and Mack Gordon. From **Smiles**, on Broadway, starring the glorious Marilyn Miller. Adamson's first hit.

1933   *Everything I Have Is Yours*. Burton Lane/Adamson. From the landmark film **Dancing Lady**, starring Clark Gable, Joan Crawford, and bandleader/singer Art Jarrett, who performed this lovely song with Crawford.

1936   *Did I Remember?* Walter Donaldson/Adamson. Given superb treatment by Billie Holiday, this ballad was performed in the film **Suzy**, starring Cary Grant and Jean Harlow.

1937   *Where Are You?* Jimmy McHugh/Adamson. Used in **Top of the Town**, a film featuring five other McHugh/Adamson songs.
       You're A Sweetheart. McHugh/Adamson. Film title song.

1938   *My Own.* McHugh/Adamson.

1939   *Seven-Twenty in the Books.* Jan Savitt and Johnny Watson/Adamson. Theme song of the Jan Savitt Band.
       It's a Wonderful World. Savitt/Adamson.

1940   *Ferry Boat Serenade* and *Woodpecker Song.* Eldo diLazzaro/Adamson (English lyrics). Both of these songs by the Italian composer were performed in a Gene Autry film, **Ride, Tenderfoot, Ride**.

1941   *We're Having a Baby, My Baby and Me.* Vernon Duke/Adamson. Written for the Eddie Cantor musical on Broadway, **Banjo Eyes**.

1942   *Manhattan Serenade.* Louis Alter/Adamson. Theme song of the popular radio show, "Easy Aces."
       Moonlight Mood. Peter DeRose/Adamson. Another Adamson lyrical hit.

1943   *Change of Heart.* Jule Styne/Adamson. Oscar nominee.
       Comin' In On a Wing and a Prayer. McHugh/Adamson. A popular World War II song and a number 1 record on the charts. Recorded early on by Eddie Cantor and the Song Spinners.
       Daybreak. Fedre Grofé/Adamson. Part of Grofé's *Mississippi Suite (Mardi Gras)*, Adamson's words were sung by Kathryn Grayson in the film, **As Thousands Cheer**.

1944   *I Couldn't Sleep a Wink Last Night; A Lovely Way to Spend an Evening*; and *The Music Stopped.* McHugh/Adamson. Three fine hits performed by Frank Sinatra in the musical movie, **Higher and Higher**. *I Couldn't Sleep* was nominated for an Academy Award.

1948   *You Say The Nicest Things, Baby.* McHugh/Adamson. For the Broadway musical, **As The Girls Go**.
       It's A Most Unusual Day. McHugh/Adamson. For the Hollywood film, **A Date With Judy**.

1951   *My Resistance Is Low.* Hoagy Carmichael/Adamson. For the film, **The Las Vegas Story**.

1955   *Ain't There Anyone Here for Love?* Carmichael/Adamson. Jane Russell belted out this one in the film version of **Gentlemen Prefer Blondes**, for which Carmichael and Adamson were chosen to write additional songs. (See also Styne and Robin, this chapter.)
       I Have a Dream. Burton Lane/Adamson.

1957   *An Affair to Remember.* Harry Warren/Adamson and Leo McCarey (film director). Film title song, with Vic Damone turning in a fine singing performance on the soundtrack.

FRED AHLERT, Composer (1892–1953)

One of the many songwriters born in New York City, Ahlert was also, like a variety of other songwriters, an attorney (such as Hoagy Carmichael, J. Fred

Coots, Arthur Schwartz, and Carl Sigman who were lawyers, or at least completed law school). Ahlert was a student at Townsend Harris, the special high school for the academically talented, and graduated from the College of the City of New York. He worked as a staff arranger with the firm of Waterson, (Irving) Berlin, and Snyder.

Chronology

1915   *Beets and Turnips*. Ahlert/Cliff Hess. Ahlert's first published song.

1920   *I'd Love to Fall Asleep and Wake Up in My Mammy's Arms*. Ahlert, Sam Lewis, and Joe Young (wm). Ahlert's first hit.

1928   *I'll Get By*. Ahlert/Roy Turk. An American popular standard.

1929   *Mean to Me*. Ahlert/Turk. Another great standard.

1930   *Walkin' My Baby Back Home*. Ahlert/Turk.

1931   *Where the Blue of the Night Meets the Gold of the Day*. Ahlert/Turk and Bing Crosby. This was Crosby's theme song.

1932   *Love You Funny Thing; I Don't Know Why*; and *I'll Follow You*. Ahlert/Turk.

1935   *I'm Gonna Sit Right Down and Write Myself a Letter*. Ahlert/Sam Lewis and Joe Young. Made popular by Fats Waller.

HARRY AKST, Composer (1894–1963)

One of the few people known to have co-written with Irving Berlin, Akst was a born and bred New Yorker. His father played violin with the Metropolitan Opera. Akst started out as a concert pianist then wrote for Broadway and Hollywood. His first song was written while he was in army basic training at Camp Upton, Long Island, during World War I. In World War II, Akst accompanied Jolson entertaining troops. Akst also did some acting.

Chronology

1918   *My Laddie*. Akst (wm). First published song written at Camp Upton.

1925   *Dinah*. Akst/Sam Lewis and Joe Young*.

1926   *Baby Face*. Akst/Benny Davis.

1929   *Am I Blue?* Akst/Grant Clarke.

1931   *Guilty*. Richard Whiting*, Gus Kahn*, and Akst (wm).

LOUIS ALTER, Composer (1902–1980)

Alter, born in Massachussetts, was a nine-year-old piano prodigy who later attended the New England Conservatory of Music. He composed for Broadway musicals and his first published song, in 1928, was heard in Earl Carroll's ***Vanities***. An early member of the Hollywood songwriting pioneers, he had a number of film scores to his credit.

Chronology

1928   *Blue Shadows*. Alter (instr.). First published composition.

1936   *You Turned the Tables on Me*. Alter/Sidney Mitchell (Chapter 4).

1941   *Dolores*. Alter/Frank Loesser.

1942   *Manhattan Serenade*. Alter/Harold Adamson. Theme song of the radio show, ''Easy Aces.''

1946   *Do You Know What It Means to Miss New Orleans?* Alter/Eddie DeLange. From the film **New Orleans**.

1952   *Nina Never Knew*. Alter/Milton Drake (Chapter 4).

HAROLD ARLEN, Composer (1905–1986)

One of the foremost composers of popular song, Arlen was born in Buffalo, New York. His real name was Hyman Arluck and his father was a *chazzan* (a cantor in a synagogue). His mother taught piano and if her son was her pupil, she did a fine job. After his stint as a choirboy—no doubt in his father's temple—Arlen was playing piano with local bands by age fifteen. He played in dance bands on New York riverboats, although these crafts were not as famed as their Louisiana counterparts, and ended up in Manhattan in 1925. He was a pianist in George White's **Scandals** and Vincent Youmans'* rehearsal pianist for another musical. While his great career really began in New York, his west coast successes may be better known.

Broadway Chronology

1930   *Get Happy*. Arlen/Koehler. Arlen's first composing job for the stage; written with Koehler for **The 9:15 Revue**, starring Ruth Etting. It is still a hit.

1931   *Between the Devil and the Deep Blue Sea*. Arlen/Koehler. This marvelous song was featured in **Rhythmania**, Cab Calloway's revue for Harlem's Cotton Club.

1932   *I've Got a Right to Sing the Blues*. Arlen/Koehler. A jazz standard and theme song for trombonist Jack Teagarden, introduced in Earl Carroll's **Vanities**. The song is sometimes titled *I Gotta Right*, etc.
       I've Got the World on a String. Arlen/Koehler. Written for the '32 Cotton Club Revue, this classic was made popular by Frank Sinatra and Woody Herman.
       It's Only a Paper Moon. Arlen/Yip Harburg and Billy Rose. From the Broadway musical, **The Great Magoo**.

1934   *You're a Builder Upper* and *Shoein' the Mare*. Arlen/Ira Gershwin. Featured in **Life Begins at 8:30**, starring Ray Bolger.

1936   *Song of the Woodman*. Arlen/Harburg. Soloed by Bert Lahr in **The Show Is On**; later reprised in the film, **The Wizard of Oz**.

1937   *Down With Love*. Arlen/Harburg. Hit from **Hooray For What?**, on Broadway.

1944   *Right as the Rain*. Arlen/Harburg. A great hit from **Bloomer Girl**.

1946   *Come Rain or Come Shine*. Arlen/Mercer. Many consider this favorite, written for the musical **Saint Louis Woman**, arguably Arlen and Mercer's finest song.

The same score also included the now familiar *I Had Myself a True Love* and *Anyplace I Hang My Hat Is Home*.

1954   *A Sleeping Bee*. Arlen/Truman Capote.
From the Broadway musical **House of Flowers**, featuring a libretto and lyrics written by one of literature's finest, Truman Capote.

1959   **Saratoga**. Arlen/Mercer. Arlen's last Broadway show.

Hollywood Chronology

1929   *Long Before You Came Along*. Arlen/Yip Harburg. Arlen's first Hollywood song and the only one he wrote for the film, **Rio Rita**, which was scored by Harry Tierney and Joe McCarthy (Chapter 1).

1932   *Kicking the Gong Around*. Arlen/Ted Koehler. Arlen had met Koehler in New York in 1929, and that was the start of a wonderful collaboration. This was their first song used in a film. It was heard in the film **The Big Broadcast** and, subsequently, recalled as a 1931 Cotton Club song from **Rhythmania**. Cab Calloway performed in both features.

1934   *Let's Fall in Love*. Arlen/Koehler. A truly beautiful ballad and film title song.

1935   *Last Night When We Were Young*. Arlen/Harburg. Cited by musicologists and musicians as one of the finest of all ballads, this song was excised from the film in which it was originally supposed to be heard, **Metropolitan**. The producers thought it was "too sad," and they knocked it out of two more films. A sad song, a wonderful song. For proof, listen to the individual arrangements done by Tony Bennett, Judy Garland, and Frank Sinatra.

1939   Songs from **The Wizard of Oz**. Arlen/Harburg. A film masterpiece, the duo wrote the Oscar-winning *Over the Rainbow*, as well as *Follow the Yellow Brick Road, The Merry Old Land of Oz, We're Off to See the Wizard, Ding Dong the Witch Is Dead*, and other delightful tunes for children of all ages.
Lydia the Tatooed Lady. Arlen/Harburg. Their contribution to the Marx Brothers' film, **At the Circus**.

1941   *Blues in the Night* and *This Time the Dream's On Me*. Arlen/Johnny Mercer. *Blues* was this great team's first collaboration and an Academy Award–nominated film title song. *This Time* was another fine ballad used in the movie, which was an excellent story about jazz musicians.

1942   *That Old Black Magic* and *Hit the Road to Dreamland*. Arlen/Mercer. From **Star Spangled Rhythm**, in Hollywood.

1943   *Cabin in the Sky* and *Happiness Is Just a Thing Called Joe*. Arlen/Harburg. Arlen and Harburg wrote the score for **Cabin in the Sky**, an all African-American cast film, directed by Vincent Minelli, with first class performances from Lena Horne, Duke Ellington, and Ethel Waters.
Stormy Weather. Arlen/Koehler. This classic film title song was introduced to moviegoers by Lena Horne. The screenplay was also written by Koehler. Performers included: the Nicholas Brothers, Bill "Bojangles" Robinson, and Cab Calloway.
One for My Baby and *My Shining Hour*. Arlen/Mercer. Two fine hits written for Fred Astaire's film, **The Sky's the Limit**.

Blues in the Night. Arlen/Mercer. Their '41 hit recycled for the film ***Thank Your Lucky Stars***, and performed—not exactly sung—by the great actor, John Garfield.

1944   *Now I Know*. Arlen/Koehler. Another Oscar-nominated song, written for Danny Kaye's first film, ***Up In Arms***.

1945   *Accentuate the Positive*. Arlen/Mercer. Introduced in the film, ***Here Come the Waves***, this Academy Award–nominated song lost the Oscar to the great Rodgers/ Hammerstein song, *It Might As Well Be Spring*. Nonetheless, *Accentuate* has become a standard.
Out of this World and *June Comes Around Every Year*. Arlen/Mercer. The title song from the film comedy, ***Out of this World***, and *June* featured Bing Crosby's voice dubbed over Eddie Bracken's.

1948   *For Every Man There's a Woman*. Arlen/Leo Robin. Academy Award–nominated song from the movie ***Casbah***, with Tony Martin. Arlen and Robin wrote three other fine songs for the film: *It Was Written in the Stars, Hooray for Love*, and *What's Good About Goodbye?*

1954   *The Man That Got Away*. Arlen/Ira Gershwin. Originally a non-musical, the classic film ***A Star Is Born*** was reprised as a musical and the Arlen/Gershwin ''dream team'' was assigned the score. The new version was a triumph for Judy Garland and James Mason. Among the film's seven Arlen/Gershwin songs, one was truly outstanding and nominated for an Oscar, *The Man That Got Away*.
The Country Girl. Arlen/Gershwin. A film with songs by Arlen and Gershwin and for the award-winning Bing Crosby, William Holden, and Grace Kelly drama.

LOUIS ARMSTRONG, Composer/Lyricist (1901–1971)

Putting aside all hyperbole, Armstrong can be called Mr. Jazz; or, if you wish, Mr. American Music. His contributions to American popular music, to singing and, of course, to one of the truest of American art forms, are incalculable. Recognized throughout the world for his influence on jazz and on trumpet playing and singing, Louis Armstrong belongs—with Duke Ellington*, George Gershwin*, and Leonard Bernstein*—among the icons.

Daniel Louis Armstrong (it has been recorded as Louis Daniel, too) was born in New Orleans and, as a homeless waif, he worked the streets as a coal deliverer. He also learned cornet at a waifs' home and played in the streets and in brothel bands. Armstrong grew into a career that included night club and musical revues; dance halls and film; radio, television, and recording studio work. He married three times: Daisy Parker, a New Orleans lady of the evening; Lil Hardin, the jazz pianist/composer; and Lucille Armstrong, whom he adored and lived with for years.

He was a unique human being. And so was his music. Armstrong's work as a soloist with King Oliver and Fletcher Henderson were early indications of his greatness. But it was his *Hot Fives* and *Hot Sevens* sessions that started him on the road to international acclaim. Tom Piazza, in *The Guide to Classic Recorded Jazz*, calls the *Hot Fives* and *Sevens* recordings ''possibly the most influential series of recordings in the history of jazz, certainly one of the very greatest and definitely one of the most enjoyable.''

A few additional notes on Armstrong: his army of admirers who truly respect his greatness prefer the name Loui*s*, instead of Loui*e*; although he was also affectionately called Satchmo or Satch, both abbreviations of what was originally ''Satchel Mouth.'' (He referred to himself as Pops, a word he used in addressing nearly everyone else.) Even though he was not, as some books would have it, born on July 4, 1900, he did not discourage the belief that he was. There are so many other interesting stories about this amazing musician; indeed, so much has been written about Armstrong by so many, it is difficult to know where to start—Gary Giddens' fine biography is recommended as a first read.

Chronology

1926 *I Want a Big Butter and Egg Man*. Armstrong and Percy Venable (wm). Written for a New York musical, *Cafe Revue*.

1927 *Struttin' with Some Barbecue*. Armstrong and Lil Hardin (wm). Some sources credit only Hardin.
Wild Man Blues. Armstrong and Jelly Roll Morton (instr.).
Someday You'll Be Sorry. Armstrong (wm).

1930 *Back O'Town Blues and Brother Bill*. Armstrong and Luis Russell (wm). Both composed in the early 1930s; exact years unknown.

1938 *Ol' Man Mose*. Armstrong and Zilner Randolph (wm).

WILLIAM "COUNT" BASIE, Composer/Bandleader (1906–1984)

Born William Basey in Red Bank, New Jersey, this major figure in American jazz studied piano, ''more or less'' with Fats Waller in New York. The Count became a master of the stride school of piano playing, and at age 21, was playing in a movie theatre in Kansas City. It was in that hotbed of jazz and swing, that the famed bandleader Benny Moten invited Basie to join his organization. In a reasonably short time, Basie organized his own group, featuring the best of the best: Lester Young, tenor sax; Buck Clayton and Harry ''Sweets'' Edison, trumpets; Dickie Wells, trombone; and Jo Jones, drums.

For thirty years, the Basie Band was the swinging model. Arrangers Ernie Wilkins, Bill Holman, and Neal Hefti helped the aggregation to maintain its consistent excitement and professionalism decade after decade. Basie's ability to hire and retain musicians who made the band great was quite significant. At various times, the Basie Band featured vocalists Billie Holiday, Joe Williams, and Jimmy Rushing; while the rhythm sections included the drum master ''Papa Jo'' Jones, guitarist Freddie Green, and pianist Basie, himself. The Basie Band was a comfortable home for the stars of jazz and swing.

Chronology

1938   *Every Tub*. Basie and Ed Durham (Chapter 4) (instr.).
         Jumpin' at the Woodside and *One O'Clock Jump*. Basie (instr.). The latter was
         Basie's theme song.

1939   *Blue and Sentimental*. Basie, Mack David, and Jerry Livingston (wm).
         John's Idea and *Sent for You Yesterday, Here You Come Today*. Basie and
         Durham (instr.).

1941   *Goin' to Chicago Blues*. Basie, Ed Durham, and Jimmy Rushing (wm).
         Two O'Clock Jump. Basie and Harry James (instr.).

1945   *Good Bait*. Basie and Tad Dameron (instr.). If you are not quite sure what
         "swinging" means, Basie's version of this song will provide the definition.

BENNIE BENJAMIN, Composer (1907–1989)

The birthplace of composer Bennie Benjamin was Christiansted, Saint Croix,
in the U.S. Virgin Islands. At age 20, Benjamin arrived in New York to study
tenor banjo and guitar. He became a sideman with popular orchestras of the
1930s; he was also a Tin Pan Alley staff writer.

Chronology

1941   *I Don't Want to Set the World on Fire*. Benjamin, Ed Durham, Eddie Seiler, and
         Sol Marcus (Chapter 4) (wm). An Ink Spots evergreen.

1942   *Strictly Instrumental*. Benjamin, Seiler, Marcus, and Edgar Battle (wm). A hit for
         Harry James.
         When the Lights Go On Again All Over the World. Benjamin, Seiler, Marcus
         (wm). A sentimental World War II number.

1945   *Oh! What It Seemed to Be*. Benjamin and Frankie Carle (bandleader) George
         David Weiss (see Bock/Harnick, Chapter 3). Frank Sinatra's recording raised this
         to hit status.

1946   *Rumors Are Flying*. Benjamin and Weiss (wm).

1952   *Wheel of Fortune*. Benjamin and Weiss (wm). Vocalist Kay Starr recorded this
         big hit.

1954   *Cross Over the Bridge*. Benjamin and Weiss (wm). A hit for Patti Page.

IRVING BERLIN, Composer/Lyricist (1888–1989)

The most often quoted description of Irving Berlin's place in American music
comes from Jerome Kern: "Irving Berlin *is* American popular music."

Israel Baline was born in the town of Temun in pre-Soviet Russia, where his
father (like Harold Arlen's) was a synagogue cantor. The family immigrated to
New York when Berlin was a small child. Uneducated, Izzy, as he was called,
sang on the streets for pennies and later moved on to become a singing waiter
in Coney Island. The name Irving Berlin first appeared on sheet music for a
song in 1907 called *Marie from Sunny Italy*, but it was composed by Nick

Michaelson, a pianist at the Pelham Cafe. It was there the young man who swept floors, waited on tables, and entertained customers, wrote the words to Michaelson's song. For his work, Izzy earned thirty-seven cents.

As the years went on, Berlin was to earn more money than any songwriter in the history of American music. By turning out hit after hit, Berlin was considered the most prolific of all composer/lyricists. He practiced his craft for more than six decades. A well-known rumor regarding this amazing productivity was that Berlin had "a little colored boy" who did much of the writing for which he took credit; but this has been denied in most Berlin biographies. One version of this rumor (heard first hand) came from a reputable pianist/entertainer who studied music with an Italian teacher of great renown. That teacher was also the mentor of Arthur Johnston* and said that Johnston was, indeed, the "ghost" for Berlin. Johnston was Berlin's pianist for a time, but the ghostwriting has never been proven.

Berlin's diverse output included ballads and novelties; holiday and patriotic songs; showtunes and, in his early career, rags. He wrote songs for singing and dancing in Hollywood; and was, of course, a highly successful musical publisher and producer. While Berlin wrote literally hundreds of ballads and lovely love songs, his fame was extended through the genre of patriotic and holiday songs, which helped him attain the prestigious status of American hero. *God Bless America, Count Your Blessings* (an Oscar winner), *Oh, How I Hate to Get Up in the Morning, Easter Parade*, and arguably the world's most popular seasonal song, *White Christmas*, are just a few of his famous patriotic and holiday compositions.

On a personal note, when Berlin was older and quite reclusive, an advertising associate of mine had an idea for a radio or television jingle for our client, the Slant/Fin heating products manufacturer. The title was *I've Got Slant/Fin to Keep Me Warm*, to the tune of *I've Got My Love to Keep Me Warm*. When we contacted Berlin's office, his longtime secretary advised us, "never, neither while Mr. Berlin is alive or after his death, will his songs be used for singing commercials!" We politely thanked the lady and wrote another jingle. Unlike the works of many other songwriters, Berlin songs are not used for commercials.

Berlin's evergreens include his first hit, *Alexander's Ragtime Band*, as well as *Blue Skies, No Business Like Show Business*, and the many others reported in the chronologies below. He also produced a number of well-known dance tunes: *Cheek to Cheek, It Only Happens When I Dance with You, Everybody Step, The Best Things Happen While You're Dancing, A Couple of Song and Dance Men*, and others. Berlin has been much admired and praised by contemporaries, critics, and fans. Three great stars of stage and screen—Fred Astaire, Ginger Rogers and Ethel Merman—acknowledged that much of their success was due to the wonderful music, rhythms, and lyrics of Irving Berlin. To close, an amusing story from Michael Feinstein, from his book, *Nice Work If You Can Get It*. Berlin was in a recording studio singing, *Oh, How I Hate to Get Up in the Morning*. One of the engineers turned to another and said, "If the guy who wrote that song heard this guy singing it, he'd turn over in his grave.'' Berlin, it should be noted, lived to be 101.

Pioneer Days Chronology

1907 *Marie From Sunny Italy*. Michaelson/Berlin.

1911 *Alexander's Ragtime Band*. Berlin (wm). Probably the most popular and most profitable ragtime song ever written. Yet, it is about ragtime, not in ragtime. *Everybody's Doing It*. Berlin (wm). Launched the Turkey Trot dance craze.

1912 *When the Midnight Choo Choo Leaves for Alabam*. Berlin (wm). An enormous hit—and the reason Berlin was made a partner in the prominent music publishing firm of Waterson, Berlin and Snyder. In the same year, Berlin married Dorothy Goetz, sister of songwriter and, later, Hollywood producer, E. Ray Goetz. On their honeymoon, she contracted typhoid fever, and after only five months of marriage, Berlin was left a deeply grieving widower, and wrote *When I Lost You*.

Broadway Chronology

1914 *Play a Simple Melody*. Berlin (wm). His big hit from a dozen songs he penned for a show he worked on with Vernon and Irene Castle, **Watch Your Step**.

1915 *I Love a Piano*. Berlin (wm). From the show, **Stop, Look and Listen**.

1919 *A Pretty Girl Is Like a Melody*. Berlin (wm). The all-time standard, introduced in the **Ziegfeld Follies**.
Oh, How I Hate to Get Up in the Morning and *Mandy*. Berlin (wm). As a rookie soldier, Berlin wrote both of these songs for his show, **Yip, Yip Yaphank**, named for the Long Island army training camp.

1921 *Say It with Music*. Berlin (wm). From **The Music Box Revue**.

1923 *Supper Time*. Berlin (wm). From **As Thousands Cheer**.

1924 *All Alone* and *What'll I Do?* Berlin (wm). From the 1924 version of the same revue.

1925 *Remember* and *Always*. Berlin (wm). Two of his greatest love songs.

1926 *Blue Skies*. Berlin (wm). Now a classic, Berlin contributed this one song to the Broadway musical **Betsy**, in which Rodgers*/Hart* wrote the rest of the songs. In the same year, Berlin married again, this time to an heiress, Ellin MacKay— much to the consternation, or worse, of her parents, since he was an uneducated, Jewish songwriter.

1927 *Shaking the Blues Away; Russian Lullaby*; and *The Song Is Ended*. Berlin (wm). The Ziegfeld **Follies** introduced *Shaking*; Bunny Berigan's recording of *Russian* is remarkable; and *The Song* is a never-ending classic.

1928 *How About Me?* Berlin (wm).

1932 *Soft Lights and Sweet Music* and *Let's Have Another Cup of Coffee*. Berlin (wm). From Broadway's **Face the Music**.
How Deep Is the Ocean and *Say It Isn't So*. Berlin (wm). Two more of his beautiful love songs; the latter sung with such tenderness by Lady Day—and very well by Sarah Vaughn.

1933 *Heat Wave* and *Easter Parade*. Berlin (wm). Introduced in **As Thousands Cheer**, which was the first stage appearance for Ethel (Zimmerman) Merman, an exstenographer. (For more of his mid-1930s hits, see the Hollywood chronology that follows.)

1940   *It's a Lovely Day Tomorrow* and *You're Lonely and I'm Lonely*. Berlin (wm). From **Louisiana Purchase**.

1942   **This Is the Army**. Berlin (wm). Conceived, written, produced, and staged by "Sgt. Irving Berlin, 1917," this blockbuster reprised much of the patriotism of World War I's *Yaphank*, and opened on July 4, 1942, as a World War II musical rally. While it only ran 113 performances on Broadway, it was a major hit on tour—with an all-army cast—until 1945. On stage in New York, wearing his 1917 uniform, Berlin sang *Oh, How I Hate to Get Up In the Morning* and *Mandy*, as well as three new songs he wrote for the show: *I'm Getting Tired So I Can Sleep, This Is the Army Mr. Jones* and *I Left My Heart at the Stage Door Canteen*.

1946   **Annie Get Your Gun**. Berlin (wm). The biggest hit of the 1946 season, **Annie** (produced by Rodgers* and Hammerstein*) was to have been scored by Jerome Kern*, who had died the previous year. The smash musical starred Ethel Merman, belting out Berlin's *I've Got the Sun in the Morning, Doin' What Comes Natur'lly, You Can't Get a Man With a Gun, I'm an Indian Too, There's No Business Like Show Business*, and *I Got Lost in His Arms*. (A fascinating anecdote about the song *There's No Business*, from Thomas Hischak's *The Theatre-goer's Almanac*: Berlin thought Rodgers and Hammerstein did not like the song, which he had written as a "curtain closer." He therefore discarded it, only to find out that the producers actually did like it. When he wanted to put it back into the show, he could not find the sheet music. After some time, with everyone frantically looking for it, a secretary located the music under a telephone book in Berlin's office. Thus *There's No Business Like Show Business*—the entertainment industry's anthem—was born.) Other fine Berlin songs in **Annie** included: *They Say It's Wonderful, Anything You Can Do (I Can Do Better)*, and *The Girl That I Marry*. A solid piece of entertainment, **Annie Get Your Gun** ran more than three years. Its road company starred Mary Martin; the film version was a winner as well.

1949   *Let's Take an Old Fashioned Walk*. Berlin (wm). From **Miss Liberty**.

1950   **Call Me Madam**. Songs by Berlin (wm). "The hostess with the mostess on the Ball" was the theme of this musical; and once again, Merman wowed 'em on Broadway with her performance patterned after the ubiquitous U.S. ambassador and partygiver extraordinare, Perle Mesta. Romantic Berlin songs included: *The Best Thing for You Would Be Me, It's a Lovely Day Today, You're Just in Love, Marrying for Love*, and *They Like Ike* (which was used in the 1952 presidential campaign) **Madam** ran for a year and a half.

1962   **Mr. President**. Songs by Berlin (wm). His last Broadway show.

Hollywood Chronology

1928   *Marie*. Berlin (wm). His contribution to the film, **The Awakening**, this song was recorded about a decade later by the Tommy Dorsey Band, and it hit the top of the charts.

1929   *Let Me Sing and I'm Happy*. Berlin (wm). Performed by Al Jolson in the film, **Mammy**.

Puttin' On the Ritz. Berlin (wm). Title song of a movie starring Harry Richman. **Cocoanuts; Hallelujah**; and **Glorifying the American Girl**. All scored by Berlin. The first film is still a Marx Brothers' favorite; the second had an all African-American cast; and the third was Florenz Ziegfeld's only movie.

1931   *Reaching for the Moon*. Berlin (wm). Another beautiful film title song.

1935   **Top Hat**. Songs by Berlin (wm). The classic Astaire and Rogers film with a fine Berlin score including *Top Hat, White Tie and Tails, No Strings (I'm Fancy Free), Cheek to Cheek, Isn't This a Lovely Day?*, and *Piccolino*.

1936   **Follow the Fleet**. Songs by Berlin (wm). Fred, Ginger, and Irving redux—with a memorable score: *Let's Face the Music and Dance, Let Yourself Go, I'm Putting All My Eggs in One Basket*, and *We Saw the Sea*.
Yiddle on your Fiddle. Berlin (wm). Sung by the original "funny girl," Fanny Brice, in the silver screen version of **The Great Ziegfeld**.

1937   *This Year's Kisses; I've Got My Love to Keep Me Warm; He Ain't Got Rhythm; Slumming on Park Avenue*; and *You're Laughing at Me*. Berlin (wm). Used in an Alice Faye film, **On the Avenue**.

1938   **Alexander's Ragtime Band**. Songs by Berlin (wm). Featuring Alice Faye and Ethel Merman, and nearly two dozen Berlin songs. *Now It Can Be Told* was introduced; *Heat Wave, Blue Skies*, and others were recycled from earlier years.
Change Partners. Berlin (wm). From **Carefree**.

1939   *I Poured My Heart into a Song*. Berlin (wm). Oscar-nominated song from a most enjoyable Fred Astaire film, **Second Fiddle**, but Arlen/Harburg's *Over the Rainbow* won the musical Academy Award that year.
Syncopated Walk. Berlin (wm). Used in the last Astaire and Rogers team-up film, **The Story of Vernon and Irene Castle**.
God Bless America. Berlin (wm). The "other national anthem" was written by Berlin in 1939 and made popular (an understatement) by singer Kate Smith. It is easier to sing and play than *The Star Spangled Banner*. It is probably not as musically fine as *America the Beautiful*. But clearly, *God Bless America* is one of the most performed patriotic songs of all time. It, no doubt, contributed to the decision by the U.S. Government to honor Irving Berlin as an American hero.

1941   *Any Bonds Today*. Berlin (wm). Written as the official song of the U.S. Treasury Department, Berlin's composition helped sell war bonds in support of the government's World War II efforts.

1942   **Holiday Inn**. Songs by Berlin (wm). The feel-good movie musical that had a motel chain named after it. **Holiday Inn** starred Bing Crosby and Fred Astaire—and the Berlin score itself, including the legendary, Academy Award–winning song, *White Christmas*, which ranks among songs played most often—*Happy Birthday* and *Star Dust* notwithstanding. Until 1997, Bing Crosby's recording of *White Christmas* was the biggest selling single of all time. It was finally topped by Elton John's *Candle in the Wind, '97*—his tribute to the late Diana, Princess of Wales. John's recording sold 35 million copies in less than a few weeks. Other Berlin songs in the film include: *Be Careful, It's My Heart, I'll Capture Your Heart Singing (Dancing), You're Easy to Dance With, Plenty To Be Thankful For, Happy Holiday*, as well as the title song. The film, played regularly on television (especially at Christmas), also includes a Berlin song introduced nine years earlier, *Easter Parade*.

1943   ***This Is the Army***. Songs by Berlin (wm). His stage production made into a movie. Berlin won another Oscar for the film's entire score.

1946   *You Keep Coming Back Like a Song; A Couple of Song and Dance Men*; and *Everybody Step*. Berlin (wm). For the Astaire and Crosby film, ***Blue Skies***. *You Keep* was nominated for an Oscar.

1947   ***Easter Parade***. Songs by Berlin (wm). The filmmakers made Berlin's song a movie title, and Judy Garland, Fred Astaire, Ann Miller, and Peter Lawford starred in this highly enjoyable motion picture. Other Berlin songs included were *Steppin' Out with My Baby, A Couple of Swells, It Only Happens When I Dance with You*, and a reprised oldie, *I Love a Piano*.

1949   *Let Me Sing and I'm Happy*. Berlin (wm). Reprised for another box office winner, ***Jolson Sings Again***.

1950   ***Annie Get Your Gun***. Songs by Berlin (wm). Ebullient Betty Hutton took the Merman part for this film version—and she was wonderful. Berlin added another wonder song, *Who Do You Love, I Hope?*

1954   ***White Christmas***. Songs by Berlin (wm). Once again a hit song became a movie title when Paramount produced ***White Christmas***. It grossed twelve million dollars, a very large piece of change for 1954, and starred Bing Crosby, Danny Kaye, and one of the best vocalists in the business, Rosemary Clooney. The songs included *Count Your Blessings (Instead of Sheep), The Best Things Happen When You're Dancing, Love, You Didn't Do Right By Me, Snow*, and reprises of several old Berlin tunes, including the title song.

LEONARD BERNSTEIN, Composer (1918–1990)

It has been argued by musicologists that had Bernstein decided to concentrate his work on musical theatre, he may very well have assumed the icon status of Kern, Rodgers, Porter, and others. Leonard Bernstein is one of America's foremost classical conductor/composers; an enormously versatile talent who wrote opera and symphony, chorale music, and Broadway show tunes. He was born in the Boston area, graduated from Harvard, and later enjoyed a long association with the New York Philharmonic. In the world of music, he brought enjoyment to people of all ages—everywhere.

Chronology

1944   *Lonely Town* and *New York, New York (It's A Wonderful Town)*. Bernstein/Betty Comden and Adolph Green. From their hit show, ***On the Town***.

1953   *Ohio (Why Oh Why Oh?)*. Bernstein/Comden and Green. For the musical play, ***Wonderful Town***, which was based on ***My Sister Eileen***, a non-musical stage show of some years previous.

1956   ***Candide***. Bernstein/John La Touche (Chapter 4) and Dorothy Parker. Story by Lillian Hellman. The genius of Bernstein was not harmed by the lack of this play's success; as a matter of fact, revivals have proven its musical beauty. The overture remains one of the most haunting pieces of music ever composed for the theatre.

1957   **West Side Story**. Bernstein/Stephen Sondheim. The most successful Bernstein show, thanks to his collaboration with Sondheim and a wonderful stage production. The award-winning Bernstein/Sondheim score includes these classics: *Somewhere, Maria, I Feel Pretty, Something's Coming*, and *Tonight*.

RALPH BLANE, Composer/Lyricist (1914–   ) and HUGH MARTIN, Lyricist (1914–   )

Blane was christened Ralph Uriah Hunsecker, hardly a name for a Broadway actor, which he became. Originally from Arrow, Oklahoma, Blane teamed up with Martin and others as a singing group called The Four Martins. They went on to Hollywood in 1943. Hugh Martin, born in Birmingham, Alabama, was a piano student and singer who got his first Broadway job as a singer in **Hooray for What?** in 1937. Martin and Blane were both vocal arrangers who wrote stage shows throughout the 1960s.

Chronology

1941   *Buckle Down Winsocki*. Blane/Martin. From the Broadway production, **Best Foot Forward**.

1944   **Meet Me in Saint Louis**. Songs by Blane/Martin. Judy Garland starred. Blane and Martin's best film; five decades later it was their best show on Broadway and included *The Boy Next Door, Trolley Song*, and *Have Yourself a Merry Little Christmas*.

1947   *Pass That Peace Pipe*. Blane/Martin and Roger Edens. For the film, **Good News**.

RUBE BLOOM, Composer (1902–1976)

New York born and raised, Bloom was already accompanying vaudeville performers on the road when he was 17. He became a composer/pianist and radio performer—and created his first serious work, *Soliloquy*, in 1923. Like Harold Arlen, he worked on Cotton Club revues. Basically a self-taught musician, he eventually wrote piano books for students and continued to compose and arrange twenty years after his first published song.

Chronology

1928   *Song of the Bayou*. Bloom (wm). His first published song.

1929   *Jumping Jack*. Bloom, Bernie Seaman, Marvin Smoler, and Herman Ruby (wm). For the Warner Brothers' musical films, **The Show of Shows**.

1935   *Truckin'*. Bloom/Ted Koehler. For a Cotton Club revue.

1939   *Day In, Day Out*. Bloom/Johnny Mercer. Bloom's first number 1 chart record. *Don't Worry 'Bout Me*. Bloom/Koehler. Perhaps his finest ballad, written for the 1939 Cotton Club **Parade**.

1940   *Fools Rush In*. Bloom/Mercer. Another hit which became a standard.

1942   *Take Me*. Bloom/Mack David. One of Bloom's beautiful compositions.

1947   *Give Me the Simple Life*. Bloom/Harry Ruby*. For the film, **Wake Up and Dream**.

1948   *Maybe You'll Be There*. Bloom/Sammy Gallop*.

1951   *Here's To My Lady*. Bloom/Mercer. Another chartbuster.

BROOKS BOWMAN, Composer/Lyricist (1913–1937)

Another famed college musical tradition is Princeton's Triangle Club. The author of one of their early 1930s revues was a future Princetonian still in high school, Brooks Bowman. From Cleveland, Bowman went on to Princeton where he authored another Triangle revue. Sadly, Bowman—on his way to California—was killed in an auto accident at age 24. At the time he was a law student who had been offered a Hollywood contract as a songwriter.

Chronology

1934   *East of the Sun*. The classic from Bowman (wm).
       Stags at Bay, Princeton Triangle Club revue.

LEW BROWN, Lyricist (1893–1958), BUDDY DESYLVA, Lyricist (1895–1950), and RAY HENDERSON, Composer (1896–1970)

One of the truly great songwriting teams had three partners, not just two. It would be difficult to write a biography of any one of them without including the other two. Brown's chronology includes their collaborative works; the Brown and Henderson chronologies list their individual works.

Lewis Brownstein, born in Russia of musical parentage, emigrated to the United States as a child. He lived and worked as a lifeguard in Rockaway Beach, Queens, played ukelele and eventually became one of the foremost musical publishers in the business. Brown also produced musicals.

George Gard "Buddy" DeSylva was born in New York City, but moved to Azusa, California, as a teenager. He attended college at the University of Southern California just prior to World War I, and while there wrote theatricals. An author, producer, and publisher—with partners Brown and Henderson—the brilliant DeSylva had his first song published in 1917, *N'Everything*, introduced by Al Jolson. On Broadway, DeSylva's first show lyrics were written for *La La Lucille*. In 1931, DeSylva started his career as a Hollywood producer, even as the publishing firm continued.

Raymond Brost, later to be known as Henderson, was born in Buffalo, New York, and trained as a concert pianist at the Chicago Conservatory of Music. He became—as did so many songwriters—a song plugger for the Leo Feist music publishing firm, and later, an arranger for the Fred Fisher company. Henderson's first published song, *Humming*, with lyrics by Lew Brown, was in the ***Greenwich Village Follies***, circa early 1920s.

Brown Chronology

1917   *I May Be Gone for a Long, Long Time*. Brown (wm). His first published song.

1919   *Oh by Jingo, Oh by Gee, You're the Only Girl for Me*. Albert Von Tilzer/Brown. Composed by Von Tilzer (Chapter 1), this song was used in a musical called ***Linger Longer, Letty***.

1920   *I Used to Love You, But It's All Over Now*. Von Tilzer/Brown.

1924   *Shine*. Ford Dabney and Cecil Mack/Brown. A racist song.

1925   *I Wanna Go Where You Go, Do What You Do*. Sidney Clare/Brown and Cliff Friend.
        Birth of the Blues and *Black Bottom*. Brown, DeSylva, and Henderson (wm). From George White's ***Scandals***, on Broadway.
        I'd Climb the Highest Mountain. Sidney Clare/Brown.
        It All Depends On You. Brown, DeSylva, and Henderson (wm). From Jolson's ***Big Boy***, on Broadway.

1927   *Varsity Drag* and *The Best Things in Life Are Free*. Brown, DeSylva, and Henderson (wm). From their Broadway musical, ***Good News***.

1928   *Button Up Your Overcoat*. Brown, DeSylva, and Henderson (wm).
        Sonny Boy. Brown, DeSylva, and Henderson (wm). From Jolson's ***Singing Fool***.
        Together. Brown, DeSylva, and Henderson (wm). A great 1928 standard.
        You're the Cream in My Coffee. Brown, DeSylva, and Henderson (wm). From ***Hold Everything***, a Broadway musical.

1929   *If I Had a Talking Picture of You* and *Sunnyside Up*. Brown, DeSylva, and Henderson (wm). The threesome writing in Hollywood for the film, ***Sunnyside Up***.
        You Are My Lucky Star. Brown, DeSylva, and Henderson (wm). Back on Broadway writing for ***Follow Thru***.

1931   *The Thrill Is Gone, Life Is Just a Bowl of Cherries*, and, *That's Why Darkies Were Born*. DeSylva/Brown (wm). From George White's ***Scandals***.

1937   *That Old Feeling*. Sammy Fain/Brown. Oscar nominated song for the film, ***Walter Wanger's Vogues of 1938***.

1938   *Oh, Ma Ma*. Paolo Citorell/Brown and Rudy Vallee.

1939   *Beer Barrel Polka*. Jaromir Vejvocla/Brown (English lyrics). A tremendous hit for the Andrew Sisters.
        Comes Love. Sammy Stept and Charles Tobias/Brown. A fine ballad.

1942   *Don't Sit Under the Apple Tree and I Came Here to Talk for Joe*. Stept and Tobias/Brown. For the movie, ***Private Buckaroo***. The Andrews Sisters had another chart topper with *Don't Sit*.

DeSylva Chronology

1920   *Look for the Silver Lining*. Jerome Kern*/DeSylva. For ***Sally***, on Broadway.

1921   *April Showers*. Louis Silvers/DeSylva. For ***Bombo***, on Broadway. Al Jolson* made it into a biggie.

1922 *Do It Again*. George Gershwin*/DeSylva. A fine classic.
I'll Build a Stairway to Paradise. G. Gershwin/DeSylva and Arthur Francis. Arthur Francis was actually Ira Gershwin* using the two first names of his other siblings as his stage name. For George White's **Scandals**, on Broadway.
Kiss in the Dark. Victor Herbert*/DeSylva. For **Orange Blossoms**.

1923 *I Won't Say I Will, But I Won't Say I Won't*. Gershwin/DeSylva and Francis.

1924 *California Here I Come*. DeSylva, Al Jolson, and Joseph Meyer* (wm). For Broadway's **Bombo**.
Somebody Loves Me. Gershwin/DeSylva and Ballard MacDonald*. One of the finest of all American popular ballads.

1925 *If You Knew Susie Like I Knew Susie*. Joseph Meyer/DeSylva. Words also credited to Jolson.

1926 *When Day Is Done*. Robert Katscher/DeSylva. Katscher also composed *Good Evening Friends* with Irving Caesar* in 1931 for **The Wonder Bar**, starring Al Jolson.

1929 *I'm a Dreamer, Aren't We All?* Henderson/DeSylva.

1932 *Eadie Was a Lady* and *You're an Old Smoothie*. Nacio Herb Brown* and Richard Whiting*/DeSylva. From **Take a Chance**, on Broadway.

1939 *Wishing (Will Make it So)*. DeSylva (wm). For the film, **Love Affair**, with Irene Dunne, who sang it so very prettily.

Henderson Chronology

1923 *That Old Gang of Mine*. Henderson/Billy Rose and Mort Dixon. From the Ziegfeld **Follies**.

1924 *Follow the Swallow*. Henderson/Dixon.

1926 *Bye, Bye Blackbird*. Henderson/Dixon.

1935 *Animal Crackers (In My Soup)*. Henderson/Ted Koehler and Irving Caesar.

NACIO HERB BROWN, Composer (1896–1964)

Ignatio Herb Brown had an interesting life, which began in Deming, New Mexico, where his father was the town sheriff. Brown was educated at the Los Angeles High School of Musical Arts and became a vaudeville pianist. From 1916 to 1920, Brown operated a successful men's store and went on from there to a financially productive career in real estate. At the same time, Brown was a highly successful composer.

Chronology

1920 *Coral Sea*. Brown/King Zany (or Zang King). Zany's real name was Jack Doll. Paul Whiteman recorded the song.

1921 *When Buddah Smiles*. Brown/Arthur Freed. A fine musical pair and Brown's first hit. First recorded by Whiteman; later by Benny Goodman*.

1929 *You Were Meant For Me*. Brown/Freed. For the first full-length movie musical.

Singin' in the Rain. Brown/Freed. Written first for **Hollywood Revue**; later converted into the dancing/singing Gene Kelly classic on film.
Pagan Love Song. Brown/Freed. For the film, **The Pagan**.

1930   *Should I?* Brown/Freed. For the movie, **Lord Byron of Broadway**.

1931   *Paradise.* Brown and Gordon Clifford (wm). For the film, **A Woman Commands**.

1932   **Take a Chance.** Songs by Brown, Buddy DeSylva, and Richard Whiting. The Ethel Merman and Jack Haley Broadway musical, including: *Eadie Was a Lady* and *You're an Old Smoothie.*

1933   *Temptation.* Brown/Freed. For the movie, **Going Hollywood**.

1934   *All I Do Is Dream of You.* Brown/Freed. A hit from the film, **Sadie McKee**, starring Joan Crawford.

1935   *Alone.* Brown/Freed. Written for the classic Marx Brothers' comedy, **A Night at the Opera**.

1936   *You Are My Lucky Star, Broadway Rhythm*, and *I've Got a Feelin' You're Foolin'.* Brown/Freed. For the movie, **Broadway Melody**.
Good Morning. Brown/Freed. For the film, **Babes in Arms** with a very young Judy Garland.

1941   *You Stepped Out of a Dream.* Brown/Gus Kahn. For the film, **Ziegfeld Girl**.

1948   *Love Is Where You Find It.* Brown/Earl K. Brent. From the film, **Kissing Bandit**.

JOE BURKE, Composer (1884–1950)

Joseph A. Burke was born in Philadelphia, attended Catholic schools in that city, and graduated from the University of Pennsylvania (one of several songwriters in this book who went to that Ivy League bastion). He was a pianist from childhood and composed while still a schoolboy. Eventually he became a professional staff member of a New York publishing house.

Chronology

1925   *Oh How I Miss You Tonight.* Burke, Benny Davis, and Mark Fisher (wm). This vaudeville tune was Burke's first hit.

1926   *Tip Toe Through the Tulips.* Burke/Al Dubin. Used in the movie, **Gold Diggers of Broadway**.

1928/29   *Carolina Moon.* Burke and Davis (wm).

1930   *I'm Dancing with Tears in My Eyes* and *Kiss Waltz.* Burke/Dubin. From the film, **Dancing Sweeties**.

1935   *A Little Bit Independent, Moon Over Miami*, and *In a Little Gypsy Tearoom.* Burke/Edgar Leslie. Bob Crosby had a number 1 chart record with *Tearoom.*

1937   *It Looks Like Rain in Cherry Blossom Lane.* Burke/Leslie. A number 1 chart record for Guy Lombardo.

JOHNNY BURKE, Lyricist (1908–1964)

A most prolific Hollywood lyricist, Burke was born in Antioch, California, and studied at the Crane College of Music in Chicago and at the University of Wisconsin. A pianist, he was also employed by publishing firms in the late 1920s. His work with James Van Heusen, and the performances of those songs by Bing Crosby, is formidable. Burke's music was remembered and celebrated recently, with the creation and staging of a 1990s Broadway production based on his work, *Swinging on a Star*.

Chronology

1930 *The Boop-Boopa Doo Trot*. George A. Little/Burke. His first film song.

1933 *Annie Doesn't Live Here Anymore*. Harold Spina (Chapter 4)/Burke and Joe Young.

1936 *Pennies From Heaven*. Arthur Johnston*/Burke. A title song and an evergreen, created for Burke's first Crosby film.

1937 *The Moon Got in My Eyes*. Johnston/Burke. Sung by Bing Crosby in the movie, *Double or Nothing*.

1938 *Between a Kiss and a Sigh*. Johnston/Burke.
An Apple for the Teacher. James V. Monaco*/Burke. For the Crosby film, *The Starmaker*.

1939 *What's New?* Bob Haggart*/Burke. Haggart was an arranger and bassist in the fine Dixieland band, the Bob Crosby Bobcats. Bob was Bing's brother. The Bobcats recorded this great standard.
Oh, You Crazy Moon. James Van Heusen*/Burke. Their first collaboration.
Scatterbrain. Frankie Masters, Keene Kahn, Carl Bean, and Burke (wm). Masters was a bandleader and this was his band's theme song.

194? *La Cucaracha*. Unknown/Burke (English Lyrics). The famous Mexican folk song—with anglo words.

1940 *Polka Dots and Moonbeams* and *Imagination*. Van Heusen/Burke. Two hits so typical of the Big Band era tunes.
Only Forever. Van Heusen/Burke. For the Bing Crosby film, *Rhythm on the River*. The song climbed to number 1 on the charts.
Too Romantic. Van Heusen/Burke. A sweet and simple ballad for Crosby's movie, *Road to Singapore*.

1941 *Humpty Dumpty Heart*. Van Heusen/Burke. For the movie, *Playmates*.

1942 *It's Always You* and *Moonlight Becomes You*. Van Heusen/Burke. For Bing Crosby in the film *Road to Zanzibar*.

1943 *Sunday, Monday or Always*. Van Heusen/Burke. For the biographical film, *Dixie*, about minstrel/songwriter Daniel Decatur Emmet, played by Bing Crosby.

1944 *It Could Happen to You*. Van Heusen/Burke. A very pretty song for the movie *And the Angels Sing*.
Suddenly It's Spring. Van Heusen/Burke. For *Lady in the Dark*, the film version

of the Gertrude Lawrence hit stage musical. Ginger Rogers played Lawrence's part in the movie.

Swinging on a Star and *Going My Way*. Van Heusen/Burke. The songwriters won an Oscar for *Swinging*, from the 1944 film **Going My Way**.

Like Someone in Love. Van Heusen/Burke. A fine ballad for the Dinah Shore film **Belle of the Yukon**.

1945 *Aren't You Glad You're You*? Van Heusen/Burke. For **The Bells of Saint Mary's**, the film sequel of sorts to the enormously popular **Going My Way**. The title song for **Bells** was written by Emmett Adams/Douglas Furber in 1917. Furber wrote *The Lambeth Walk* in 1937 with Noel Gay (wm) and *Limehouse Blues* (Phillip Braham/Furber) in 1924.

1946 *Personality* and *It's Anybody's Spring*. Van Heusen/Burke. Two more fine hits, for the Crosby and Hope film, **Road to Utopia**. Johnny Mercer had a big hit with *Personality*.

1948 *But Beautiful, You Don't Have to Know the Language*, and *My Heart Is a Hobo*. Van Heusen/Burke. For the movie, **Road to Rio**.

1953 *Here's That Rainy Day*. Van Heusen/Burke. Written for the Broadway musical **Carnival in Flanders**. It may have been their best ballad, ever. It certainly was a classic for Sinatra and others.

1954 *Misty*. Errol Garner*/Burke. An absolutely wonderful collaboration.

IRVING CAESAR, Lyricist (1859–1996)

Caesar was not related to Julius or Sid. Isidor Caesar was a graduate of CCNY in New York and became an automobile dealer, a stenographer, and a friend of George Gershwin*. He wrote for stage shows, radio, and film. Caesar's honor and whatever fame came from it, however, was derived from his lyrics for children's safety songs.

Chronology

1919 *Swanee*. George Gershwin/Caesar. For Al Jolson's Broadway musical, **Sinbad**.

1924 *Tea For Two*. Vincent Youmans/Caesar. For the show, **No No Nannette**.

1925 *Sometimes I'm Happy*. Youmans/Caesar. From **A Night Out**, a stage production that did not make it past Philadelphia. However, Youmans recycled the song, putting it into the 1927 musical, **Hit the Deck**.

1928 *Crazy Rhythm*. Joseph Meyer*/Caesar and Roger Wolfe Kahn.

1930 *Just a Gigolo*. Leonello Casucci/Caesar (English lyrics). Originally written in Italy, Ted Lewis brought this song up to number 1 on the charts. Bing Crosby also had a hit with it, as did Louis Prima and spouse, Keely Smith, many years later.

1935 *Animal Crackers (In My Soup)*. Ray Henderson/Caesar and Ted Koehler. For the Shirley Temple film, **Curly Top**.

1936 *Is It True What They Say About Dixie*? Sammy Lerner, Gerald Marks, and Caesar (wm). For a Deanna Durbin movie, originally. Jolson made it into a standard.

SAMMY CAHN, Lyricist (1913–1983)

New York City-born Cahn loved to talk with people, but that did not keep him from being an extremely productive and successful songwriter. Featured onstage as a violinist when he was very young, Cahn met up with Saul Chaplin* and began to lead local bands. Songwriting with Chaplin, Cahn followed the lead of Arlen*/Koehler and wrote for the Cotton Club revues. Early on, in 1933, Cahn teamed up with Jule Styne* in Hollywood, and began one of the outstanding songwriting partnerships in American music.

Broadway Chronology

1944 *Guess I'll Hang My Tears Out to Dry*. Jule Styne/Cahn. Haunting ballad from the Broadway production, **Glad to See Ya**. That title was the longtime greeting of burlesque, film, and television veteran, Phil Silvers.

1945 *Nancy (With the Laughing Face)*. James Van Heusen/Cahn and Phil Silvers. Although not used in the theatre or on film, the trio wrote this tribute for Frank Sinatra for his daughter.

1947 *Papa, Won't You Dance With Me?* and *I Still Get Jealous*. Styne/Cahn. Two of the most engaging songs from the musical hit of that season, another Phil Silvers show, **High Button Shoes**. Nannete Fabray was Silvers' co-star.

1965 *Everybody Has a Right to Be Wrong*. Van Heusen/Cahn. For **Skyscraper**, the Broadway musical version of Elmer Rice's *Dream Girl*.

1966 *Walking Happy*. Scored by Van Heusen/Cahn. A happy title song for a rather unhappy twenty-week Broadway musical.

1970 *Look to the Lillies*. Scored by Cahn. His last attempt on Broadway was a musical version of **Lillies of the Field**.

Hollywood and Tin Pan Alley Chronology

1933 *Five Minutes More*. Jule Styne/Cahn. For the B-movie, **The Sweetheart of Sigma Chi**. Frank Sinatra (Chapter 4) converted the tune and made it into a hit when the film was re-made in 1946.

1934 *Rhythm Is Our Business*. Cahn, Saul Chaplin, and Jimmie Lunceford (wm). It became Lunceford's (the famed swinging bandleader) theme song.

1935 *Shoe Shine Boy*. Cahn, Chaplin, Mann Holiner, and L. E. Freeman (wm). A hit.

1937 *If It's the Last Thing I Do*. Chaplin/Cahn.
Bei Mir Bist Du Schoen (To Me You're Pretty). Chaplin/Cahn. Remake of a Yiddish song by Secunda/Jacobs; a super World War II–era hit for the Andrews Sisters.

1938 *Please Be Kind*. Chaplin/Cahn.

1942 *It Seems to Me I've Heard That Song Before*. Styne/Cahn. An Oscar nominee from the film, **Youth on Parade**, losing to the classic, *White Christmas*.

1944 *I'll Walk Alone*. Styne/Cahn.
There Goes That Song Again and *Poor Little Rhode Island*. Styne/Cahn. For the film, **Carolina Blues**.

1945   *I Fall in Love Too Easily* and *The Charm of You*. Styne/Cahn. From the movie, ***Anchors Aweigh***. *I Fall* was a Sinatra smash and got an Academy Award nomination, but lost to Rodgers and Hammerstein's *It Might As Well Be Spring*.
I Should Care. Axel Stordahl and Paul Weston/Cahn. A lovely ballad for the film, ***Thrill of a Romance***.
Day by Day. Stordahl and Weston/Cahn. A winner for Sinatra in 1945; done well by Carmen McRae later.
Can't You Read Between the Lines? Styne/Cahn.
Let It Snow, Let It Snow, Let It Snow. Styne/Cahn.

1946   *Things We Did Last Summer*. Styne/Cahn.

1948   *It's Magic* and *It's You or No One*. Styne/Cahn. For the film, ***Romance on the High Seas***. *It's Magic* was a very popular ballad for Doris Day and the third Oscar-nominated song for Styne and Cahn.

1950   *Melancholy Rhapsody*. Ray Heindorf/Cahn. From the Kirk Douglas film, ***Young Man with a Horn***; a favorite for trumpet player/writers.
Be My Love. Nicholas Brodzsky/Cahn. Fourth Oscar nomination for Cahn, from the film ***Toast of New Orleans***; sung by Mario Lanza.
Wonder Why. Brodzsky/Cahn. For the 1950 film, ***Rich, Young and Pretty***.

1951   ***Two Tickets to Broadway***. Film Story by Cahn. Cahn teamed up with Bob Crosby for the film's forgettable tune *Let's Make Comparisons*; and with Styne and Leo Robin for two other unmemorable movie songs.
Because You're Mine. Nicholas Brodzsky/Cahn.

1952   ***April in Paris***. Songs by Vernon Duke/Cahn. Six songs within their movie musical score.

1955   *Three Coins in the Fountain*. Styne/Cahn. Film title song—and the Academy Award winner that year.
Pete Kelly's Blues. Heindorf/Cahn. Fine film and fine Cahn title song.
Our Town. Songs by James Van Heusen and Cahn. An interruption in Cahn's movie works, this Thornton Wilder classic was produced for television. Frank Sinatra played Wilder's Announcer and established the score's *Love and Marriage* as a standard.
The Tender Trap. Van Heusen/Cahn. Their television success made them believe there really was something to their new partnership. This film title song seemed to confirm it when Sinatra busted the charts with it.
I'll Never Stop Loving You. Brodzsky/Cahn. Another Oscar-nominated song, from the film ***Love Me or Leave Me***.
Same Old Saturday Night. Frank Reardon/Cahn. Written for Frank Sinatra. Overall 1955 was a very good year for Cahn: from all of the above to lyrics for film scores written by the likes of Bronislaw Kaper and Alfred Newman.

1956   ***Written on the Wind***. Soundtrack by Victor Young/Cahn.
Somebody Up There Likes Me. Soundtrack title song by Bronislaw Kaper and Cahn. A film starring Paul Newman.
Hey Jealous Lover. Bee Walker and Kay Twomey/Cahn.

1957   *All the Way*. Van Heusen/Cahn. An Oscar winner from the film, ***The Joker Is Wild***, an excellent story about Joe E. Lewis. Sinatra acted and sang the main part.

1958 *Some Came Running*. Van Heusen/Cahn. Soundtrack title song for this Sinatra
      film.
      Only the Lonely. Van Heusen/Cahn. A haunting and beautiful song, which mavens
      like Will Friedwald consider Cahn's best.

1959 *High Hopes*. Van Heusen/Cahn. His third Oscar winner, from the film *A Hole
      in the Head* starring Frank Sinatra, Edward G. Robinson, and Thelma Ritter. It
      became John F. Kennedy's 1960 presidential campaign theme song.
      When No One Cares. Van Heusen/Cahn. Sinatra's last recorded saloon song for
      Capitol Records.
      The Best of Everything. Alfred Newman/Cahn. Film title song. Johnny Mathis
      recorded it well.

1960 *The Second Time Around*. Van Heusen/Cahn. From the film, *High Time*. Cahn
      was recently divorced from his wife when he wrote these lyrics.

1961 *By Love Possessed*. Elmer Bernstein/Cahn. Soundtrack title song lyrics.
      A *Pocketful of Miracles* and *All My Tomorrows*. Van Heusen/Cahn. The *Pocketful*
      film title song and *Tomorrows* were two more Sinatra hits.

1962 *Call Me Irresponsible*. Van Heusen/Cahn. Oscar winner number four from the
      film, *Poppa's Delicate Condition*.

1964 *My Kind of Town (Chicago Is)*. Van Heusen/Cahn. Academy Award–nominated
      song from a "Rat Pack" baddie, *Robin and the 7 Hoods*.
      Love Is a Bore. Van Heusen/Cahn. Written for Barbra Streisand.

1965 *September of My Years*. Van Heusen/Cahn. Album title song for the balladeer
      who sang so many Van Heusen and Cahn songs, Francis Albert Sinatra.

1968 *Star!* Neil Hefti/Cahn. Nominated for an Oscar, from the film *The Odd Couple*.
      Lost to Legrand/Bergmans' (Chapter 3) *Windmills of Your Mind*.

1972 *A Touch of Class*. Songs by George Barrie/Cahn. Barrie was then Chairman of
      Fabergé.

1973 *Let Me Try Again*. Paul Anka (Chapter 5)/Cahn.

HOAGY CARMICHAEL, Composer/Lyricist (1899–1981)

Hoagland Howard Carmichael was a musical genius, jazz pianist, performer,
and Hoosier. He was born in the college town of Bloomington, Indiana, where
his mother, a fine ragtime pianist herself, influenced his interest in music. Carmichael was a passionate jazzman early on; he played throughout high school
and college (at Indiana University), where he earned a law degree. His education, however, was periodically interrupted by his musical traveling. A member
of the Wolverines, a fine aggregation of jazz musicians, Carmichael also played
with Paul Whiteman. He became one of the New York "expatriates" of the
jazz world, playing Dixieland with the likes of Eddie Condon and Bix Beiderbecke—a dear friend and idol of Carmichael's. It was during Carmichael's short-
lived practice of law that he composed *Star Dust*, a song that has been recorded
thousands of times. He also wrote tunes with his old Woverine friends, Dick

Voynow and Stuart Gorrell. *"Sometimes I Wonder Why,"* Carmichael's 1965 autobiography, was written with Stephen Longstreet.

Chronology

1924   *Riverboat Shuffle*. Carmichael, Dick Voynow, and Irving Mills (wm). It seems that Irving Mills, the publisher, took creative credit for far too many Carmichael songs.

1927   *Washboard Blues*. Carmichael/Fred B. Callahan. This song was recorded by Paul Whiteman with Bix Beiderbecke on cornet and, for the first time on record, Carmichael singing. Mills apparently put his name on this one a year later.

1928   *Star Dust*. Carmichael/Mitchell Parish*. Carmichael composed this classic while playing piano one night at the Book Nook on the Indiana campus. Gorrell suggested Hoagy had written a "stomp" (a jazz tune for dancing marked by a driving rhythm). In his book, *Tin Pan Alley*, David Jasen reports that on October 31, 1927, Carmichael recorded *Star Dust* with Elmer Seidel's band (which they called Hoagy Carmichael and His Pals) on the Gennett label. It was then published by Mills Music as an instrumental number. In May 1929, Parish added the words. Isham Jones' orchestra recorded *Star Dust* in 1930; it was a hit for Jones and his pianist/arranger, Victor Young. In 1936, Benny Goodman's version, arranged by Fletcher Henderson, and Tommy Dorsey's arrangement, with a vocal by Edythe Wright, on the flip side of the same 78—came out. In 1941, Artie Shaw made a classic recording of the song with Billy Butterfield's fine trumpet solo. While Jasen calls the Carmichael/Seidel band recording the best, my preference is Shaw's—or Nat King Cole's later vocal.

1929   *Rockin' Chair*. Carmichael (wm). Carmichael and Louis Armstrong recorded this bluesy evergreen.

1930   *Georgia on My Mind*. Carmichael/Stuart Gorrell. This song became the anthem for its southern state namesake.

1931   *Lazy River*. Carmichael and Sidney Arodin (wm).

1933   *Lazy Bones*. Carmichael/Johnny Mercer. This collaboration started a lifelong friendship between these two fascinating artists.
       One Morning in May. Carmichael/Parish.

1936   *Little Old Lady*. Carmichael/Stanley Adams. Used in the Broadway musical, ***The Show Is On***.

1938   *Small Fry*, *Two Sleepy People*, and *Heart and Soul*. Carmichael/Frank Loesser. The third song was written for the film, ***Sing You Sinners***.

1939   *I Get Along Without You Very Well*. Carmichael/Jane Brown Thompson.
       Blue Orchids. Carmichael (wm).

1940   *The Nearness of You*. Carmichael/Ned Washington. One of the prettiest of all ballads.

1942   *Skylark*. Carmichael/Mercer.
       Lamplighter's Serenade. Carmichael/Paul Francis Webster.

1944   *Baltimore Oriole*. Carmichael/Webster. A quirky song, sung so well by Carmen McRae.

How Little We Know. Carmichael/Mercer. For the Bogart and Bacall film, **To Have and To Have Not**. Carmichael sang it in the movie, toothpick in mouth, fingers on the piano keys, and all.

1945 *Memphis in June.* Carmichael/Webster.

1946 *Ole Buttermilk Sky.* Carmichael/Jack Brooks. For the movie, **Canyon Passage**.

1947 *Ivy.* Carmichael (wm). Film title song.

1951 *In the Cool, Cool, Cool of the Evening.* Carmichael/Mercer. An Academy Award–winning song from their score for the film, **Here Comes the Groom**. Bing Crosby sang it.
      My Resistance Is Low. Carmichael/Harold Adamson. For the film, **Las Vegas Story**.

SAUL CHAPLIN, Composer (1912–1997)

Born Saul Kaplan, in New York, he was the bandleading, songwriting partner of lyricist Sammy Cahn*. Chaplin was a vocal arranger and highly regarded composer/musical director in Hollywood, with such films to his credit as **An American in Paris, Cover Girl, The Jolson Story**, and **Summer Stock**.

Chronology

1934 *Rhythm Is Our Business.* Chaplin/Cahn. For bandleader Jimmie Lunceford.

1936 *Shoe Shine Boy,* Chaplin/Cahn.
      Until the Real Thing Comes Along. Chaplin, Mann Holiner, L. E. Freeman, and Cahn (wm).
      Dedicated to You. Chaplin, Hy Zaret and Cahn (wm).

1937 *If It's the Last Thing I Do.* Chaplin/Cahn.

1938 *Please Be Kind.* Chaplin/Cahn.

1946 *Anniversary Song.* Chaplin and Al Jolson (Chapter 1) (wm). This was a Chaplin adaptation, not a composition, from *Danube Waves.* From **The Jolson Story** film.

1950 *You, Wonderful You.* Chaplin and Harry Warren*/Jack Brooks.

GEORGE M. COHAN, Composer/Lyricist (1878–1942)

George Michael Cohan was born in Providence, Rhode Island, to a very active show business family. He was supposedly taken on stage before he could walk or talk. As one of The Four Cohans, he played fiddle in vaudeville at age 4 and wrote sketches for the family's act at age 11. Cohan became one of the world's foremost entertainers, director/producers, and stage authors. He was the star of many of his own shows and a partner of Broadway mogul Sam Harris. Cohan starred as an actor in **Ah Wilderness** in 1934 and in **I'd Rather Be Right** in 1937. The 1986 *Grove Dictionary of American Music* dubbed Cohan "Mr. Broadway."

While he may well have been placed in Chapter 1, his prominence and influence on popular song, especially in the patriotic genre, is such that he is included in the main body of the book. Cohan wrote more than 500 songs. In a near perfect imitation of Cohan, film actor James Cagney sang and danced his way through the fine biopic of Cohan, **Yankee Doodle Dandy**.

Chronology

1904   *Yankee Doodle Boy* and *Give My Regards to Broadway*. Cohan (wm). From the stage musical, **Little Johnny Jones**, with story, music, and lyrics by Cohan.

1905   *Mary's a Grand Old Name*. Cohan (wm). For the production, **Forty-Five Minutes to Broadway**.

1906   *You're a Grand Old Flag*. Cohan (wm). From **George Washington, Jr**.

1907   *Harrigan*. Cohan (wm). From **Fifty Miles From Boston**.

1917   *Over There*. Cohan (wm). The classic World War I song.

CY COLEMAN, Composer (1929–   )

Seymour Kaufman, who took the stage name Cy Coleman, was born in the Bronx, New York, and by the time he was in his early 20s he wrote a hit song. A child prodigy pianist, Coleman has performed in concert, on records, and in night clubs. His prominence as a Broadway composer in the popular idiom— albeit much of it gained at the end of, and after, the Golden Age—places him among the great songwriters of that genre.

Chronology

1952   *Why Try to Change Me Now?* Coleman/Joseph McCarthy, Jr. McCarthy was the son of Joseph McCarthy, Sr. (Chapter 1).

1957   *Witchcraft* and *I Walk a Little Faster*. Coleman/Carolyn Leigh*.

1958   *Firefly*. Coleman/Leigh. A big hit for Tony Bennett.

1959   *The Best Is Yet to Come*. Coleman/Leigh.

1960   *Hey Look Me Over* and *Give Me a Little Whistle*. Coleman/Leigh. From their Broadway musical, **Wildcat**.

1962   *I've Got Your Number* and *Real Live Girl*. Coleman/Leigh. From their Broadway production, **Little Me.**
        Pass Me By. Coleman/Leigh. For the fine Cary Grant film, **Father Goose**.

1964   *When in Rome*. Coleman/Leigh. Another Tony Bennett hit.

1965   **Sweet Charity**. Scored by Cy Coleman and Dorothy Fields. Their wonderful musical included these two Broadway standards: *Hey Big Spender* and *If My Friends Could See Me Now*.

1980   *The Colors of My Life*. Coleman/Michael Stewart. For the Broadway musical, **Barnum**.

BETTY COMDEN, Lyricist (1915–   ) and
ADOLPH GREEN, Lyricist (1915–   )

These extraordinarily talented New Yorkers both went to New York University and teamed up, first, as entertainers in nightclubs; their act, *The Revuers*, also featured Judy Holliday. Comden and Green began their Broadway career in the mid-1940s and were still writing librettos and lyrics fifty years later—and entertaining, too. Working only with each other as lyricists and scriptwriters, many people believe them to be husband and wife. Not so; Green is married to comedienne Phyllis Newman.

Chronology

1944 **On the Town**. Leonard Bernstein/Comden and Green. The show, based on Robbins' memorable ballet, *Fancy Free*, included these great songs: *Lonely Town; Some Other Time; New York, New York (It's a Wonderful Town)*, and *Lucky To Be Me*. The music in the film version five years later, with new songs by Roger Edens and Comden and Green, somehow was just not the same.

1945 **Billion Dollar Baby**. Morton Gould/Comden and Green. A Broadway run of seven months, no more.

1947 *The French Lesson*. Edens/Comden and Green. The duo's only song for their own first Hollywood screenplay, **Good News**.

1949 *The Right Girl for Me, Strictly USA*, and *It's Fate Baby, It's Fate*. Edens/Comden and Green. Their lively score for the Frank Sinatra (Chapter 4) and Gene Kelly hit film **Take Me Out to the Ball Game**. Only the title song was written by someone else.

1952 *Moses Supposes*. Edens/Comden and Green. These songwriters' only music in Gene Kelly's classic film, **Singin' in the Rain**.

1954 **Wonderful Town**. Bernstein/Comden and Green. The second "town" show for this trio, featuring the songs, *O-HI-O* and *Conga*.
      Neverland and *Hook's Waltz*. Jule Styne*/Comden and Green. These two songs were commissioned by the producers of **Peter Pan** and were memorable additions to the original score by Mark Charlap and Carolyn Leigh.

1955 **It's Always Fair Weather**. Songs by Andre Previn/Comden and Green. Probably the best-known song from this excellent Gene Kelly musical motion picture is *I Like Myself*.

1956 **Bells Are Ringing**. Songs by Styne/Comden and Green. This Broadway smash hit starred Comden and Green's old pal from their *Revuer* days, Judy Holliday. The fine songs included: *Just in Time, The Party's Over*, and *It's a Perfect Relationship*.

1958 **Say Darling**. Styne/Comden and Green. More Broadway music.

1960 **Do Re Mi**. Songs by Styne/Comden and Green. *Make Someone Happy* is the sentimental standard from this Broadway musical.

1961 *Come Once in a Lifetime*. Styne/Comden and Green. A nice ballad from Broadway's **Subways Are for Sleeping**.

1964   *Fade Out, Fade In*. Styne/Comden and Green. Still more Broadway music.

1967   *Now's the Time*. Styne/Comden and Green. From their *Hallelujah, Baby* on Broadway.

1974   *Lorelei*. Styne/Comden and Green.

1978   *On The Twentieth Century*. Cy Coleman/Comden and Green. A new team—and more music for Broadway.

CON CONRAD, Composer/Lyricist (1891–1938)

In musical anthologies, Conrad's real name has been spelled Konrad A. Dobert and Conrad Dober. Born in New York, he began his musical career as a pianist and entertainer. On to Hollywood, he was the first composer to win an Academy Award.

Chronology

1912   *Down in Dear Old New Orleans*. Conrad and Jay Whidden (wm). His first published song.

1918   *Oh! Frenchy*. Conrad (wm). His first hit.

1920   *Margie*. Conrad and J. Russel Robinson (Chapter 1)/Benny Davis.
       Singing the Blues. Conrad and Robinson/Sam Lewis and Joe Young.

1921   *Ma, He's Making Eyes at Me*. Conrad/Sidney Clare (Chapter 4). A huge Eddie Cantor hit.

1923   *Barney Google (With His Great Big Google-y Eyes)*. Conrad and Billy Rose (wm). Based on a popular comic strip of the time.
       You've Got to See Mama Ev'ry Night (Or You Can't See Mama At All). Conrad and Rose (wm). A typical number for—and introduced by—Sophie Tucker.

1931   *You Call It Madness (And I Call It Love)*. Conrad (wm). Crooner Russ Columbo's theme song.

1934   *Champagne Waltz*. Conrad, Milton Drake, and Ben Oakland (wm).
       The Continental. Conrad/Herb Magidson. The first song winner of the Academy Award.

J. FRED COOTS, Composer (1897–1985)

John Frederick Coots was born in Brooklyn, New York, and was a childhood composer and piano prodigy. He worked on Tin Pan Alley as a stock clerk, then worked his way up to song demonstrator and, finally, as a staff composer for shows and revues. Coots began his Broadway composing career in 1922 and contributed to such musicals as *Sally, Irene and Mary, Spice of 1922, Hanky Panky, Hello to Everybody*, and *Greenwich Village Follies*. In 1924, teaming up with Sigmund Romberg, Coots co-composed the score for *Artists and Models*.

Chronology

1928 *Doin' the Racoon*. Coots/Herb Magidson and Raymond Klages. His first hit—it happened in Hollywood, composing for the film, **The Time, the Place and the Girl**. Raymond Klages wrote the words to Jesse Greer's music for *Just You, Just Me* in 1929.

1929 *A Precious Thing Called Love*. Coots/Lou Davis. For the film, **Shopworn Angel**—it sold two million copies of sheet music. *Why (Is There a Rainbow in the Sky)*? and *Cross Your Fingers*. Coots, Benny Davis and and Arthur Swanstrom (wm). From the Broadway stage musical, **Sons O'Guns**. Four years later, Swanstrom and Louis Alter wrote *Come Up and See Me Sometime* for the film, **Take a Chance**. Interestingly, *Come Up* was introduced by Lillian Roth—not Mae West.

1932 *I Wouldn't Trade the Silver in My Mother's Hair for All the Gold in the World*. Coots and "Little Jack" Little (wm). Possibly one of the longest titled songs in musical history.

1934 *For All We Know*. Coots/Sam Lewis. A classic and beautiful ballad. Another song with the same title was written and performed by the Carpenters in 1970, and attained considerable popularity.

1936 *Until Today*. Coots and Oscar Levant/Benny Davis. Fletcher Henderson penned a very fine arrangement of this one. *Doin' the Suzie Q* and *Frisco Flo*. Coots/Davis. For the **Cotton Club Parade**.

1938 *You Go To My Head*. Coots/Haven Gillespie. A classic performed by so many of our best musicians. It is often mistaken as a Cole Porter song, perhaps because of its beautiful melody and outstanding lyrics.
Santa Claus Is Coming to Town. Coots/Gillespie. Certainly a different kind of hit—demonstrating this duo's versatility.

1942 *Goodbye Mama, I'm Off to Yokahoma*. Coots (wm). A popular World War II novelty-cum-ballad.

SAM COSLOW, Composer/Lyricist (1902–1982)

Coslow was born in Brooklyn, New York. He graduated from Erasmus Hall High School (a secondary school whose famous alum include singer Barbra Streisand and quarterback Sid Luckman); eventually he became a writer, a publisher, and a Hollywood producer. Coslow was also in partnership with James Roosevelt, FDR's son, in an enterprise known as Soundies. These short films, based on popular songs, were way ahead of their time—and did not succeed in their marketplace the same way music videos have in ours. As a film producer, Coslow won an Oscar for **Heavenly Music**. He wrote a number of original scripts and the songs for the film, **Copacabana**. Several undated songs had lyrics added by Coslow. *Juanita*, a Spanish folk song composed in 1850, and *Kitten on the Keys*, a 1921 instrumental by Zez Confrey, were lyricized by Coslow. *Mr. Pagannini (If You Can't Sing/Swing It)* is also credited to Coslow.

Chronology

1930   *Sing You Sinners*. Coslow and W. Franke Harling (wm). For the film, ***Honey***.

1931   *Just One More Chance*. Coslow and Arthur Johnston (wm). Bing Crosby made into a number 1 hit.

1932   *(Sweet) Moon Song*. Coslow and Johnston (wm). It sounds so very Irving Berlinesque.

1933   *Thanks* and *The Day You Came Along*. Coslow and Johnston (wm). For the film, ***Too Much Harmony***, with Bing Crosby*.
       Down the Old Ox Road. Coslow and Johnston (wm). For the movie, ***College Humor***.

1934   *My Old Flame*. Johnston/Coslow. Film song for ***Belle of the '90s***, starring Mae West.
       Cocktails for Two. Johnston/Coslow.

1946   *Song of the South*. Johnston/Coslow. Coslow's title song contribution to Johnston's soundtrack for this Disney movie.

NOEL COWARD, Composer/Lyricist (1899–1973)

A quadruple threat of the entertainment business, British-born Noel Pierce Coward was a playwright, producer, director, composer, and lyricist. The stories, films, and song hits from this true renaissance man continue to be enjoyed throughout the world.

Chronology

1929   *I'll See You Again*. Coward (wm). Written for his opera, ***Bittersweet***.

1930   *Someday I'll Find You*. Coward (wm). For his play, ***Private Lives***.

1931   *Mad Dogs and Englishmen*. Coward (wm). For Broadway's third ***Little Show***.

1934   *I'll Follow My Secret Heart*. Coward (wm). Written for his musical, ***Conversation Piece***.

1935   *Mad About the Boy*. Coward (wm). From his musical, ***Words and Music***.

BING CROSBY, Lyricist (1904–1977)

The legendary crooner, christened Harry Lillis Crosby, was born in Spokane, Washington. He attended Gonzaga College in Spokane and later its law school. Crosby began his magnificent career as a singer with the Delta Rhythm Boys. Crosby and his partners, Harry Barris (Chapter 4) and Al Rinker (the latter was Mildred Bailey's brother), sang in a jazz style. They were hired by Paul Whiteman* and Bing made some fine cuts with the so-called King of Jazz. Crosby went on to great fame as an actor and made an enormous fortune in such areas as frozen orange juice and other enterprises. He was once a part owner of the Pittsburgh Pirates baseball franchise. Honored with award after award, Crosby has been called (along with Louis Armstrong*) the most influential of all popular singers.

Chronology

1931 *Where the Blue of the Night Meets the Gold of the Day.* Fred Ahlert*/Crosby and Roy Turk*.

1932 *(I Don't Stand a) Ghost of a Chance with You.* Victor Young*/Crosby and Ned Washington*.

MACK DAVID, Composer/Lyricist (1912–   )

Mack David is the older of the two songwriting brothers (Hal David is known for his collaboration with Burt Bacharach, Chapter 3). He has written more than one thousand songs. A New Yorker who attended Cornell University and Saint John's Law School, David wrote his first song while studying to become a lawyer. In Hollywood for several decades, he wrote television scores as well. Most memorable is his work for the top vocalists of the Big Band era. While primarily known as a lyricist, Mack David has composed, arranged, and adapted music. In 1939, he and conductor Andre Kostalanetz did just that to Tchaikovsky's *Fifth Symphony*, turning it into *Moon Love*. In 1940 they converted Petr Ilyich's *Andante Cantabile* to *On the Isle of May*.

Chronology

1939 *Blue and Sentimental.* Count Basie*/David and Jerry Livingston*.

1940 *Falling Leaves.* Frankie Carle/David. Introduced by one of the schmaltziest of the big bands, Horace Heidt and His Musical Knights.

1942 *Take Me.* Rube Bloom*/David.
      Sinner Kissed an Angel. Ray Joseph/David.

1944 *Candy.* Alex Kramer and Joan Whitney (Chapter 4)/David. Johnny Mercer/Pied Pipers hit. David wrote a number of film scores with this husband and wife team.

1945 *I'm Just a Lucky So and So.* Duke Ellington*/David.

1946 *La Vie En Rose.* Alex Louigay/David. This French-American collaboration is now a standard.
      Chi Baba Chi Baba. Jerry Livingston*, Al Hoffman*, and David (wm). A Perry Como hit.

1949 *Bibbi-Di, Bobbi-Di Boo, The Work Song,* and *A Dream Is a Wish Your Heart Makes.* Livingston, Hoffman, and David (wm). For the Disney/RKO co-production, **Cinderella.** *Bibbi-Di* was an Oscar nominee.

1951 *Cherry Pink and Apple Blossom White.* Alex Louigay/David. A soundtrack theme for the film **Underwater**. It was a number 1 Billboard chart record as played by Prez Prado.

1953 *Baby, Baby, Baby.* Livingston and David (wm).

1959/ *77 Sunset Strip, Surfside 6,* and *Hawaiian Eye.* Livingston and David (wm). The
  60 duo wrote the soundtrack title songs for these three popular television series.

1965 *The Ballad of Cat Ballou.* Livingston/David. The film's title song.
      Walk on the Wild Side. Elmer Bernstein/David. David's collaboration with this composer of many well-known film scores and title songs. Film title song.

BENNY DAVIS, Lyricist (1895–1979)

Although he was born in Brooklyn, New York, Benny Davis grew up in Portland, Oregon. By the age of fourteen he was already a vaudeville singer and dancer. He acted, was an emcee for a variety of productions in show business, and also managed a few night clubs in Atlantic City and Philadelphia. Davis was known to have helped many young performers in their careers.

Chronology

1917 *Goodbye Broadway, Hello France.* Billy Baskette/Davis and C. Francis Reisner. A big World War I hit.

1920 *Margie.* J. Russel Robinson (Chapter 1) and Con Conrad/Davis.

1921 *I'm Nobody's Baby.* Davis, Lester Santly, and Milton Ager (Chapter 4) (wm).

1924 *Oh, How I Miss You Tonight.* Joe Burke and Mark Fisher/Davis. Fisher was a co-composer of the universally known song, *When You're Smiling,* along with Larry Shay and Joe Goodwin.

1926 *Baby Face.* Harry Akst*/Davis.

1928 *Carolina Moon.* Burke/Davis.

1930 *I Still Get a Thrill.* J. Fred Coots/Davis.

1942 *All I Need Is You.* Davis, Peter DeRose*, and Mitchell Parish* (wm).

1943 *There Goes My Heart.* Abner Silver/Davis. From the film, *The Heat's On*. Silver co-wrote *No, No, A Thousand Times, No* with Al Sherman and Al Lewis.

EDGAR DELANGE, Composer/Lyricist (1904–1949) and WILL HUDSON, Composer (1908–1981)

DeLange was born in Long Island City, Queens, New York, and attended the University of Pennsylvania. His first career was as a Hollywood stunt man; he left that strange world and became an organizer and leader of dance bands. For a while, his co-leader was Hudson. Will Hudson, of Barstow, California, was educated in Detroit, Michigan. He began his musical career as an orchestra arranger and eventually formed his own band. He also worked as a staff composer at a music publishing company. Hudson served in World War II and after that, enrolled as a composition student at the Julliard School of Music, in New York. He wrote for McKinney's Cotton Pickers, Andy Kirk, Earl "Fatha" Hines, Fletcher Henderson, Louis Armstrong, Don Redman, and Jimmie Lunceford.

Chronology

1934 *Moonglow.* DeLange and Hudson/Irving Mills.

1935 *Hobo on Park Avenue.* DeLange and Hudson (wm). Their own band's theme song.

1936 *Organ Grinder's Swing.* Hudson/Mitchell Parish and Irving Mills. A hit.

1938 *Deep in a Dream.* James Van Heusen*/DeLange.

1939   *All This and Heaven, Too.* Van Heusen/DeLange. From ***Swingin' the Dream*** on Broadway.

1940   *Shake Down The Stars.* Van Heusen/DeLange.
Heaven Can Wait. Van Heusen/DeLange.

1942   *String of Pearls.* Jerry Gray/DeLange.
Along the Navajo Trail. DeLange, Larry Markes, and Dick Charles (wm). Markes and Charles also wrote *Mad About Him, Sad About Him, How Can I Be Glad Without Him* in 1941.
Just As Though You Were Here. J. Benson Brooks/DeLange.

1946   *Do You Know What It Means to Miss New Orleans?* Louis Alter/DeLange. For the film, ***New Orleans***.

GENE DEPAUL, Composer (1919–1988) and DON RAYE, Lyricist (1909–   )

DePaul was born in New York City; graduated from Benjamin Franklin High School; and went on to become a pianist, vocal arranger, and composer. He had a swinging, lively, and easily recognizable style of music. Raye was born in Washington, DC, and christened Donald MacRae Wilhoite, Jr. A champion dancer—and in vaudeville from 1924 to 1926—he won prizes for his Black Bottom and Charleston performances. In 1937, Raye started his studies in advertising at New York University and, whether successful in that noble profession or not, he did write some fine lyrics.

Chronology

1937   *For Dancers Only.* Sy Oliver/Raye and Vic Schoen. An early Raye hit and Jimmie Lunceford's theme song.

1940   *Your Red Wagon.* Richard Jones/Raye. A big Count Basie hit.
I Love You Much Too Much. Alex Olshey and Chaim Towber (Original wm); Raye (English lyrics). Adapted from Olshey and Towber's Yiddish song.
Rhumboogie. Hughie Prince/Raye. From the film, ***Argentine Nights***. A big Andrews Sisters hit.
Beat Me Daddy Eight to the Bar. Prince and Eleanor Sheehy/Raye. Will Bradley and Ray McKinley had a hit with this boogie woogie tune.

1941   *Cow Cow Boogie.* Gene DePaul, Raye, and Benny Carter (wm). Introduced in the film, ***Reveille with Beverly***, this song was a chart buster for Ella Mae Morse and Ella Fitzgerald.
I'll Remember April. DePaul, Raye, and Pat Johnson (wm). Written for the movie, ***Ride'em Cowboy***.
You Don't Know What Love Is. DePaul/Raye. A fine ballad for the film, ***Keep'em Flying***.
The Boogie Woogie Bugle Boy of Company 'B'. Prince/Raye. A sensational hit for LaVerne, Patty, and Maxine Andrews.

1942   *Mr. Five By Five.* DePaul and Raye (wm). For the film, ***Behind the Eight Ball***. A popular tribute to Basie vocalist Jimmy Rushing.

1943 *He's My Guy* and *Star Eyes*. DePaul and Raye (wm).

1944 *Milkman, Keep Those Bottles Quiet*. DePaul and Raye (wm). A big hit for the duo, first heard in the film, **Broadway Rhythm**.

1946 *House of Blue Lights*. Freddie Slack and Raye/(wm). An Ella Mae Morse biggie, with Slack's accompaniment.

1953 *Teach Me Tonight*. DePaul/Sammy Cahn.

PETER DEROSE, Composer (1900–1953)

Born and raised in New York City, DeRose attended public schools and was initially a pianist and song contributor to Broadway shows. In the early days of radio, with his wife May Singhi Brun (or Breen)—known as "the ukelele girl''—DeRose hosted a popular show called *Sweethearts of the Air*. DeRose worked in Hollywood up to the time of his death.

Chronology

1930 *When Your Hair Has Turned to Silver I Will Love You Just the Same*. DeRose/ Charles Tobias. DeRose's first published song was introduced by crooner Rudy Vallee.

1934 *Wagon Wheels* and *Rain*. DeRose/Billy Hill. From **Ziegfeld Follies**, a show that had most of its songs written by Vernon Duke and E. Y. Harburg. The 1934 **Follies** production was an attempt by actress Bille Burke to recoup debts incurred by her late husband, Flo Ziegfeld. She convinced the Shuberts to produce the show, but, unfortunately, it failed financially.
Deep Purple. DeRose/Mitchell Parish*. This lovely ballad took about five years to become a hit, thanks to the Larry Clinton Band and its "girl singer," Bea Wain.
Lilacs in the Rain. DeRose/Parish.

1938 *On a Little Street in Singapore*. DeRose/Hill.

1939 *The Lamp Is Low*. DeRose and Bert Shefter/Parish. This beautiful song was adapted from Ravel's *Pavane Pour Une Infante Defunte* and recorded by Tommy Dorsey, as well as Larry Clinton.

1940 *Starlit Hour*. DeRose/Parish. A very pretty song recorded by Glenn Miller and by Ella Fitzgerald.

1942 *All I Need Is You*. DeRose, Benny Davis, and Parish (wm).
Moonlight Mood. DeRose/Harold Adamson.

1945 *Autumn Serenade*. DeRose/Sammy Gallop. DeRose's last published hit.

HOWARD DIETZ, Lyricist (1896–1983)

Acknowledged as one of the premier popular song lyricists, Dietz, a New York City native, was also a man of diverse talents and successes. Like his fellow songwriters Arthur Schwartz* (his longtime partner), Richard Rodgers, Oscar Hammerstein, and others, he graduated from Columbia University. He became a newspaper columnist, a publicist, a high-level advertising executive, and, in Hollywood, the head of advertising at MGM and the publicity director of Loews. Somewhere along the line, Dietz also produced films.

Broadway Chronology

1923   *Poppy*. Arthur Samuels/Howard Dietz. Samuels and Dietz wrote three unrecollected songs for this 1920s show.

1927   *Merry Go Round*. Jay Gorney and Henry Souvaine/Morris Ryskind and Dietz. Ryskind and Dietz also wrote the sketches for this revue with no real hits.

1929   *I Guess I'll Have to Change My Plan*. Schwartz/Dietz. Supposedly their first collaboration, this song was a big hit. It was written for *The Little Show*. It was originally a summer camp song by Schwartz and Lorenz Hart, with the campy title, *I Love to Lie Awake in Bed* or *The Pajama Song*. Dietz rewrote the words in 1929.
        Moanin' Low. Ralph Rainger/Dietz. Introduced by Libby Holman in *The Little Show*.

1930   *Something to Remember You By*. Schwartz/Dietz. Written for the musical, *Three's a Crowd*, the same show which, earlier in London, had introduced the Green-Heyman-Sour-Byton classic, *Body and Soul*.

1931   *The Bandwagon*. Songs by Schwartz and Dietz. This delightful musical had sketches by Dietz, as well as his lyrics to such enjoyable songs as *I Love Louisa*, *New Sun in the Sky*, and the classic, *Dancing in the Dark*.

1932   *Flying Colors*. Songs by Schwartz and Dietz. *Alone Together, A Shine On Your Shoes*, and *Smokin' Reefers* were highly praised songs from this production.

1934   *Revenge with Music*. Schwartz/Dietz. The partners' first non-musical ''book'' show did feature the moving ballad, *You and the Night and the Music* and *If There Is Someone Lovelier Than You*.

1935   *Love Is a Dancing Thing*. Schwartz/Dietz. A nice tune for the musical, *At Home Abroad*.

1937   *I See Your Face Before Me; By Myself;* and *Triplets*. Schwartz/Dietz. For *Between the Devil*, with the libretto by Dietz, too.

1940   *The Love I Long For*. Vernon Duke/Dietz. From *Sadie Thompson*.
        Jackpot. Songs by Duke/Dietz.

1948   *Inside USA*. Songs by Schwartz/Dietz. Included *Haunted Heart* and *Rhode Island Is Famous for You*.

1950   *Die Fledermaus*. Johann Strauss/Dietz. (English lyrics).

1961   *Magic Moment*. Schwartz/Dietz. For the show, *The Gay Life*.

1963   *Jennie*. Songs by Schwartz and Dietz. Mary Martin and cast did eighty-two performances of this story about the life of Sir Winston Churchill's mother.

Hollywood Chronology

1929   *What Makes My Baby Blue* and *Housekeeping for You*. Jay Gorney/Dietz. For Gertrude Lawrence's talking picture debut, *The Battle of Paris*, with a score by Cole Porter.

1936   *Under Your Spell*. Schwartz/Dietz. Title song and two others for this film.

1948   *The Dickey Bird Song*. Sammy Fain*/Dietz. According to Clive Hirschhorn in *The Hollywood Musical*, this was the only "durable" song in the movie, ***Three Darling Daughters***.

1949   ***Dancing in the Dark***. Schwartz/Dietz. This 20th-Century film release was based on the Broadway play, ***The Bandwagon***, and featured a number of Schwartz/Dietz evergreens.

1953   *That's Entertainment*. Schwartz/Dietz. This song, now a show business anthem, was the only new Schwartz/Dietz number in MGM's movie masterpiece, ***The Bandwagon***. With a screenplay by Betty Comden and Adolph Green—and tour de force performances from a wonderful cast headed by Fred Astaire—this film and its music can be enjoyed over and over again.
       Two Faced Woman. Schwartz/Dietz. This was a production number in ***Torch Song***, a comeback film for Joan Crawford. It had been excised from ***The Bandwagon***, perhaps for good reason.

MORT DIXON, Lyricist (1892–1956)

Mort Dixon, of New York City, was a streetcar conductor who became a vaudeville performer. He also worked as a bank clerk and, in World War I, toured France as a director of musical shows.

Chronology

1923   *That Old Gang of Mine*. Ray Henderson*/Billy Rose* and Dixon. For the Ziegfeld's ***Follies***.

1924   *Follow the Swallow*. Henderson/Rose and Dixon.

1926   *Bye Bye Blackbird*. Henderson/Dixon.

1927   *I'm Looking Over a Four Leaf Clover*. Harry McGregor Woods*/Dixon.

1928   *Nagasaki*. Harry Warren*/Dixon. A fine jazz standard.

1930   *Would You Like to Take a Walk?* Warren/Rose and Dixon. From the Broadway revue, ***Sweet and Low***.

1931   *You're My Everything*. Warren/Rose and Dixon. A standard from the Broadway revue, ***Laugh Parade***.
       I Found a Million Dollar Baby (In a Five and Ten Cents Store). Warren/Rose and Dixon. Still an evergreen, written for Billy Rose's revue, ***Crazy Quilt***.
       River Stay Away from My Door. Woods/Dixon. Used in the Broadway revue, ***Mums the Word***.

1933   *Marching Along Together*. Edward Pola and Franz Steininger/Dixon.

1934   *Flirtation Walk*. Allie Wrubel and Dixon (wm). Film title song.

1935   *The Lady in Red*. Wrubel/Dixon. For the film, ***In Caliente***.

WALTER DONALDSON, Composer/Lyricist (1891–1947)

Donaldson was Brooklyn-born and followed the same path as his contemporaries: Tin Pan Alley songplugging, then on to writing songs. Donaldson also spent a few years after high school as a Wall Street broker, but by his early twenties he had found his musical career. His early songs were published by the firm where he plugged: Waterson, Berlin, and Snyder.

Chronology

1915   *We'll Have a Jubilee in My Old Kentucky Home*. Donaldson (wm). His first published song.

1918   *The Daughter of Rosie O'Grady*. Donaldson/Monty Brice. Written just after Donaldson served as an army recruit at Camp Upton, on Long Island.

1919   *How Ya Gonna Keep 'Em Down on the Farm?* Donaldson, Sam Lewis*, and Joe Young* (wm). A hit.

1921   *My Mammy*. Donaldson/Lewis and Young. This song was commissioned by Al Jolson.

1924   *My Blue Heaven*. Donaldson/George Whiting. Some reference sources say this was composed in 1927.

1925   *Yes, Sir, That's My Baby* and *At Sundown*. Donaldson/Gus Kahn.

1926   *What Can I Say Dear, After I Say I'm Sorry?* Donaldson/Abe Lyman.

1928   *Makin' Whoopee* and *Love Me or Leave Me*. Donaldson/Kahn. For the Broadway revue, **Whoopee**.

1930   *My Baby Just Cares for Me*. Donaldson/Kahn. For the film adaptation of **Whoopee**.
       You're Driving Me Crazy. Donaldson/Kahn. For the Broadway revue, **Smiles**.

1935   *When My Ship Comes In*. Donaldson/Kahn. Written for the Eddie Cantor film, **Kid Millions**.
       Tender Is the Night. Donaldson/Harold Adamson.* For the movie, **Here Comes the Band**.
       Did I Remember? Donaldson/Adamson*. A beautiful ballad made even more beautiful by Billie Holiday. It was written for a Jean Harlow film, **Suzy**.
       Little White Lies Donaldson (wm).

1936   *You, Gee But You're Wonderful You*. Donaldson/Adamson. For the film, **The Great Ziegfeld**.

1940   *Mister Meadowlark* and *On Behalf of the Visiting Firemen*. Donaldson/Johnny Mercer. Two delightful tunes with equally enjoyable words.

ERVIN DRAKE, Composer/Lyricist (1919–1998)

Drake, whose real name was Ervin Maurice Druckman, was born in New York City, the son of a furniture manufacturer. A graduate of the prestigious Townsend Harris High School and CCNY, Drake was an art/lithography/printing student. He did not follow that career, nor one in the furniture business, which he also tried. With show business in his blood (his mother appeared in two Hollywood films), he opted for music. Like Lorenz Hart*, Yip Harburg*, and other City College alumni, he composed scores for the school's varsity shows and became a musical staff writer at CBS, where he wrote special material for the network.

Chronology

1942   *Perdido*. Juan Tizol/Drake and H. J. Lengsfelder. This great instrumental (the lyrics were added), by the superb trombonist who played in Duke Ellington's band, became an Ellington classic. To fully appreciate it, listen to Ella Fitzgerald's rendering of the words to the music—even when she forgets some of them.
Hayfoot, Strawfoot. Paul McGrane/Drake and Harry Link.

1944   *Tico Tico*. Zequinha Abreu/Drake (English lyrics). This novelty song was written by the South American composer for the "toon" film, *Saludos Amigos*.

1946   *Good Morning Heartache*. Drake, Irene Higginbotham, and Dan Fisher (wm). Billie Holiday made an absolutely beautiful recording of this one.

1951   *Castle Rock*. Al Sears/Drake and Jimmy Shirl. Done jazz style by Johnny Hodges (another Ellington connection) and Sinatra style by Sinatra.

1953   *I Believe*. Drake, Shirl, Al Stillman, and Irvin Graham (wm). A hit written for a CBS television network special with Jane Froman.

1961   *Al Di La*. Carlo Donida/Drake (English lyrics). An Italian ballad used in the film, *Rome Adventure*.
It Was a Very Good Year. Drake (wm). This nostalgic song won a NARAS award for Sinatra.

1964   *A Room Without Windows*. Drake (wm). Sung by Steve Lawrence in the Broadway musical, *What Makes Sammy Run?*

DAVE DREYER, Composer (1894–1967)

A pianist who accompanied Al Jolson* and Sophie Tucker—among others—Dreyer was born in Brooklyn. He became a film score composer and music publisher. Songwriting credited to Al Jolson could well have been composed by Dreyer.

Chronology

1925   *Cecilia*. Dreyer/Herman Ruby (see Sam Stept*).

1927   *Me and My Shadow*. Dreyer and Jolson/Billy Rose*. From *Harry Delmar's Revue* on Broadway.

1928   *Back in Your Own Backyard* and *There's a Rainbow Round My Shoulder*. Dreyer, Rose, and Jolson (wm). From *The Singing Fool*.

1931   *Wabash Moon*. Dreyer and singer Morton Downey (wm).

AL DUBIN, Lyricist (1891–1945)

Born in Zurich, Switzerland, Dubin came to the United States as a youngster. He began as a composer but made a most formidable career as a wordsmith. Had it not been for his early death, Dubin could have been on the list as one of the most prolific and successful of popular songwriters. He was the writing partner of such eminent composers as James McHugh*, Harry Warren*, Sammy Fain*, Joe Burke*, James Monaco*, and opera composer Victor Herbert*.

Chronology

1924 *Nobody Knows What a Red-Headed Mama Can Do*. Sammy Fain/Dubin. Dubin's first published song, for which Irving Mills also took credit as co-lyricist.

1925 *The Lonesomest Girl in Town*. James McHugh/Dubin.

1926 *A Cup of Coffee, a Sandwich and You*. Joseph Meyer (Chapter 4)/Billy Rose* and Dubin. For the Broadway musical, **Andre Charlot's Revue**.
Tip Toe Through the Tulips. Joe Burke/Dubin. A 1926 film song for **Gold Diggers**, which was originally on Broadway. About a half century later, this popular novelty tune was revived by Tiny Tim, a ukulele-strumming character who sang in a grating falsetto. It was pure camp. Tim went on the road with his tip-toeing act, but unfortunately, died at an early age.

1929 *What Has Become of Hinky Dinky Parlay Vous?* McHugh/Dubin and Mills. Used in the Lawrence Stallings and Maxwell Anderson film, **This Cockeyed World**, a comedy sequel to **What Price Glory?**
If Your Best Friends Won't Tell You and *Painting the Clouds with Sunshine*. Burke/Dubin. Some sources say *Painting* was introduced in **Gold Diggers of 1929**.
Your Love Is All I Crave. Perry Bradford, Jimmy Johnson, and Dubin (wm). Both *If Your Best Friends* and *Your Love* were included in the film, **Show of Shows**. *Painting* was written for George M. Cohan's film version of **Little Johnny Jones**. The Jimmy Johnson writing with Bradford and Dubin could be James P. Johnson, composer of *If I Could Be With You One Hour Tonight* (1926) and *Don't Cry Baby* (1929). The name Johnson, like Smith, Jones, Williams, Steward, Scott and other common names, abounds in anthologies about the world of songwriting and performing and thus, makes misinterpretations possible.

1930 *I'm Dancing With Tears in My Eyes* and *Kiss Waltz*. Burke/Dubin. These two song were written for the film, **Dancing Sweeties**.
For You. Burke/Dubin. This became the theme song of the Casa Loma Orchestra.

1932 *Three's a Crowd*. Harry Warren/Kahal and Dubin. For the film, **The Crooner**.

1933 **42nd Street**. Songs by Warren and Dubin. The seminal Hollywood musical, with this songwriting duo's title song—plus *Shuffle Off to Buffalo, You're Getting to Be a Habit with Me*, and more.
Gold Diggers of '33. Songs by Warren and Dubin. Hits included: *We're in the Money, I've Got to Sing a Torch Song, Shadow Waltz*, and more.
Roman Scandal. Warren/Dubin. Six more songs for this film.

1934 *I Only Have Eyes for You*. Warren/Dubin. The title song and this one were written for the movie, **Dames**.

1935 *Lullaby of Broadway*. Warren/Dubin. The year's Oscar winner, from **Gold Diggers of 1935**.
About a Quarter to Nine and *Latin from Manhattan*. Warren/Dubin. The songwriters penned these two, plus five more, for the movie, **Go into Your Dance**. *I Love You Much Too Much, Muchacha*. Warren/Dubin. For the film, **In Caliente**. *Lulu's Back in Town*. Warren/Dubin. For the movie, **Broadway Gondolier**. *Don't Give Up the Ship*. Warren/Dubin. For the motion picture, **Shipmates Forever**.

1936 *Hearts Divided, Colleen*, and *Sing Me a Love Song*. Songs by Warren and Dubin.
      The duo wrote dozens of songs for these three films.
      Shadow Waltz. Warren/Dubin. For the movie, *Cain and Mabel*.

1937 *September in the Rain*. Warren/Dubin. Warren composed the music two years
      earlier for *Stars Over Broadway*. Dubin added the lyrics for the film, *Melody for
      Two*, and wrote *Melody*'s title song.

1938 *Girlfriend of the Whirling Dervish*. Warren/Johnny Mercer and Dubin. The best
      of about a dozen songs the three wrote together that year.

1939 *Indian Summer*. Victor Herbert/Dubin. A lovely song that became a big band hit.

1940 *South American Way*. Jimmy McHugh/Dubin. For the film, *Down Argentine
      Way*.

1941 *Anniversary Waltz*. Dave Franklin and Dubin (wm).

1943 *We Mustn't Say Goodbye*. James V. Monaco/Dubin. An Oscar-nominated song,
      one of eight written by Monaco and Dubin, for *Stage Door Canteen*, the big
      United Artists' tribute to the American Theatre Wing's contribution to armed
      forces personnel on leave and liberty in New York. *We Mustn't* lost out to another
      song for the same film, *You'll Never Know*, written by none other than Harry
      Warren, this time with Mack Gordon*.

1946 *A Cup of Coffee, a Sandwich and You*. Meyer/Rose and Dubin. The twenty-year-
      old hit, used this time in the 20th Century Fox film, *Margie*.
      About a Quarter of Nine. Warren/Dubin. Reprised for the movie, *The Jolson
      Story*. It had been a Jolson hit eleven years earlier.

1948 *Feudin', Fussin' and Fightin'*. Burton Lane/Dubin. For the film of the same name.

VERNON DUKE, Composer/Lyricist (1903–1969)

   Vladimir Dukelsky was a Russian composer of classical and ballet music who,
in 1930, came to the United States and became a composer of premier songs.
Two years after his arrival in the States, Duke composed the score for his first
Broadway stage musical, *Walk a Little Faster*; not surprising, coming from the
same creative talent, who at age 8 had already scored a ballet. It was about this
time, in the early 1930s, that George Gershwin* took Duke under his wing. In
a 1985 poll conducted by radio station WNEW-AM, then one of New York's
top popular music stations, *I Can't Get Started* by Duke and Ira Gershwin* was
voted the best of all popular recordings—ahead of *Star Dust*. This was surely
because of the great quality of the music and words, as well as Bunny Berigan's
classic rendition. Vernon Duke was, indeed, one of the finest jazz experimenters.

Chronology

1930 *I'm Only Human After All*. Duke/Ira Gershwin*. Duke's first ballad, for the revue,
      Garrick Gaities.

1932 *April in Paris*. Duke/Yip Harburg*. The renowned musicologist/composer Alec
      Wilder called *April* ''the perfect theatre song.'' It was written for *Walk a Little
      Faster*, Duke's first Broadway musical.

1934   *What Is There to Say?* and *I Like the Likes of You.* Duke/Harburg. For the ***Ziegfeld Follies***.
 Autumn in New York. Duke (wm). For the musical, ***Thumbs Up***.

1936   *I Can't Get Started.* Duke/Ira Gershwin. Duke's third great ballad in a couple of years, it was written for the ***Follies*** and sung by Bob Hope. The 1937 and 1938 Bunny Berigan versions are a little bit better than marvelous.

1938   *Spring Again.* Duke/Ira Gershwin. Duke got his citizenship in 1938; and wrote this song for ***The Goldwyn Follies*** in Hollywood.

1940   *Taking a Chance on Love.* Duke/Ted Fetter and John LaTouche (Chapter 4). *Taking* and the title song for the Broadway musical ***Cabin in the Sky*** were hits.

1941   *We're Having a Baby, My Baby and Me.* Duke/Harold Adamson* and LaTouche. Written for Eddie Cantor's Broadway musical, ***Banjo Eyes***.

1943   *Cabin in the Sky.* Duke/Fetter and LaTouche. The musical was made into a movie and Lena Horne turned the title song into a hit—again.

1946   *Sweet Bye and Bye.* Duke/Ogden Nash. Title song for the Broadway show with lyrics by the poet/humorist.

1952   ***The Male Animal.*** Scored by Duke and Sammy Cahn*. The duo wrote a half dozen tunes for this movie version of the Broadway musical.
 April in Paris. Duke/Harburg. The recycled title song was the one big hit from this film, also scored by Duke and Cahn.

MICHAEL EDWARDS, Composer (1893–1962) and BUD GREEN, Lyricist (1897–1981)

Edwards, born in Pennsylvania, was a flutist, concert violinist, and an arranger. He conducted vaudeville orchestras, and on Tin Pan Alley, edited and arranged music. Edwards was a highly successful Hollywood composer with a folio of songs for choruses and cartoons. A renowned classical musician, composer, and arranger, *Once in a While* was his only hit. It is now a classic. Green was probably not Bud's real name—nor was Bud, we presume. He was born in Austria, and moved to New York City in his childhood, where he grew up and got his education. Another Tin Pan Alley staffer, Green began in that metaphorical place as a gofer. He started writing lyrics when he was eighteen years old.

Chronology

1925   *Alabamy Bound.* Ray Henderson/Buddy DeSylva and Green.
 I Love My Baby and My Baby Loves Me. Harry Warren/Green. Warren and Green wrote quite a few songs together in the 1920s.

1928   *That's My Weakness Now.* Sam Stept/Green.
 I'll Always Be in Love with You. Stept/Herman Ruby and Green. This song was used in the film ***Syncopation***, and was played by the legendary Bunny Berigan.

1937   *Once in a While.* Edwards/Green. A very lovely standard—and their biggest hit— *Once* was recorded first by Tommy Dorsey.

1938   *Flat Foot Floogie.* Slam Stewart and Slim Gaillard/Green. The great jazz bassist, Stewart and his partner/guitarist, Gaillard, had a huge hit with this composition.

1944   *Sentimental Journey.* Les Brown and Ben Homer/Green. Another major Green chartbuster, thanks to Brown's recording with a fine vocal performance by Doris Day.

DUKE ELLINGTON, Composer (1899–1974)

Edward Kennedy Ellington shares the songwriting crown for American popular music with the Gershwins and, perhaps, a few others. But his unique style of composition, blended with the arrangements performed by his magnificent orchestras, sets him apart from all others. His interpretation of African-American melody, rhythm, and style—known as "Ellingtonia"—continues to thrill and delight music lovers all over the world, and will do so for as long as music is played. This brilliant artist and gentleman of elegance, style, class, sophistication, and professionalism has no peers. Passionately devoted to his craft—composing, leading, arranging, and performing—Ellington worked until his death. Few composers and leaders of orchestras are honored to have a society named for them; Ellington is one. The Duke Ellington Society keeps his memory and music alive.

What also sets him apart, much to his credit, is that he composed for his musicians. Ellington wrote to their talent so they could share the joy in soloing to his songs: Johnny Hodges, Harry Carney, Ray Nance, Ben Webster, Cootie Williams, and many others. These were the best musicians in the world and they stayed with Ellington forever—or came back to his band after leaving it. Ellington and his musicians arrived in New York in 1919. Soon after, Duke began to compose his music and the reputation of the Ellington band for interpretation, orchestration, and performance—especially by some of the great soloists—was earned quickly. They became the premier band of the Cotton Club.

Ellington's orchestrations, with much thanks to Billy Strayhorn*, are seminal works for musicologists to marvel at through the ages. Further study of the man and his legendary compositions and performances can be found in the writings of Stanley Dance, Ellington's friend and biographer. As for the chronology that follows, only about forty songs are cited, but there are hundreds more of his excellent compositions: ballads, blues, tone poems, cantatas, suites, show tunes, movie scores, and jazz.

Chronology

1927   *Black and Tan Fantasy* and *East Saint Louis Toodle-O.* Ellington and Bubber Miley (instr.). The latter composition was Ellington's first theme song; Miley was the Ellington band's first trumpet soloist. (Some spell it "Toodle-oo.")

1929   *The Mooche.* Ellington. The same year, Flo Ziegfeld tapped Ellington to conduct for the George Gershwin* musical, **Show Girls**. Irving Mills took co-composer credit.

1930   *Ring Dem Bells.* Ellington/Mills. The same year that this song was introduced, Ellington's band was becoming a big hit at Harlem's famed Appollo Theatre.

1931   *Rockin' in Rhythm*. Ellington/Mills.
       Mood Indigo. Ellington and Albany "Barney" Bigard. Mitchell Parish* was most probably the real lyricist of this classic; he bitterly quit writing when Irving Mills* "appropriated" the *Mood Indigo* lyricist title. Parish, the lyricist of *Star Dust, Moonlight Serenade* (Glenn Miller/Parish), and more, left his temporary career as a court stenographer to return to songwriting. Bigard was the Ellington band's soprano saxophone/clarinet soloist.

1932   *It Don't Mean a Thing if It Ain't Got that Swing*. Ellington/Mills. An American swing standard—and still a hit.
       Drop Me Off in Harlem. Ellington/Nick Kenny. Kenny was the Broadway columnist for the *New York Daily Mirror*. He was referred to as the king of the soppy poets; he and his brother, Charles, wrote the words to J. Fred Coots' composition, *Love Letters in the Sand*.

1933   *Sophisticated Lady*. Ellington/Parish and Mills. A classic.

1934   *Solitude*. Ellington/Edgar DeLange and Mills? Another absolute masterpiece.
       Daybreak Express. Ellington (instr.).

1935   *In a Sentimental Mood*. Ellington (wm).

1936   *Echoes of Harlem*. Ellington (instr.). performed by trumpet soloist Cootie Williams, a wonderful example of how Duke composed for his musicians.

1937   *Caravan*. Ellington and Juan Tizol/Mills. Tizol (1900–1984) was Ellington's long-time featured trombonist.
       Diminuendo in Blue. Ellington (instr.).
       I've Got to Be a Rug Cutter. Ellington (wm).

1938   *I Let a Song Go Out of My Heart*. Ellington/Henry Nemo (Chapter 4), John Redmond, and Mills.
       Prelude to a Kiss. Ellington/Irving Gordon and Mills. A gorgeous ballad; Johnny Hodges' solo is pure musical beauty.
       Jeep's Blues. Ellington (instr.). Johnny Hodges, one of the finest alto saxophonists of all time, had two nicknames: "Rabbit" and "Jeep." Thus, the title of this instrumental.
       Boy Meets Horn. Ellington/Mills. Duke wrote this for erudite trumpeter Rex Stewart.

1939   *I'm Checking Out, Goombye*. Ellington and Strayhorn (wm). The very close relationship between Duke and "Swee' Pea," as Strayhorn was called, began about this time—and stayed that way until Strayhorn's early demise in 1967. *I'm Checking* was a fun song Rosemary Clooney did well some years later.
       Something to Live For. Ellington/Strayhorn. A grand ballad.
       Crescendo in Blue. Ellington (instr.). Composed in 1939, *Crescendo* was a sequel to *Diminuendo*; eighteen years later, at the Newport Jazz Festival, Ellington performed the piece. At that festival and on record, tenor saxophone player Paul Gonzalves played one of the most exciting—and definitely one of the longest—of all sax solos.

1940   *All Too Soon*. Ellington/Carl Sigman. There are two gem performances recorded by Ellington and by Ella Fitzgerald.

Concerto for Cootie (Williams). Ellington (instr.). Written in 1940 and retitled in 1943.

Cottontail and *In a Mellow Tone*. Ellington (wm). Two more hits.

1941 *Day Dream*. Ellington and Strayhorn/LaTouche. Another fine ballad sung so beautifully by Ella Fitzgerald.

I Got It Bad (And That Ain't Good). Ellington/Paul Francis Webster. Written for the unstaged but mightily publicized Ellington musical, **Jump for Joy**. The show was touted as the greatest African-American musical of all time, but neither Broadway nor Hollywood moguls supported it.

Just a Sittin' and a Rockin'. Ellington/Lee Gaines. Another hit.

1942 *C-Jam Blues*. Ellington (instr.).

Don't Get Around Much Any More. Ellington/S. K. (Bob) Russell*. One of Duke's best.

1943 *Do Nothing 'Til You Hear from Me*. Ellington/Russell. The re-titled *Concerto for Cootie*. Ellington and Woody Herman had hit recordings.

1944 *I Ain't Got Nothing But the Blues*. Ellington/Don George.

I Didn't Know About You. Ellington/Russell. Adapted from Ellington's tone poem, *Sentimental Lady*.

I'm Beginning to See the Light. Ellington, Johnny Hodges, and Harry James/George. Certainly a very interesting combination of musician-writers.

Main Stem. Ellington (instr.).

1945 *I'm Just a Lucky So and So*. Ellington/Mack David. Recorded by vocalist Al Hibbler.

1946 *Just Squeeze Me*. Ellington and Strayhorn/Lee Gaines. Not to be confused with Fats Waller's *Squeeze Me*.

Take Love Easy. Ellington/John LaTouche. Highly praised song from **Beggar's Holiday**, LaTouche's version of **The Beggar's Opera**, which only had a run of fourteen weeks.

1958 *Satin Doll*. Ellington and Strayhorn/Johnny Mercer. The classic written three decades after Ellington's first hit, *Black and Tan Fantasy*

RAY EVANS, Composer/Lyricist (1915–) and JAY LIVINGSTON, Composer/Lyricist (1915–)

Evans, from upstate New York, and Livingston, from Pennsylvania, were college roommates at the University of Pennsylvania where they began a long-term partnership at the college's Mask and Wig Club. They went on together to write many hits for Hollywood and American popular music. Their friendship continues in California, where they both now live.

Chronology

1946 *To Each His Own*. Evans and Livingston (wm). Film title song and on the Billboard charts.

1947 *Golden Earrings*. Victor Young/Evans and Livingston. Having arrived in

Hollywood near the end of World War II, the partners wrote the words for this film title song, their first hit.

1948   *Buttons and Bows*. Evans and Livingston (wm). A novelty piece—and an Oscar winner—from the film, ***Paleface***.

1949   *Mona Lisa*. Evans and Livingston (wm). Another year, another Academy Award for this song from ***Captain Carey, USA***. Nat King Cole did some job on this classic.

1950   *Silver Bells*. Evans and Livingston (wm). For the film, ***The Lemon Drop Kid***.

1951   *A Place in the Sun*. Franz Waxman/Evans and Livingston. Film title song. Waxman won the Oscar for best film score.

1955   *Que Sera, Sera*. Evans and Livingston (wm). A third Oscar for the talented pair and a big hit for Doris Day. From the film, ***The Man Who Knew Too Much***.

1960   *Mr. Lucky*. Henry Mancini (Chapter 3)/Evans and Livingston. The title song of a popular television series by the same name.

1964   *Dear Heart*. Mancini/Evans and Livingston. A film title song.

1965   *In the Arms of Love*. Mancini/Evans and Livingston. From the film, ***What Did You Do in the War, Daddy?*** In Evans and Livingston's case they seemed to have learned how to write Oscar songs.

SAMMY FAIN, Composer (1902–1989)

Sammy Fain was born in New York City, the son of Rabbi Menachem Feinberg, a clergy/cantor. Fain started to compose while still a schoolboy, sang in vaudeville, and was a songplugger in Tin Pan Alley, as were so many of his contemporaries. During the 1940s, 1950s, and 1960s, Fain wrote several scores for Broadway shows, including ***Christine***, with lyricist Oscar Hammerstein. Fain's last show was ***Something More*** in 1964. In a Hollywood career that spanned three decades, he wrote beautiful music and was also credited for the words and music in songs with his collaborators. Fain worked with the great names of songwriting: Yip Harburg*, Harry Warren*, Al Dubin*, Sam Coslow*, Lew Brown*, and Irving Kahal*. He wrote or co-wrote more than twenty songs for more than a half dozen films.

Chronology

1927   *Let a Smile Be Your Umbrella*. Fain, Harry B. Smith, and Francis Wheeler/Irving Kahal. Introduced in vaudeville and later used in the 1930 film, ***It's A Good Life***.

1929   *Wedding Bells Are Breaking Up That Old Gang of Mine*. Fain and Willie Raskin/Kahal. A most popular song.

1930   *You Brought a New Kind of Love to Me*. Fain, Pierre Norman Connor, and Kahal (wm). Used in the film, ***The Big Pond***.

1933   *By a Waterfall*. Fain/Kahal. From the movie, ***Footlight Parade***.

1938   *That Old Feeling*. Fain and Lew Brown (wm). For the film, ***Vogues of 1938***, this song became an American standard.
         I Can Dream, Can't I, and *I'll Be Seeing You*. Fain and Kahal (wm). Two songs

with everlasting appeal that came from a revue that lasted two short weeks, ***Right This Way***.

1939   *Are You Having Any Fun?* Fain/Jack Yellen. For George White's ***Scandals***, on Broadway.

1944   *Mississippi Dream Boat*. Fain/Ralph Freed. Back in Hollywood, writing for the film, ***Swing Fever***.

1945   *Please Don't Say No, Say Maybe*. Fain/Freed. Their hit from the movie, ***Thrill of a Romance***.

1950   *Dear Hearts and Gentle People*. Fain/Bob Hilliard. A hit for Bing Crosby, Dinah Shore, and others. In 1950 and 1951, Fain teamed up with lyricist Mack Gordon, he wrote eight songs with Hilliard for Disney's ***Alice in Wonderland***; and he wrote his first song with the fine lyric writer Paul Francis Webster, although it did not get released until used as the title song for the 1962 film, ***Tender Is the Night***.

1953   *Secret Love*. Fain/Sammy Cahn. Used in ***Calamity Jane***, it won the Academy Award. Fain and Cahn wrote four more songs in 1953, for ***Peter Pan***.

1955   *Love Is a Many Splendored Thing*. Fain/Paul Francis Webster. This popular film title song won the Oscar.

1957   *April Love*. Fain/Wheeler. Another film title song.

1958   *A Very Precious Love*. Fain/Wheeler. From the movie, ***Marjorie Morningstar***.

1959   *Once Upon A Dream*. Fain/Jack Lawrence. From the film, ***Sleeping Beauty***.

DOROTHY FIELDS, Lyricist (1905–1974)

Born in New Jersey, just outside of New York City, Dorothy Fields was the daughter of Lew Fields, the famous vaudevillian and later a major producer on Broadway. Her brothers, Herbert and Joseph, were also in the business as librettists and playwrights. As peer songpluggers for Mills Music on Tin Pan Alley, Fields and Jimmy McHugh formed a long-lasting partnership in songwriting. Fields and McHugh began their great run in Hollywood in 1930, writing songs for MGM. They really did not have any hits until five years later. From 1939 through 1944, Fields collaborated with composers like Arthur Schwartz. She also wrote lyrics and librettos for several Broadway shows with her brother, Herbert.

Broadway Chronology

1926   *I Can't Give You Anything But Love*. McHugh/Fields. It was dropped from ***Harry Delmar's Revels***.

1928   *I Must Have That Man* and *Diga Diga Doo*. McHugh/Fields. These two songs—plus *I Can't Give You Anything But Love*—were used in the musical, ***Blackbirds***. A controversy arose over *I Can't* when songwriters Fats Waller and Andy Razaf said they sold it to McHugh and Fields for a pittance and they wanted their royalties. Never adjudicated in court, rumor had it that there was some settlement as a result of the song's great popularity.

1930   *On the Sunny Side of the Street* and *Exactly Like You*. McHugh/Fields. Written for **The International Revue**, which only had a twelve-week run. The songs are still playing.

1931   **Rhapsody in Black**. Scored by McHugh and Fields. This production starred Ethel Waters, but closed after ten performances.

1933   *Don't Blame Me*. McHugh/Fields. A beautiful balled for **Clowns in Clover**. Other 1930s shows this songwriting team contributed music and lyrics to include **Shoot the Works** and **Singin' the Blues**.

1945   *Close as Pages in a Book*. Sigmund Romberg/Fields. Used in the big Mike Todd hit, **Up in Central Park**.

1946   **Annie Get Your Gun**. Irving Berlin (score)/Dorothy and Herbert Fields (libretto). A one-of-a-kind classic.

1950   *There Must Be Something Better Than Love*. Morton Gould/Fields. The big song from **Arms and the Girl**, sung by Pearl Bailey.

1951   *Make the Man Love Me, He Had Refinement, Love Is the Reason,* and *Look Who's Dancing*. Arthur Schwartz/Fields. Fine songs for the fine musical, **A Tree Grows in Brooklyn**, based on the award-winning novel. It starring Shirley Booth, who captured the hearts of theatregoers and critics alike. Not long after, Booth had the starring role in Schwartz/Fields' **By the Beautiful Sea**, a 270-performance play, with music that included the memorable song, *Alone Too Long*. In 1959, Fields collaborated with composer Albert Hague for the Broadway musical, **Redhead**. Hague had composed the hit *Young and Foolish* in 1955 with lyrics by Arnold Horwitt for the stage musical **Plain and Fancy**.

1966   **Sweet Charity**. Songs by Cy Coleman and Fields. Story by Neil Simon. A take-off on a Fellini film that took off on Broadway, **Charity** had an excellent score and superb performances by husband and wife stars, Bob Fosse and Gwen Verdon. The now classic songs included: *Hey Big Spender, If They Could See Me Now, Baby Dream Your Dream*, and the title song. Three years later, the film version seemed less engaging.

1973   *It's Not Where You Start*. Coleman/Fields. From Field's last Broadway musical **Seesaw**, a stage version of the William Gibson prize-winning play **Two for the Seesaw**.

Hollywood Chronology

1935   **Roberta**. Songs by Jerome Kern/McHugh, and Fields. A top moneymaker for RKO starring Fred Astaire and Ginger Rogers. The songs included *Lovely to Look At* and new Fields lyrics to a Kern/Hammerstein song written for a London show some years before, *I Won't Dance*. *Lovely* was an Oscar nominee, but lost to *Lullaby of Broadway*.
   I'm in the Mood for Love. McHugh/Fields. An all-time American standard.
   I Feel a Song Coming On. George Oppenheimer/Fields. For the film, **Every Night at Eight**. McHugh and Fields wrote the movie's title song, *Speaking Confidentially* and *Take It Easy*, the latter not be confused with the 1943 Cugat/ Lina Romay hit.
   Hooray for Love. McHugh/Fields. Film title song. They wrote six more for the movie.

1936   *The Way You Look Tonight*. Kern/Fields. This still popular song won the Academy Award. Kern and Fields wrote it for **Swing Time**, in which Astaire and

Rogers sang and danced to *Pick Yourself Up, A Fine Romance, Waltz in Swing Time, Bojangles of Harlem*, and *It's Not in the Cards*.
Stars in My Eyes. Fritz Kreisler/Fields. From Columbia's operetta film, **The King Steps Out**. Fields rewrote lyrics for several Kreisler songs used in this musical movie.

1937   *Our Song* and *The Whistling Boy*. Kern/Fields. For the film, **When You're in Love**, starring Grace Moore and Cary Grant.

1938   *You Couldn't Be Cuter*. Kern/Fields. A hit from the movie, *Joy of Living*, starring Irene Dunne and Douglas Fairbanks.

1940   *Remind Me*. Kern/Fields. Written for the Abbott and Costello picture, **One Night in the Tropics**, which also featured songs by Oscar Hammerstein* and Otto Harbach*. *Remind Me* is a lesser known ballad, but highly respected by musicians. One of the most engaging versions is by veteran vocalist David Allyn.

1952   *I'll Be Hard to Handle*. Bernard Dougal/Fields. For the MGM **Roberta** remake; story adapted by songwriter Harry Ruby. Other Fields songs included *You're Devastating* and *The Most Exciting Night* (with Harbach) and *Layfayette* (with Kern).

DORIS FISHER, Composer/Lyricist (1915–   ) and ALAN ROBERTS, Composer/Lyricist (1905–1966)

Doris Fisher, the daughter of songwriter Fred Fisher (Chapter 1), was born in New York and became a nightclub and radio singer. She also produced nightclub shows and became a Hollywood contract songwriter. Her brother Marvin (1916–1993) wrote *When Sunny Gets Blue* (see Jack Segal, Chapter 3). Marvin and another brother, Dan, became the top executives of Fred Fisher Music, founded by their father. Roberts, born in Brooklyn, began his career as an accountant but rapidly changed to comedy songwriting, working for the likes of Sid Caesar, Red Buttons, Eddie Cantor, and Mike Todd.

Chronology

1940   *Whispering Grass*. Doris and Fred Fisher (wm). Her first composition, turned into a hit by the Ink Spots.

1944   *Into Each Life Some Rain Must Fall*. Fisher and Roberts (wm). Another Ink Spots hit.
Angelina (The Waitress at the Pizzeria). Fisher and Roberts (wm). A perfect number for clowning Louis Prima.
What's the Good Word (Mr. Bluebird)? Fisher and Roberts (wm).
You Always Hurt the One You Love. Fisher and Roberts (wm).

1945   *Tampico*. Fisher and Roberts (wm). A sensational arrangement was performed by the exciting Stan Kenton Band.

1946   *Put the Blame on Mame*. Fisher and Roberts (wm). This song was "performed" by Rita Hayworth in the film, **Gilda**. Voice-over Anita Ellis really did the singing, but Hayworth's body interpretation of the song evoked a sensuality contemporary performers like the Spice Girls can only hope to emulate.

CHET FORREST, Composer/Lyricist (1915–) and ROBERT WRIGHT, Composer/Lyricist (1914–)

George Forrest Chichester, known as George or Chet Forrest, was born in Brooklyn, New York. Robert Wright was from Daytona Beach, Florida. The two met while they were both students at the University of Miami. Forrest was a stage director as well as a songwriter. This creative team, long active in Hollywood, also wrote two popular Broadway shows. Forrest and Wright worked together for more than six decades—some kind of record in the music business.

Chronology

1923   *Donkey Serenade*. Rudolph Friml* and Herbert Stothart/Forrest and Wright. Written for the film, *The Firefly*—and sung by Allan Jones (Jack Jones' father)—this was Forrest and Wright's first lyrical hit.

1937   *Always and Always*. Edward Ward/Forrest and Wright. From the film, *Manequin*, starring Joan Crawford.

1939   *At the Balalaika*. George Posford and Stothart/Forrest and Wright. From the movie, *Balalaika*.
       It's a Blue World. Forrest, Wright, and Eric Maschwitz (wm). From the film, *Music in my Heart*. Maschwitz also went by the name of Holt Marvel*.

1942   *Jersey Bounce*. Bobby Plater, Tiny Bradshaw, and Edward Johnson/Forrest and Wright. The partners began to swing—just listen to Benny Goodman's version.

1944   *Strange Music*. Grieg, Forrest and Wright (wm). Adapted from an Edvard Grieg theme for their Broadway musical play, *Song of Norway*.

1953   *Kismet*. Alex Borodin, Forrest; and Wright (wm). Their second, and no doubt, best play with music *adapted from a theme* by Borodin. Their own words and music produced real chart movers: *And This Is My Beloved; Baubles, Bangles, and Beads*; and *Stranger in Paradise*.

ARTHUR FREED, Lyricist (1894–1973)

Freed's real name was Arthur Grossman. He was born in Charleston, South Carolina, and, after attending Phillips Exeter Academy, was a World War I army sergeant. After the war, Freed first went into vaudeville as a partner of Louis Silvers, another future songwriter; then he became a writer for impressario Gus Edwards; and eventually became one of Hollywood's foremost musical producers. In 1928 Freed produced *Broadway Melody*, and the rest, as they say, is history. From 1939 through 1958, Freed was the man responsible for producing: *Babes in Arms; Cabin in the Sky; Girl Crazy; Meet Me in Saint Louis; The Harvey Girls; Ziegfeld Follies '46; The Pirate; On the Town; Take Me Out to the Ballgame; Show Boat* (third screen version); *Singin' in the Rain; The Band Wagon*; and *Gigi*—and we may have missed a few.

Chronology

1921   *When Buddha Smiles*. Nacio Herb Brown/Freed.

1923   *I Cried for You*. Gus Arnheim, Abe Lyman, and Freed (wm).

1928 *You Were Meant for Me*. Brown/Freed. From Freed's ***Broadway Melody***, the first score ever conceived and written exclusively for the screen.

1929 *Pagan Love Song*. Brown/Freed. From the movie, ***The Pagan***.
Singin' in the Rain. Brown/Freed. From ***Hollywood Revue***, the first no-plot musical film.
Broadway Melody. Brown/Freed. Film title song.

1930 *Should I?* Brown/Freed. For the motion picture, ***Lord Byron of Broadway***.

1933 *Temptation*. Brown/Freed. Written for ***Going Hollywood***, starring Bing Crosby.

1934 *All I Do Is Dream of You*. Brown/Freed. For the film, ***Sadie McKee***.

1935 *Alone*. Brown/Freed. From the zany Marx Brothers classic, ***A Night at the Opera***.
You Are My Lucky Star and *I've Got a Feeling You're Fooling*. Brown/Freed. From ***Broadway Melody of '36***.

1939 *Good Morning*. Brown/Freed. Written for ***Babes in Arms***, it was not really a hit until recycled into the film ***Singin' in the Rain*** some years later.

1940 *Our Love Affair*. Roger Edens/Freed. For the movie, ***Strike Up the Band***, Freed's first time without music by Nacio Brown.

1946 *This Heart of Mine*. Harry Warren/Freed. Freed collaborating with the film composer extraordinaire for ***The Ziegfeld Follies***.

RALPH FREED, Lyricist (1907–1973)

Born in Canada and raised in Seattle, Washington, Ralph Freed moved to southern California as a young man. He began writing for the movies at age 27. His lyrics were written to the music of Burton Lane*, James McHugh*, Sammy Fain*, Victor Herbert*, and a number of the other top Hollywood composers.

Chronology

1934 *Little Dutch Mill*. Harry Barris/Freed. This became a number 1 chart record for Bing Crosby, a fellow Delta Rhythm Boys member with Barris.

1936 *Hawaiian War Chant*. Johnny Noble and Leleiohaku/Freed. Became a big hit for the Tommy Dorsey Band a few years later.
Sandman. Bonnie Lake/Freed. Theme of the (Tommy and Jimmy) Dorsey Brothers Orchestra.

1939 *You Leave Me Breathless*. Frederick Hollander/Freed.
A fine ballad for the film, ***Cocoanut Grove***. Hollander also composed *Falling in Love Again (Can't Help It)* with lyrics by Sammy Lerner for the film ***The Blue Angel*** in 1930.

1941 *How About You?* Lane/Freed. Probably Freed's best lyric and surely the most "standard," it was unfortunately nominated for for an Academy Award the same year *White Christmas* won.

1944 *Mississippi Dream Boat*. Fain, Lew Brown, and Freed (wm). The hit song from the film, ***Swing Fever***.
Young Man with a Horn. George Stoll and Freed (wm). The title song of a fine film by one of Hollywood's best regarded composers.
In a Moment of Madness. Jimmy McHugh/Freed. Performed in the MGM musical film, ***Two Girls and a Sailor***.

1945   *Please Don't Say No, Say Maybe*. Fain/Freed. A fine hit from ***Thrill of Romance***. Fain and Freed wrote more movie songs through 1948, but no real hits.

1948   *Fleurette*. Victor Herbert/Freed. For the film, ***Three Darling Daughters***.

CLIFF FRIEND, Composer/Lyricist (1893–1974)

Coming from a musical family in Cincinnati, Cliff Friend began his career as a pianist and eventually moved on to Broadway as a partner of Billy Rose*. Before New York, Friend toured the world in vaudeville and worked with Buddy DeSylva; then, from 1920 to 1931, he wrote Broadway scores, including ***Bombo*** and Earl Carroll's ***Vanities***. In the 1930s Friend went on to Hollywood where he wrote for films and became a test pilot.

Chronology

1922   *You Tell Her I Stutter*. Friend/Billy Rose. Friend's first song, but not his first hit.

1924   *Just Give Me a June Night*. Abel Baer (Chapter 4) Friend. This one was a hit.
       Big Butter and Egg Man. Friend (wm). A jazz tune popularized by Jack Teagarden.

1925   *I Wanna Go Where You Go, Do What You Do*. Friend/Sidney Clare and Lew Brown.

1936   *When My Dream Boat Comes Home*. Friend and Dave Franklin (wm).

1937   *The Merry Go Round Broke Down*. Friend and Franklin (wm).

1941   *We Did It Before and We Can Do It Again*. Friend and Franklin (wm).

1944   *Time Waits for No One*. Friend and Charles Tobias (wm).

RUDOLPH FRIML, Composer (1879–1972)

Born in Prague, Czechoslovakia, Friml is one of several operetta composers included in this book (along with Victor Herbert* and Sigmund Romberg*). Having studied composition with Antonín Dvořák, Friml arrived in the United States in 1907, became a touring concert pianist, and composed concertos and suites. Friml actually succeeded Herbert on the opera that was to become ***The Firefly***.

Chronology

1912   *Gianina Mia*. Friml/Otto Harbach. Friml's first major U.S. composition in the pop genre, from the opera ***The Firefly***.

1922   *L'Amour Toujour, L'Amour*. Friml/Catherine Chisholm.

1923   *Donkey Serenade*. Friml/Chet Forrest and Robert Wright*. For the film, ***The Firefly***.

1924   *Rose Marie*. Friml/Oscar Hammerstein and Otto Harbach. The title song for the famous operetta, reprised as a film in 1936. *Indian Love Call* is the other evergreen from this score.

1925   ***The Vagabond King***. Friml/Brian Hooker.

Love Me Tonight, Only a Rose, and *Song of the Vagabonds* were all composed for this operetta.

SAMMY GALLOP, Lyricist (1915–1971)

Gallop was from Duluth, Minnesota, and went to school there, studying engineering and drafting at Duluth Junior College. He moved to songwriting while still in his 20s. Gallop wrote for New York nightclub revues and Broadway musicals.

Chronology

1941 *Elmer's Tune*. Dick Jurgens, Elmer Albrecht, and Gallop (wm).

1943 *Holiday for Strings*. David Rose/Gallop. Gallop simply added words to this well-known instrumental.

1945 *Autumn Serenade*. Peter DeRose/Gallop.

1946 *Shoo Fly Pie and Apple Pan Dowdy*. A folk song that Guy Wood (Chapter 4) and Sammy Gallop ''updated.''

1948 *Maybe You'll Be There*. Rube Bloom/Gallop.

1950 *Count Every Star*. Bruno Coquatrix/Gallop.

1952 *Somewhere Along the Way*. Kurt Adams/Gallop.

1955 *Wake the Town and Tell the People*. Jerry Livingston/Gallop.

KIM GANNON, Lyricist (1900–1974)

James Kimball Gannon was another of a long line of Brooklyn-born songwriters who first went to law school and passed the bar, then decided to write lyrics. He became a composer for the movie industry.

Chronology

1940 *The Five O'Clock Whistle*. Gannon and Joseph Myrow* (wm).

1941 *Moonlight Cocktail*. Lucky Roberts/Gannon. A big Glenn Miller hit and a number 1 chart record.
      Autumn Nocturne. Myrow/Gannon. This lovely composition became a hit song for the Claude Thornhill Orchestra.

1942 *Always in My Heart*. Ernesto Lecuona/Gannon (English lyrics). A film title song.

1943 *I'll Be Home for Christmas*. Gannon, Buck Ram, and Walter Kent (wm). A huge hit for Bing Crosby.

1949 *Dreamer's Holiday*. Mabel Wayne*/Gannon. A hit for Perry Como and for Buddy Clark.

1953 *Under Paris Skies*. Hubert Giraud/Gannon (English lyrics).

ERROLL GARNER, Composer (1921–1977)

Writers on music continue to put forth that Garner, a Pittsburgh-born jazz pianist, could not read music. True or not, he was the composer of several instrumentals prior to his great hit ballad, *Misty*. Garner was Art Tatum's re-placement in New York when the latter couldn't perform any longer. In the late 1940s, Garner's first published instrumental was *Erroll's Bounce*.

Chronology

1954   *Misty*. Garner/Johnny Burke*. A classic. The twist here is that this is a song about which a movie (*Play Misty For Me*, with Clint Eastwood) was written, rather than the reverse. *Misty* was first recorded by a trio led by Garner.

1961   *Dreamstreet* Garner (instr.).

GEORGE GERSHWIN, Composer (1898–1937) and IRA GERSHWIN, Lyricist (1896–1983)

No songwriters in the history of popular music can compare in musical quality and lyrical beauty to the Gershwin brothers. Coming from an immigrant New York City family, Ira and George (named Israel Gershowitz and Jacob Gersh-wine at their births—after several re-namings, the family became Gershwin) made a perfect team; yet they were totally unalike in personality.

Ira, the eldest of four children, was an excellent student who was accepted to the prestigious Townsend Harris High School for gifted young people. He was a reporter on the school newspaper and also wrote lyrics and poetry, sometimes with his friend Izzy Hochberg (who became the lyricist E. Y. Harburg*). In 1917, Ira wrote his first song, *You May Throw All the Rice You Desire*, which was never published and, unfortunately, the musical composition itself was lost. Later that same year, Ira and brother Jacob wrote another song, *You Are Not the Girl*, which also was never published.

The first published Gershwin song, *The Real American Folk Song (It's a Rag)*, was introduced in 1918 by stage star Nora Bayes. Some music history books contradict that, and state the Gershwins' first published song was *Waiting for the Sun to Come Out*. There were no immediate hits for the brothers, but the enthusiastic acceptance of their music was coming—quickly. In the meantime, Ira enrolled at the City College of New York. George was of a different mold—mischievous, athletically active, and a "wild kid" who was in no way interested in traditional education. But when the family got its first piano, George found the channel for his passions. He was able to play the keyboard in a very short time; and play he did, constantly. Very few discs of George Gershwin's piano playing were produced; at age 15 he traveled out to East Orange, New Jersey, to make piano rolls, earning the munificent sum of thirty-five dollars a week. At about the same time, he earned another fifteen a week as a demo pianist for the Jerome H. Remick publishing house—the sassy street kid did all right for himself. Gershwin played/recorded more than 125 piano rolls, which, according to Michael Montgomery in *The Gershwins*, "constitute the largest and most significant legacy of Gershwin's performing style."

A composer of ballads and preludes, rhapsodies and ballets, and music of so many kinds, George Gershwin crowded a full life's worth of work into a short amount of time, less than twenty years of songwriting. Like later musicians

Tony Bennett and Miles Davis, George was a prodigious artist/painter. He was also an art collector, perhaps emulating a hero, Jerome Kern*. His death, from a brain tumor in 1937, was mourned throughout the world of music and by the millions and millions of people who loved his songs.

Ira wrote just about the finest poetry ever set to music, and he did it for more than thirty years with his beloved brother George and other fine composers. Ira Gershwin published early on under the name Arthur Francis, which he adopted from the names of his brother Arthur and sister Francis. (Incidentally, the middle initial in Ira B. Gershwin's signature was taken from his mother's maiden name: Bruskin.)

The Gershwins never won an Academy Award. In 1937, the year George and Ira wrote the music for two films, **Shall We Dance?** and **Damsel in Distress**, their songs, *They Can't Take That Away From Me, They All Laughed* and *Let's Call the Whole Thing Off* were nominated—but lost to *Sweet Leilani*. At last count, there were at least ten biographies of the Gershwin brothers. In Kimball and Simon's handsome 1973 coffee table book, *The Gershwins*, there is a quote from composer Richard Rodgers summing up the Gershwins' work by writing "three musical notes on a bar of music; S'Wonderful; then the phrase, 'and it was Ira who wrote the perfect words.'" The chronology lists some of their greatest hits and is followed by a separate list of George's classical works.

Chronology

1919   *Swanee*. G. Gershwin/Irving Caesar. Sung by Al Jolson in **Sinbad**.

1922   *I'll Build a Stairway to Paradise*. G. Gershwin/Arthur Francis and George Gard "Buddy" DeSylva*. DeSylva was a close friend of the Gershwins who became a highly successful songwriter, publisher, and producer. The song was in George White's **Scandals** on Broadway.

1923   *I Won't Say I Will, But I Won't Say I Won't*. G. Gershwin/Francis and DeSylva. From **Little Miss Bluebird** on the New York stage. Sarah Vaughn did a fine job on a recording three decades later.

1924   *Fascinating Rhythm, Oh, Lady Be Good*, and *The Man I Love*. George/Ira Gershwin. The first two songs were in **Lady Be Good** on Broadway. *The Man* was dropped from the show—and dropped again from **Strike Up the Band** in 1930—but, nonetheless, it is a classic.
Somebody Loves Me. G. Gershwin/DeSylva and Ballard Macdonald*.

1925   *Sweet and Lowdown*. George/Ira Gershwin. From **Tip Toes** on Broadway.

1926   **Oh Kay!** Songs by George/Ira Gershwin. This production starred Gertrude Lawrence and included the songs *Do, Do, Do, Clap Yo' Hands, Someone to Watch Over Me*, and *Maybe*.

1927   **Funny Face**. Songs by George/Ira Gershwin. Starring Adele and Fred Astaire and featuring *S'Wonderful, He Loves and She Loves, My One and Only*, and *How Long Has This Been Going On?*

1928   *I've Got a Crush on You.* George/Ira Gershwin. For **Treasure Girl**. Lee Wiley slowed it down; Frank Sinatra* helped maintain it as a musical treasure.

1929   *Liza.* George/Ira Gershwin. From **Show Girl** on Broadway.
Soon. George/Ira Gershwin. Used in **Strike Up the Band**. Not to be confused with the Rodgers and Hart hit, *Soon*, from the 1935 Bing Crosby film **Mississippi**.

1930   **Girl Crazy**. Songs by George/Ira Gershwin. This incredible Broadway musical starred Ginger Rogers and Ethel Merman. The songs included *Bidin' My Time, Sam and Delilah, But Not for Me, I Got Rhythm*, and what is often considered to be the greatest of the Gershwin ballads, *Embraceable You*.

1931   **Of Thee I Sing**. Songs by George/Ira Gershwin. The title song, *Who Cares*, and *Love Is Sweeping the Country* were hits from this musical. *Of Thee* was introduced by a hoofer, later to become a Hollywood actor and a U.S. Senator from California, George Murphy.

1933   *Isn't It a Pity?* George/Ira Gershwin. From **Pardon My English**.
Mine and *Wintergreen for President (Tweedledee)*. George/Ira Gershwin. From **Let 'em Eat Cake**, again on Broadway.

1935   **Porgy and Bess**. Geroge/Ira Gershwin and DuBose Heyward (wm). The classic American opera, from Heyward's book, included: *Bess, You Is My Woman, I Got Plenty o'Nuttin', I Loves You, Porgy, It Ain't Necessarily So* and *Summertime*.

1936   *I Can't Get Started (With You)* and *By Strauss*. Vernon Duke*/I. Gershwin. Both songs were heard in **The Show Is On**, on Broadway. *I Can't Get Started* is one of the great ballads of all time. Bunny Berigan (trumpeter, leader, and singer), helped make it one of the most popular songs ever, thanks to his classic recording. In 1951, *By Strauss* was sung again in **An American in Paris**, by Gene Kelly, Oscar Levant, and Georges Guetary.

1937   **Shall We Dance?** Songs by George/Ira Gershwin. The movie starred Fred Astaire and Ginger Rogers and the songs *They All Laughed, Hi-Ho, They Can't Take That Away from Me, Beginner's Luck*, and more.
Damsel in Distress. Songs by George/Ira Gershwin. The brothers' second magnificent film score in 1937 (again starring Fred Astaire and Ginger Rogers), this time featuring, *Things are Looking Up, Nice Work If You Can Get It*, and *A Foggy Day*. According to music historians, Ira supposedly wrote the lyrics to *A Foggy Day* in just forty minutes, while riding in a cab in London, England.

1938   **The Goldwyn Follies**. Songs by Vernon Duke/George and Ira Gershwin. Ella Logan, a fine singer, introduced *Love Walked In* and *I Was Doing Alright*. The film score also included *Love Is Here to Stay*.

1941   **Lady in the Dark**. Songs by Kurt Weill/I. Gershwin. The memorable song from this Broadway production was *My Ship*.

1944   **Cover Girl**. Songs by Jerome Kern/I. Gershwin. *Long Ago and Far Away* and *A Sure Thing* were two of the songs in this brilliant and highly successful film starring Gene Kelly and Rita Hayworth.

1946   *For You, For Me, For Ever More*. Kay Swift/I. Gershwin. From the non-musical movie, **The Shocking Miss Pilgrim**. Swift (Chapter 4) was a protégé of the Gershwins.

1954   *A Star Is Born*. Songs by Harold Arlen/I. Gershwin. The first musical version of
the renowned American film starred Judy Garland—and the song that became a
blues classic, *The Man That Got Away*.

Classical George Gershwin

1924   *Rhapsody in Blue*. On February 12, Paul Whiteman presented and conducted *An
Experiment in Modern Music*. This legendary concert featured two pianists, Zez
Confrey, composer of *Kitten on the Keys*, and George Gershwin. Whiteman led
the Palais Royal Orchestra in eleven numbers; one of the last was Gershwin's
Rhapsody in Blue, featuring the young composer at the piano. Although it
received a standing ovation, criticisms were mixed—and still are. The
composition was arranged by Ferde Grofé, a fine composer himself. The
performance soloists included trumpeter Henry Busse, saxophonist Don Clark,
and clarinetist Ross Gorman. It was Gorman who, in rehearsal, played a glissando
introduction to *Rhapsody* with an ascending slide, which he claimed to have done
whimsically—that haunting introductory wail has been played and heard ever
since. Lyrics were written for *Rhapsody in Blue*—I heard a vocalist singing them
with the old Whiteman band back in the 1930s.

1925   *Concerto in F* and *Song of the Flame*.

1926   *Prelude for Piano*.

1929   *An American in Paris*.

1935   *Cuban Overture* and *Porgy and Bess*.

RAY GILBERT, Lyricist (1912–1976)

Gilbert was born in Hartford, Connecticut, and grew up in Chicago. He became a writer for famed vaudevillian Sophie Tucker and for Earl Carroll's *Vanities* on Broadway. Gilbert went on to Hollywood and was under contract for
his songwriting, with the Disney studios in particular.

Chronology

1926   *Muskrat Ramble*. Edward "Kid" Ory/Gilbert. A jazz classic.

1941   *Zoot Suit*. Bob O'Brien/Gilbert.

1943   *You Belong to My Heart*. Augustin Lara/Gilbert (English) lyrics.

1945   *Zip-a-Dee-Doo-Dah*. Allie Wrubel/Gilbert. An Oscar winner from the Disney
film, *Song of the South*.

1946   *Sooner or Later*. Charles Wolcott/Gilbert. Also from *Song of the South*.

HAVEN GILLESPIE, Lyricist (1888–1975)

Gillespie was a Kentucky-born newspaperman who eventually landed a job
on the *New York Times*. The wonderful song to which he wrote wonderful
words, *You Go to My Head*, is reminiscent of Cole Porter.

Chronology

1925 *Drifting and Dreaming.* Egbert Van Alstyne (Chapter 1), Erwin Schmidt, Loyal Curtis, and Gillespie (wm). It became the theme song of an orchestra led by Orrin Tucker.

1926 *Breezin' Along with the Breeze.* Richard Whiting/Gillespie and Seymour Simons (Chapter 4).

1934 *Santa Claus Is Coming to Town.* Fred Coots/Gillespie. Might well be the most popular children's Christmas song of all time.

1938 *You Go to My Head.* Coots/Gillespie. His marvelous lyrics include the line "you intoxicate my soul with your eyes."

1949 *That Lucky Old Sun.* Beasley Smith/Gillespie.

BENNY GOODMAN, Composer (1909–1986)

Benjamin David Goodman was one of twelve children whose parents were poor immigrants. But their family was rich in music—and young Benny was a prodigy at age 11, having already studied clarinet at the famous Hull Settlement House in Chicago. By age 13, Benny was playing professionally. He used his developing talent to support his family early on in life, after his father was killed in an automobile accident.

Benny Goodman was the best clarinetist of all time, bar none. He was a jazz master and played classical music with the most renowned of the classicists—symphonic, chamber and the rest. And Goodman was one of the inventors of swing (with considerable help from the great Fletcher Henderson). Having started in Chicago with Ben Pollack's orchestra and played with Bix Beiderbecke and others, Goodman moved on to New York in the early 1930s, and went into the "pit" bands, playing with roommates Glenn Miller and Tommy Dorsey. Influenced by jazz clarinetist Jimmy Noone (they studied under similar teachers, but Noone was out there first), Goodman added to the Chicago jazz style wherever he played with a phrasing and tone that no other musician ever brought to that reed instrument.

Beyond his playing, he was a brilliant and sometimes irascible organizer and leader; such stars as pianist Jess Stacy and vocalist Helen Forrest were known to have been victims of Goodman's wrath. Both expressed considerable dislike for Goodman and his fierce "ray," a look that made musicians feel awfully small when, indeed, all they had done was play a note that might not quite have pleased Benny. Despite much malignity, Benny Goodman did do kind things—obviously, for his family, but for others, too. For example, he was known to have paid the medical bills when Fletcher Henderson was hospitalized with a terminal illness. The historical importance of Goodman and his wonderful bands of the mid-1930s and beyond cannot be ignored. There may be only one or two other instrumentalists (e.g., Louis Armstrong and Charlie Parker come to mind) who can placed at the very top of the performers list along with Benny Goodman.

Chronology

1934   *If Dreams Come True*. Goodman and Edgar Sampson (Chapter 4)/Irving Mills. *Stompin' at the Savoy*. Goodman, Sampson, and Chick Webb/Andy Razaf.

1938   *Don't Be That Way*. Goodman and Sampson/Mitchell Parish.

1941   *Flying Home*. Goodman and Lionel Hampton/Sid Robin. Robin also wrote the lyrics to Charlie Shavers' song, *Undecided*. Hampton's vibes instrumental version is still famous.
Air Mail Special. Goodman, Charlie Christian, and Jimmy Mundy (Chapter 4) (instr.) Christian was a great electric guitarist in the Goodman band.
Two O'Clock Jump. Goodman, Count Basie and Harry James (instr.). A sequel to the earlier *One O'Clock Jump*.

MACK GORDON, Lyricist (1904–1959)

Morris Gittler, who became songwriter Mack Gordon, was born in Poland and came to the United States as a child. He was a boy soprano who sang in minstrel shows before becoming a vaudevillian/actor. After years of successfully performing comedy, Gordon began writing special comedic material for the movies. He then went on to an even more prestigious career as a lyricist. Gordon's first Hollywood lyrics were written to songs composed by Maurice Abrahams, Max Rich, George Weitz, and others. Unfortunately, there were no hits for Gordon in his inaugural year (1929) out West. In 1930, Gordon and co-lyricist Harold Adamson provided the words to Vincent Youmans' big hit *Time on My Hands*, for **Smiles** on Broadway. In 1931, he and composer Harry Revel wrote the songs for the **Ziegfeld Follies**. Revel and Gordon also wrote the music and lyrics for two more New York shows: **Smiling Faces** and **Marching By**.

Hollywood Chronology

1930   *Aint'cha*. Max Rich/Gordon. From the film, **Painted Heels**. Gordon wrote another nine movie songs that year with Harry Revel, Abner Silver, and Ted Snyder.

1933   *Did You Ever See a Dream Walking?* Revel/Gordon. Their first real hit, from the movie, **Sitting Pretty**.

1934   *Love Thy Neighbor*. Revel/Gordon. From **We're Not Dressing**, a movie musical take-off of **The Admirable Chrichton**. Bing Crosby sang this hit.
With My Eyes Wide Open, I'm Dreaming. Revel/Gordon. From the film, **Shoot the Works**.
Stay As Sweet As You Are. Revel/Gordon. The duo's third hit of the year, from the film, **College Rhythm**.

1935   *Love in Bloom*. Revel/Gordon. Film title song, first sung by Dixie Lee (Bing Crosby's first wife). It later became a gag theme for Jack Benny. The film also included *Lookie Lookie Lookie Here Comes Cookie* by Gordon (wm).
Without a Word of Warning and *From the Top of Your Head to the Tip of Your Toes*. Revel/Gordon. Two hits from the movie, **Two for Tonight**, sung by Bing Crosby to/with Joan Bennett.

1936   *I Feel Like a Feather* and *The Animal in Me*. Revel/Gordon. From **The Big**

Broadcast of '36, starring Ethel Merman, with film acting performances by both Gordon and Revel. *I Feel* actually premiered in *Collegiate*, an earlier Betty Grable picture which featured a total of eight Revel/Gordon songs.

Good Night My Love and *One Never Knows, Does One*? Revel/Gordon. For *Stowaway*, starring Ginger Rogers. Revel and Gordon also wrote one song for the movie, *Palm Springs*, and seven more tunes for a Shirley Temple film that year.

1937   *Wake Up and Live*. Songs by Revel/Gordon. The writing team really scored with the title song, *There's a Lull in My Life, I Love You Much Too Much, Muchacha, Never in a Million Years* and four others for this Alice Faye film.

1938   *You Can't Have Everything*. Songs by Revel/Gordon. Another Faye movie with great songs including the title tune, *Afraid to Dream, Please Pardon Us*, and *We're in Love*.

In Old Chicago. Revel/Gordon. Film title song.

Love and Hisses. Revel/Gordon. Title song of a film in which Revel/Gordon also wrote, *I Want to Be in Winchell's Column*. The late Walter Winchell, an infamous gossip columnist and former vaudevillian, played himself in the film.

An Old Straw Hat. Revel/Gordon. For the Shirley Temple classic, *Rebecca of Sunnybrook Farm*.

I've Got a Date With a Dream. Revel/Gordon. This chart topping song was written for the film, *My Lucky Star*.

1940   *Down Argentine Way*. Songs by Harry Warren/Gordon. Carmen Miranda sang the Oscar-nominated title song, and helped Don Ameche and Betty Grable through *Two Dreams Met. Down Argentine* lost the Academy Award to *When You Wish Upon a Star*.

Adored One. Alfred Newman/Gordon. From the biographical film, *Lillian Russell*.

Young People. Songs by Warren/Gordon. This score was Warren's first music composed for Fox (after having left Warners' with a fine career there). *Young People* starred an aging 20-year-old Shirley Temple.

1941   *Chattanooga Choo Choo*. Warren/Gordon. From the movie, *Sun Valley Serenade*, this Academy Award-nominated song lost to the classic by Kern and Hammerstein, *Last Time I Saw Paris. Sun Valley* also had lots of Glenn Miller ever-greens, including: *It Happened in Sun Valley, Kiss Polka*, and *I Know Why and So Do You*.

I Yi, Yi, Yi, Yi, (I Like You Very Much). Warren/Gordon. A Miranda special from the film, *That Night in Rio*. Gordon wrote fourteen more songs with Warren in 1941.

1942   *Orchestra Wives*. Songs by Warren/Gordon. This *Sun Valley* follow-up film featured the Oscar-nominated *I Got a Gal in Kalamazoo, At Last*, and *Serenade in Blue. I Got*, which has become an American standard, lost in the Academy Awards to *White Christmas*.

Springtime in the Rockies. Songs by Warren/Gordon. This Big Band movie, one of many abounding at the time, featured Harry James, with vocalist Helen Forrest (Fogel) warbling *I Had the Craziest Dream*.

There Will Never Be Another You. Warren/Gordon. From the film, *Iceland*.

1943 *You'll Never Know*. Warren/Gordon. Perhaps Warren and Gordon's loveliest and most memorable song; from **Hello Frisco, Hello**.
Sweet Rosie O'Grady. Songs by Warren/Gordon.

1944 *I'm Making Believe*. James V. Monaco/Gordon. Benny Goodman played it in a movie; Ella Fitzgerald and the Ink Spots made it a number 1 Billboard chart record. Monaco and Gordon also wrote six songs that year for the movie, *Pin Up Girl*.

1945 *I Wish I Knew* and *The More I See You*. Warren/Gordon. Sung by Betty Grable in the film **Billy Rose's Diamond Horseshoe**.
I Can't Begin to Tell You. Monaco/Warren. Written for the film, **The Dolly Sisters**, this song was an Oscar nominee, losing to the Warren and Mercer classic, *On the Atchison, Topeka and the Santa Fe*.

1946 *3 Little Girls in Blue*. Songs by Josef Myrow*/Gordon. This film's music included two hits, *You Make Me Feel So Young* and *On the Boardwalk in Atlantic City*. The multitalented Gordon also produced this movie for Fox.

1947 **Mother Wore Tights**. Songs by Myrow/Gordon. This movie's songs included the Oscar-nominee *You Do*, as well as *Kokomo, Indiana*, and *Tra La La*. *You Do* lost to *Zip-a-Dee-Doo-Dah*.
Mam'selle. Edmund Goulding/Gordon. Written for the film, **The Razor's Edge**.

1949 *You Go Your Way and I'll Go Crazy*. Revel/Gordon. For the movie, **Make Mine Laughs**.

1950 *Wilhelmina*. Myrow/Gordon. Written for the Betty Grable film, **Wabash Avenue**, this nominee lost the Academy Award to *Mona Lisa*. That same year, Warren and Gordon wrote six songs for **Summer Stock**, starring the great Judy Garland.

1955 *You My Love*. Jimmy Van Heusen/Gordon. Written for the sad film **Young at Heart**, it was performed, as only he could do it, by Frank Sinatra*.

1956 **Bundle of Joy**. Songs by Josef Myrow/Gordon. Seven songs from this wonderful songwriting team were written for this movie, but none is remembered now.

JOHNNY GREEN, Composer (1908–1989)

All evidence points to the fact that this great composer of golden age music, a gentleman of class and formality, preferred to be addressed as John, rather than Johnny. John W. Green was born in New York City, educated in private schools, and received an AB degree in economics from Harvard. After working on Wall Street for a short time, Green moved into the field of his great success— as an orchestra leader, an arranger, a pianist, a recording artist, and a composer. A prodigious contributor of Hollywood film scores, he began his songwriting career on Broadway.

Broadway Chronology

1929 *Coquette*. Green and Guy Lombardo/Gus Kahn. Green was only 21 years old when he co-composed this music.

1930 *Body and Soul*. Green/Edward Heyman*, Frank Eyton, and Robert Sour. Written for the Schwartz/Dietz revue on Broadway, ***Three's a Crowd***, and sung by Libby Holman. Heyman was the original wordsmith, and Eyton and Sour "appended" it, some say to the consternation of Green. In 1939, tenor sax player Coleman "Bean" Hawkins made a magnificent instrumental recording of this classic of classics and, in 1943, Hawkins reprised his own solo. It remains one of the great jazz recordings of all times. Although little is known about Robert Sour and Frank Eyton, it is fair to say that they contributed words to one of the greatest of all popular songs, *Body and Soul*. In Michael Feinstein's book, *Nice Work If You Can Get It: My Life in Rhythm and Rhyme*, he recounts the story that several different lyricists tried to write words to *Body and Soul*, including the famous Howard Dietz*. Feinstein goes on to say that John Green, the composer of the song, "was very specific about the lyrics he wanted performed [Edward Heyman's]." Robert Sour also wrote *We Could Make Such Beautiful Music Together* (composed by Henry Manners) and *Walkin' by the River* (composed by Una Mae Carlisle) in 1940, and *I See a Million People But All I Can See Is You* (Carlisle/Sour) in 1941.

Out of Nowhere. Green/Heyman. This second classic was taken to first place on the charts by Bing Crosby; it has been played consistently since then by jazz musicians. In 1957, Harry Harris wrote new lyrics to the song for the film, ***The Joker Is Wild***.

1933   *Weep No More My Baby*. Green/Heyman. For Earl Carroll's ***Murder at the Vanities*** on Broadway.

I Cover the Waterfront. Green/Heyman. Another classic.

Hollywood Chronology

1937   *I'm Yours*. Green/E. Y. Harburg. For the swell film, ***Second Chorus***.

Don't Look Now. Green/Irving Kahal. For the Paramount film, ***Double or Nothing***.

1943   *Take It and Git*. Green/James T. Marshall. This non-Green type swinger was written for the movie, ***Sleepy Lagoon***.

1944   *I'll Take the High Note*. Green/Harold Adamson. For the film, ***Bathing Beauty***.

1946   *Easy to Wed*. Green/Ted Duncan. Green composed the music for this MGM film's title song, along with *It Shouldn't Happen to a Duck* (words by Robert Franklin) and *Gonna Fall in Love with You* (lyrics by Ralph Blane).

1947   ***Something in the Wind***. Songs by Green and Leo Robin. The songs in this film included *Turntable Song, You Wanna Keep Your Baby Lookin' Right, It's Only Love, Happy Go Lucky and Free*, and the title tune.

1952   *Like Monday Follows Sunday*. Green, Clifford Grey, Rex Newman, and Douglas Furber (wm).

Serenade for a New Baby. Green (wm). All three of these songs were written for the film, ***Everything I Have Is Yours***.

BOB HAGGART, Composer (1914–   )

Robert Sherwood Haggart was born in New York and began his career as a guitarist, studying that instrument with George Van Epps. A professional musician by the time he reached his late teens, Haggart gained early fame as a founding member of Bob Crosby's Bobcats, side-by-side with swinging sideman Ray McKinley and others. In the late 1930s and early 1940s, Haggart was one of the busiest studio musicians working and did arrangements for Billie Holiday, Louis Armstrong*, and Duke Ellington*.

In the 1950s and 1960s, Haggart and trumpeter Yank Lawson formed a modern version of the Original Dixieland Jazz Band, the "World's Greatest Jazz Band." Their group was also known as the Lawson-Haggart Band. In 1996, Haggart, at age 82, was playing bass at a well-known Manhattan jazz club.

Chronology

1938   *South Rampart Street Parade*. Haggart/Ray Bauduc. Bauduc was a drummer in Crosby's band.
       I'm Prayin' Humble. Haggart (wm). For Crosby's band.
       Dogtown Blues. Haggart (wm).

1939   *What's New*? Haggart/Johnny Burke. Originally titled, *I'm Free*, this number was introduced by the Bobcats. I prefer Frank Sinatra's slower, more poignant version.

1940   *Big Noise from Winnetka*. Haggart and Bauduc/Gil Rodin and Bob Crosby. Arguably the most popular of Haggart's tunes, its fame is also due to the swinging arrangement performed by the Crosby band, with Bauduc and Haggart doing their respective musical thing, including Haggart whistling quite wonderfully.

OSCAR HAMMERSTEIN, Lyricist (1895–1960)

This musical giant—and the most romantic of all lyricists—was christened Oscar Greeley Clendenning Hammerstein, II. A librettist whose words are truly treasured in the world of songwriting and beyond, Hammerstein's integrity and decency are remembered as well; perhaps the essence of this special man is best documented in Hugh Fordin's fine 1960 Hammerstein biography, *Getting to Know Him*.

Born to wealth, on 116th Street in New York City, Oscar had a famous grandfather and namesake. Oscar I was a successful inventor of cigar-making equipment who invested in apartment houses and backed the construction of a dozen Broadway theatres; he was the founder/builder of the Harlem Opera House, later known as the Apollo Theatre. Well-known for his pioneering presentations of opera, Oscar I was also famous for suing people. William Hammerstein was Oscar II's father. A highly regarded and successful Broadway theatre manager, one of his well-known musical palaces was the Victoria Vaudeville House, also in Manhattan.

Oscar II was a Columbia University graduate who wrote plays and words to the compositions of operatic masters such as Herbert Stothart and Sigmund Romberg. He was a protégé of Otto Harbach* and co-wrote with the giants of popular music: Jerome Kern*, Vincent Youmans*, and of course, Richard Rodgers*, with whom he had his greatest successes. Hammerstein and his lyricist colleague, Lorenz Hart*, wrote their first songs for a musical revue, *Always You*, in 1920. Twice during the next quarter century, Hammerstein helped make history with new categories of musical theatre: with Kern and *Show Boat* and with Rogers and *Oklahoma*. He began contributing to films in 1929 with lyrics to the Broadway operetta, *The Desert Song*.

This genius was the "surrogate father" of young Stephen Sondheim and the greatest influence on Sondheim's life and career. Sondheim said of Hammerstein, "If Oscar had been an engineer, I would have been an engineer." Hammerstein died of cancer in 1960. As Mary Martin would no doubt sing in praise of Oscar Hammerstein, "he was a wonderful guy." He was a giant of American musical theatre and film—as a writer, a lyricist, and a producer. He was a man of taste, and despite detracting accusations of being "too sugary" and "too soppy," he was a fine poet.

Broadway Chronology

1920   *Always You*. ?/Hammerstein. Hammerstein had tried writing and staging non-musicals, but that had not worked out, so he wrote the lyrics for this Broadway show; the composers, interestingly, are not referenced in my sources.
Tickle Me and *Jimmie*. Herbert Stothart/Otto Harbach, Frank Mandel, and Hammerstein. These two songs were written for a musical production Stothart staged. Harbach was one of Hammerstein's mentors. Also, the stage manager for these two 1920 productions was Arthur Hammerstein, Oscar's uncle.

1922   *Daffy Dill*. Songs by Stothart/Hammerstein. Story by Guy Bolton. This show ran nine weeks.
Queen of Hearts. Lewis Gensler/Hammerstein. Nora Bayes starred in this Broadway production.

1923   *Wildflower*. Songs by Vincent Youmans and Hammerstein. Story by Otto Harbach and Hammerstein. *Bambalina* was this show's hit song.
Mary Jane McKane. Songs by Youmans/Hammerstein. The duo's second musical stage collaboration that year.

1924   *Rose Marie*. Rudolph Friml/Harbach and Hammerstein. Libretto by Harbach and Hammerstein. This production was presented at the beginning of what music historian Gerald Bordman calls "the Golden Age of the American Musical Theatre." The show ran 557 performances, astonishing for that time, and featured the beloved classic, *Indian Love Call*.

1925   *Sunny*. Songs by Jerome Kern/Harbach and Hammerstein. The big song from this first Kern and Hammerstein collaboration was *Who*.

1926   *Wild Rose*. Friml/Harbach and Hammerstein. The last musical this trio wrote together; it ran two months.
Desert Song. Sigmund Romberg/Harbach and Hammerstein. Book by Frank Mandel (co-producer), Harbach, and Hammerstein. This Broadway production, really a Vienese opera, was a 471-performance smash hit; it included the songs *One Alone* and *The Riff Song*.

1927   *Golden Dawn*. Songs by Stothart, Harbach, and Hammerstein. This production had a limited 181 performances run.
Show Boat. Songs by Kern and Hammerstein. Original story by Edna Ferber; stage adaptation by Hammerstein. This Ziegfeld production was the landmark musical of the era and has enjoyed four revivals, with its magnificent songs

including: *Ol' Man River, Can't Help Lovin' Dat Man, Why Do I Love You?* and *Make Believe*.

1928 **Good Boy**. Songs by Stothart, Kalmar, Ruby, Meyers, and Hammerstein.
  Rainbow. Songs by Romberg/Harbach and Hammerstein. This one only ran five weeks.
  New Moon. Songs by Romberg/Harbach and Hammerstein. This Broadway musical gave us the songs *Softly, As in a Morning Sunrise, Stouthearted Men, One Kiss, Lover Come Back to Me*, and *Wanting You*.

1929 *Why Was I Born?* and *Don't Ever Leave Me*. Kern/Hammerstein. From **Sweet Adeline**, a production that ran seven months.

1932 *I've Told Ev'ry Little Star* and *The Song Is You*. Kern/Hammerstein. From the duo's successful Broadway production, **Music in the Air**.

1935 *I Won't Dance*. Kern/Hammerstein. The hit from the London-based musical, **Three Sisters**. It was rewritten for the film, **Roberta** with Dorothy Fields lyrics.

1939 *All the Things You Are*. Kern/Hammerstein. Alec Wilder, the brilliant songwriter and musicologist, called this ''the perfect love song.'' For many, *All* is the most beautiful of all Kern/Hammerstein ballads, even though it came from a Broadway musical that ran only 59 times, **Very Warm for May**.

1943 **Oklahoma!** Songs by Richard Rodgers/Hammerstein (lyrics and libretto). The beginning of the great Rodgers and Hammerstein partnership—and another Broadway milestone. **Oklahoma**'s music, sets, choreography, directing, singing, and acting were done to perfection. Just like **Showboat** sixteen years earlier, this masterpiece, based on Lynn Riggs' book *Green Grow the Lilacs*, changed the face of American musical theatre forever. Included the songs *Out of My Dreams, Surrey with the Fringe on Top, People Will Say We're in Love, Kansas City, Oh, What a Beautiful Morning, I Cain't Say No*, the title song, and more.
  Carmen Jones. Songs by Rodgers/Hammerstein. Hammerstein's rewrite of Bizet's opera, staged with an all African-American cast, was a Broadway success—a 500-plus performance run.

1945 With **Oklahoma**'s established success on Broadway and growing international acclaim from road company stagings, Rodgers collaborated with Hammerstein on another smash hit, **Carousel**. Their superb score included evergreens: *If I Loved You, Soliloquoy, You'll Never Walk Alone* and *June Is Busting Out All Over*.

1947 **Allegro**. Rodgers/Hammerstein (Original story and lyrics). A fine musical play that had a one-year run and these two hit songs: *A Fellow Needs a Girl* and *The Gentleman Is a Dope*.

1948 **South Pacific**. Songs by Rodgers and Hammerstein. The writing duo astounded critics and audiences alike with their tremendous stage version of James A. Michener's Pulitzer Prize–winning *Tales of the South Pacific*—the second musical in history to also win the Pulitzer Prize. Joshua Logan directed and Mary Martin and Ezio Pinza headed a superb cast of the original 2,000 performance production, which is still a worldwide favorite from junior high schools to professional summer stock presentations. Hammerstein's beautiful message of tolerance and decency was balanced with comedy, exuberance, and music. The list of wonderful hit songs includes *There Is Nothing Like a Dame, Dites Moi, Happy Talk,*

Cockeyed Optimist, Bali Ha'i, Honey Bun, You've Got to be Carefully Taught, This Nearly Was Mine, I'm Gonna' Wash That Man Right Out of My Hair, Younger Than Springtime, and *Some Enchanted Evening*.

1951 **The King and I**. Songs by Rodgers/Hammerstein. Their fifth team hit was based on the book, *Anna and the King of Siam*. Hammerstein created a musical tale that was made to order for Gertrude Lawrence and launched the career of Yul Brenner. The original production ran four years and has been revived several times. Just listing the songs is to lovingly recall the continuously played music: *Hello, Young Lovers; I Whistle a Happy Tune; We Kiss in a Shadow; Getting to Know You; Something Wonderful*; and *Shall We Dance?*

1953 **Me and Juliet**. Songs by Rodgers/Hammerstein. Not a runaway hit, but Hammerstein still wrote fine lyrics; Rodger's haunting score, including *No Other Love*, was used again—more successfully—in the television series, *Victory at Sea*. Rodgers' original title was *Beneath the Southern Cross*.

1955 **Pipe Dream**. Songs by Rodgers/Hammerstein. A one-season run with beautiful music that included the song, *All at Once You Love Her*.

1958 **Flower Drum Song**. Songs by Rodgers/Hammerstein. A really enjoyable musical with the hit songs *Love Look Away* and *I Enjoy Being a Girl*.

1959 **The Sound of Music**. Songs by Rodgers/Hammerstein. Rodgers and Hammerstein's list of classics was topped, in many ways, by this musical based on the real-life experiences of the Von Trapp family of Austria. While rooted in fact, this stage extravaganza—not totally pleasing to New York's hardbitten critics—will go down in Broadway history as a Cinderella-type fantasy for children "nine to ninety-three." This grand production starred Mary Martin and was produced by Rodgers, Hammerstein, Leland Hayward, and Richard Halliday (Mary Martin's husband). The songs were grand, too: *Edelweiss, Climb Every Mountain, My Favorite Things, Do Re Mi, Sixteen Going on Seventeen*, the title song, and more.

Hollywood Chronology

1930 Hammerstein wrote the lyrics for three Youmans' songs for the film, **Song of the West**, and words for eight Sigmund Romberg* compositions for the movie, **Viennese Nights; Sunny** was put on film in Hollywood.

1931 Romberg/Hammerstein wrote eight more songs for **Children of Dreams**.

1935 **The Night Is Young**. Songs by Romberg/Hammerstein. Original Story by Vicky Baum. This film operetta was really Hammerstein's first experience with lyrics written expressly for the Hollywood genre. In addition to the title song, Hammerstein's lyrics to *When I Grow Too Old to Dream* contributed to the film becoming a classic.

1936 **Rose Marie**. Friml/Harbach and Hammerstein (lyrics and libretto). This MGM movie ignored the original Broadway plot, but it was a big hit—and a vehicle— for the popular Jeanette McDonald and Nelson Eddy team. Two new actors also appeared: David Nivins (eventually Niven) and James Stewart. *Rose Marie* and *Indian Love Call* remained in the score from the 1924 stage version.

Show Boat. Songs by Kern/Hammerstein. Clive Hirschhorn was right in calling the film version of *Show Boat* "an undisputed musical masterpiece." It came from the stage to the screen with a number of the original cast (Robeson as Joe, in particular), and featured movie superstars of the day, including Irene Dunne, Charles Winninger, Allan Jones, Helen Morgan, and Hattie McDaniel. The reprised hit songs included *Make Believe, Ol' Man River, Can't Help Lovin' Dat Man, You are Love*, and *Bill. Why Do I Love You?* was, unfortunately, omitted. ***Give Us This Night***. Songs by Erich Wolfgang Korngold/Hammerstein. Another operatic film. Korngold was a somewhat renowned opera composer of the day.

1937   ***High, Wide and Handsome***. Songs by Kern/Hammerstein. Screenplay by Hammerstein. A fine western musical with Irene Dunne, Randolph Scott, and Dorothy Lamour. Historians call it ''*Oklahoma's* preview.'' It featured the unique American ballad, *The Folks Who Live on the Hill*.
I'll Take Romance. Ben Oakland/Hammerstein. The title song is much finer than its namesake film.

1938   *A Mist Over the Moon*. Oakland/Hammerstein. Written for the film, ***The Lady Objects***, this Oscar-nominee lost to *Thanks for the Memory*.
The Great Waltz. Songs by Richard Strauss/Hammerstein. Hammerstein wrote lyrics to Strauss' music for this highly regarded biographical film of the great waltzmaster.

1940   ***The New Moon***. Songs by Romberg/Frank Mandel, Lawrence Schwab, and Hammerstein. The MGM motion picture version of the operetta, starring Jeanette McDonald and Nelson Eddy. The lovely Romberg melodies include *Lover Come Back to Me, Softly, As in a Morning Sunrise, Stout Hearted Men, One Kiss*, and *Wanting You*.
One Night in the Tropics. Scored by Kern and Hammerstein. Yes, they wrote the songs for this Abbott and Costello picture. The best song from the film was Kern and Dorothy Field's *Remind Me*.
The Last Time I Saw Paris. Kern/Hammerstein. Used in the film, ***Lady Be Good***, a screen adaptation that did not quite resemble the Gershwin stage musical. This Oscar-winning song was particularly moving at the time, since the Nazis had recently occupied Paris.

1941   ***Sunny***. Songs by Kern/Harbach and Hammerstein. The Broadway musical was first filmed in 1930 and made into a movie once more, this time starring Ray Bolger and still featuring the beautiful song, *Who*.

1943   ***Desert Song***. Songs by Romberg/Hammerstein. Originally a Broadway operetta written by Frank Mandel, Lawrence Schwab, and Hammerstein, it was filmed for the first time in 1929. The second time, Hollywood made it into a World War II thriller, but kept the same Romberg/Hammerstein songs, especially *One Alone* and the title song.

1944   ***Broadway Rhythm***. Songs by Kern and Hammerstein. The West Coast take-off on *Very Warm for May*, and the first film in which *All The Things You Are* was heard.

1945   *It Might as Well Be Spring*. Rodgers/Hammerstein. This Academy Award winner came from the songwriting duo's first film collaboration, ***State Fair***. The movie was a musical version of a 1933 Will Rogers' picture; although Rodgers and Hammerstein and others were not happy with it, I thought it was delightful—

especially the Oscar-winning song and two others: *That's for Me* and *It's a Grand Night for Singing*.

1946   *All Through the Day*. Kern/Hammerstein. An Oscar-nominated song written for the film, **Centennial Summer**. It was Kern's last song; he died soon after the film was released. But the music continued: many of Hammerstein's collaborative standards, as well as non-standards, were heard in the musicals of the late 1940s and 1950s.

1951   *A Kiss to Build a Dream On*. Kalmar/Ruby and Hammerstein. Used in the film, **The Strip**, and nominated for an Academy Award. The songwriters penned it in 1935.
Show Boat. Songs by Kern and Hammerstein. Presented by MGM—in color this time—with the addition of dances by Marge and Gower Champion.

1952   *I Won't Dance*. Kern/Hammerstein. Their song reprised, again, from the original London musical **Three Sisters**, to the 1935 film **Roberta**, to this remake movie **Lovely to Look At**.

1955   **Oklahoma!** Songs by Rodgers and Hammerstein. Filmed—beautifully.

1956   **The King and I**. Songs by Rodgers/Hammerstein. Won the Academy Award for the best film score. Marni Nixon's voice was beautifully dubbed in for actress Deborah Kerr. Yul Brenner was excellent once again—and so was the music.

1957   **Cinderella**. Rodgers/Hammerstein. They wrote *Do I Love You Because You're Beautiful* for this Disney film.

1958   **South Pacific**. Songs by Rodgers and Hammerstein. Starring the highly talented Mitzi Gaynor and a wonderfully solid singer named Rossano Brazzi. She was great and his singing was superb—especially *This Nearly was Mine*. The critics were not impressed by the movie.

1961   **Flower Drum Song**. Songs by Rodgers/Hammerstein. Universal made a ton of money from this movie which received mixed reviews. The music, like the original Broadway production, was fine, particularly *Love Look Away* and *I Enjoy Being a Girl*.

1965   **The Sound of Music**. Songs by Rodgers and Hammerstein. The movie surpassed the reviews and acclaims it received on Broadway—and has now earned more than $100,000,000. It starred Julie Andrews, one of the most charming singer/ actors of this generation, and Christopher Plummer, an actor's actor and star in his own right. The child actors delighted audiences—and frozen in time on film, continue to do so. Most of all, the sound of the Oscar-winning music stays alive in *My Favorite Things, Do Re Mi, Sixteen Going on Seventeen, Edelweiss, Climb Every Mountain*, the title song, and the others.

OTTO HARBACH, Lyricist (1873–1963)

Research sources indicate that Hauerbach may have been his original name, but whatever it was, Otto Harbach wrote fine operettas and musical plays for the Broadway stage. He also was Oscar Hammerstein's mentor. Born in Salt Lake City, Utah, Harbach earned a Ph.D. in English from Columbia University in New York, then became an English teacher and a successful advertising professional. His musical career was launched in 1908; from 1912 to 1919, he collaborated with Rudolph Friml* and Oscar Hammerstein*. Harbach also wrote with Gus Kahn*, Vincent Youmans*, Burt Kalmar and Harry Ruby*, Irving Caesar*, Herbert Stothart*, Joe McCarthy, and others.

Chronology

1908 *Cuddle Up a Little Closer*. Karl Hochsna/Harbach. From Harbach's first play, **Three Twins**.

1912 *Gianina Mia*. Rudolph Friml/Harbach. Written for **Firefly**.

1924 *Rose Marie* and *Indian Love Call*. Friml/Oscar Hammerstein and Harbach. Written for the highly successful Broadway musical **Rose Marie**—and later reprised in the 1936 MGM film version.

1925 *Sunny*. Jerome Kern/Hammerstein and Harbach. Title song from their Broadway production.

1926 *Desert Song* and *One Alone*. Sigmund Romberg/Hammerstein and Harbach. From the smash hit musical, **Desert Song**.

1931 *The Night Was Made for Love*. Kern/Harbach. Written for the production, **Cat and the Fiddle**.

1933 *Smoke Gets in Your Eyes*. Kern/Harbach. The most famous of Harbach's lyrics; written for the musical, **Roberta**. Also from that production, *The Touch of Your Hand, Yesterdays*, and the title song.

E. Y. "YIP" HARBURG, Lyricist (1896–1981)

Israel Hochberg was nicknamed "Yip" because of his small size and speed as a child (Yip is short for *yipsel*, which in Yiddish means squirrel). Born in New York City, Harburg attended Townsend Harris High School for gifted students, where he met and became close friends with Ira Gershwin. Both young men were wonderful writers who wrote for their high school newspaper; later, at City College, they put together skits for the school's amateur shows. Much Harburg lore from this time of his life and beyond is contained in the enjoyable biography, *Who Put the Rainbow in the Wizard of Oz?*, written by Harold Meyerson and Ernie Harburg.

E. Y. Harburg (the E stood for Erwin in the Anglicized version of his given name) was more than a lyricist: he was a powerful fount of ideas, a librettist, and a creator of stories for theatre and film. In addition, he was a man known for his integrity, decency, and fairness. "[H]is profound sense of empathy to his fellow man," from the *Smithsonian American Songbook Series*, is an apt phrase that well describes Yip Harburg. That sense is evident in many of his lyrics, too.

Broadway Chronology

1929–32   Working with several partners, Harburg wrote for Earl Carroll's **Sketchbook** and **Vanities**; for **Garrick Gaities**; for **The Vanderbilt Revue**; and for an early Bob Hope musical, **Ballyhoo of '32**.
Brother Can You Spare a Dime? Jay Gorney/Harburg. Written for **Americana**, this was the perfect theme song for the ongoing economic depression in 1932. Russian-born Gorney (Gornetsky, 1896–1964) wrote several Broadway scores, but *Brother* was his only big hit. It is still a popular standard and remains a big Bing Crosby evergreen.

1934   *April in Paris.* Vernon Duke/Harburg. Introduced in the Broadway revue, **Walk a Little Faster**, this memorable piece of Harburg poetry remains one of the most popular of all ballads. It has been recorded over a thousand times by vocalists, big bands, and jazz ensembles—Count Basie did the exciting big band swing version. A film was made using the same title.
What Is There to Say. Duke/Harburg. *To the Beat of the Heart.* Samuel Pokrass/Harburg. These two songs were written for the **Ziegfeld Follies of 1934**, a show financially backed by the Schuberts and produced by Billie Burke to pay off the debts of her late husband, Flo Ziegfeld. *What Is There* was the production's crowning achievement and *To the Beat* was Harburg's first protest song (it introduced by Everett Marshall, who would later go on to act in film and television, and achieve success as E. G. Marshall).
You're a Builder Upper. Arlen/Ira Gershwin and Harburg. Written for the Broadway production, **Life Begins at 8:40**.
Fun to Be Fooled. Arlen/I. Gershwin and Harburg.

1937   *Down with Love.* Arlen/Harburg. From the musical, **Hooray for What**, introduced by Vivian Vance (of later *I Love Lucy* television fame).

1940   *There's a Great Day Coming.* Burton Lane*/Harburg. Written for **Hold On to Your Hats**, which ran twenty weeks and featured the singing of Al Jolson.

1944   *Right as the Rain, The Eagle and Me*, and *Evelina.* Arlen/Harburg. Written for *Bloomer Girl*, starring Celeste Holm. This production was considered Arlen and Harburg's answer to the previous year's blockbuster, **Oklahoma!**
Blue Holiday. Songs by Ellington/Harburg. Yip and the Ellington band contributed to this Ethel Waters show, but it still only ran one week.

1946   **Finian's Rainbow**. Songs by Lane/Harburg. One of the finest of all musicals— with a powerful message as well. Ella Logan and David Wayne were the stars in this clever and convincing production. The musical was on Broadway for two years; the film version was in and out of the movie theatres; but the Lane/ Harburg songs keep going and going: *How Are Things in Glocca Morra?; When I'm Not Near the Girl That I Love, I Love the Girl That I'm Near; Something Sort of Grandish; If This Isn't Love; That Old Devil Moon; The Begat;* and *That Great Come and Get it Day.*

1951   *Here's to Your Illusions.* Sammy Fain*/Harburg. From the Broadway production, **Flahooley**.

Hollywood Chronology

1929   *What I Wouldn't Do for That Man*. Jay Gorney (Chapter 4)/Harburg. From the critically acclaimed film, ***Applause*** (no connection to the later Broadway show), and sung by Helen Morgan.

1933   *It's Only a Paper Moon*. Arlen/Billy Rose* and Harburg. Used in the movie, ***Take a Chance***.

1936   *Last Night When We Were Young*. Arlen/Harburg. One of the finest love songs of all times was actually removed from the film, ***Broadway Melody***. The producers thought it was too sad. Arlen and Harburg tried to have it used in other films, with the same reaction.

1939   ***The Wizard of Oz***. Scored by Arlen/Harburg. This Academy Award–winning film was a Yip Harburg brainchild and a Judy Garland *tour de force*. The MGM production featured a cast of just under 10,000 people, including 150 munchkins, Ray Bolger, Bert Lahr, Jack Haley, Margaret Hamilton, and Frank Morgan. The immortal words and music include *Over the Rainbow, We're Off to See the Wizard, Ding Dong the Witch Is Dead*, and *Yellow Brick Road*.
Lydia the Tatooed Lady. Arlen/Harburg. Groucho sang it so well in the Marx Brothers' ***At the Circus***.

1941   ***Babes in Arms***. Arlen and Roger Edens/Harburg. This film featured several songs by the trio.
I'm Yours. Johnny Green/Harburg. This song was used in the movie ***Second Chorus***.

1942   ***Rio Rita*** and ***Panama Hattie***. Songs by Arlen/Harburg. These two popular films had a number of the duo's songs, but none of them became hits.

1943   *Happiness Is (Just) a Thing Called Joe*. Arlen/Harburg. This Oscar-nominated ballad was presented in the film version of ***Cabin in the Sky***.
Meet the People. Songs by Lane/Harburg. Harburg also produced this movie.

1944   *Make Way for Tomorrow*. Jerome Kern*/I. Gershwin and Harburg. Written for the lovely film, ***Cover Girl***, and sung by Phil Silvers, Gene Kelly, and Rita Hayworth.
Hollywood Canteen. Harburg wrote the words for a number of songs for this movie.
Can't Help Singing and *Cal-I-for-Ni-Yay*. Kern/Harburg. The songwriting team wrote the *Can't Help* title tune and the Oscar-nominated *Cal-I* for this Deanne Durbin film.

1946   *Cinderella Sue*. Kern/Harburg. This song was written for ***Centennial Summer***, the last film Kern composed for—with Harburg and Oscar Hammerstein—who co-wrote *All Through the Day*, the big song from this movie.

1953   *I'm Yours*. Johnny Green/Harburg. Used in the Dean Martin and Jerry Lewis movie, ***The Stooge***. This fine ballad was originally written for the 1930 Broadway musical, ***Simple Simon***.

1962   ***Gay Purr-ee***. Songs by Arlen/Harburg. This cartoon film featured some famed voices, but no famed songs.

1963   *I Could Go On Singing*. Arlen/Harburg. Judy Garland sang this film title song.

Ironically, given the song's title, it was the last time these three artists worked together.

1968   *Finian's Rainbow*. Songs by Lane and Harburg. Fred Astaire starred, the critics panned, and the music prevailed—and remains intact, just fine.

LORENZ HART, Lyricist (1895–1943)

Hart was born in New York City and attended classes at Columbia University. It was there he began to write with Richard Rodgers*, thus beginning a highly successful, though tumultuous, relationship. Hart was a brilliant linguist and in his early twenties began to show his enormous talent as a lyricist on Broadway. Ranked as one of the three best lyricists of all time (Ira Gershwin* and Cole Porter* the other two), his personal life was tragic and short. But despite that hardship and brevity, Hart left a beautiful legacy of style that lyricists will try to emulate for a long, long time. The melodies and the lyrics of Richard Rodgers and Lorenz Hart have been—and will continue to be—heard in the movies. In 1948, Arthur Freed wrote a fictitious biographical screenplay based on the lives of these two great songwriters. MGM produced it, with a tremendous cast— Gene Kelly and Sid Charisse danced *Slaughter on Tenth Avenue* and Perry Como and Mel Tormé sang. The film was filled with Rodgers and Hart's best works, resulting in a most entertaining joy to see and hear.

Broadway Chronology

1919   *Any Old Place With You*. Rodgers/Hart. Written for the play, *A Lonely Woman*, wherein that demonstrated his exceptional talent for writing clever lyrics.
        Romeo. Songs by Rodgers/Hart. This Broadway production had the same songs the partners had written for their Columbia University show, *Fly with Me*.

1920   *Poor Little Ritz Girl*. Songs by Rodgers/Hart. The first Broadway show with all Rodgers/Hart songs.

1924   *Manhattan* and *Sentimental Me*. Rodgers/Hart. Their first two real hit songs, from *Greenwich Village Follies*.

1925   *Garrick Gaieties* and *Dearest Enemies*. Songs by Rodgers/Hart. No evergreens from these two revues, but *Here in My Arms* and *Bye and Bye*, from *Dearest Enemies*, were popular in their day.

1926   *Blue Room*. Rodgers/Hart. The hit song from *The Girl Friend*.
        Mountain Greenery. Rodgers/Hart. Audiences applauded this one, written for the 1926 edition of *Garrick Gaieties*, a revue full of fun and spoofs.
        Heaven Will Protect the Working Girl. Rodgers/Hart. A clever pop tune written for *Peggy Ann*.
        This Funny World. Rodgers/Hart. Written for the musical *Betsy*.

1927   *My Heart Stood Still* and *Thou Swell*. Rodgers/Hart. From their Broadway musical adaptation of Mark Twain's classic, *A Connecticut Yankee in King Arthur's Court*.

1928   *You Took Advantage of Me*. Rodgers/Hart. Sung in *Present Arms* on Broadway.

1929   *With a Song in My Heart*. Rodgers/Hart. From the show, *Spring Is Here*.

A Ship Without a Sail. Rodgers/Hart. A fine piece from their score for the musical, **Heads Up**, starring Victor Moore.

1930 *Ten Cents a Dance*. Rodgers/Hart. For Broadway's **Simple Simon**, produced by Flo Ziegfeld—who excised another popular song they wrote for the show, *Dancing on the Ceiling*.

1931 **America's Sweetheart**. Songs by Rodgers/Hart. Book by Herbert Fields. This musical was a spoof on Hollywood and starred Harriet Lake, who later went to Hollywood, changed her name to Ann Southern, and became one of the "American sweethearts" the Broadway show satirized. As Lake, she sang *I've Got Five Dollars*. Fields had been writing librettos for Rodgers and Hart musicals since the mid-1920s, and they had all done quite well in Manhattan, with Flo Ziegfeld producing many of their shows. But the promise of even bigger bucks lured the trio—as it did writers of all kinds—to the land of milk and honey and the home of "Tinseltown."

1935 *The Most Beautiful Girl in the World; Little Girl Blue*, and *My Romance*. Rodgers/Hart. These hit songs were written for the Billy Rose stage production **Jumbo**, starring Jimmy Durante.

1936 *Glad to Be Unhappy* and *There's a Small Hotel*. Rodgers/Hart. For Broadway's **On Your Toes**.

1937 **Babes in Arms**. Book, music, and lyrics by Rodgers/Hart. This was truly a unique musical with a great cast, including Alfred Drake, Mitzi Green, and Dan Dailey. The show's songs are practically all evergreens, including *I Wish I Were in Love Again, Where or When, The Lady Is a Tramp, Johnny One-Note*, and perhaps the most popular Rodgers and Hart song of all, *My Funny Valentine*.

1939 **I Married an Angel**. Songs by Rodgers/Hart. This production ran ten months on Broadway, and had two big hit songs, the title tune and *Spring Is Here*.
Too Many Girls. Rodgers/Hart. This musical's hits included *I Didn't Know What Time It Was* and *Give It Back to the Indians*.

1940 *It Never Entered My Mind*. Rodgers/Hart. From their Broadway production, **Higher and Higher**. Listen to Frank Sinatra's version.
Pal Joey. Songs by Rodgers/Hart. Story by John O'Hara. The prolific author's play became the prizewinner of 1940—with these Rodgers and Hart songs: *Bewitched, I Could Write a Book, Zip*, and *Him*. Gene Kelly debuted on Broadway in **Pal Joey**.

1942 **By Jupiter**. Songs by Rodgers/Hart. Their last Broadway collaboration included the hits *Ev'rything I've Got (Belongs To You)* and *Wait Till You See Her*.

1943 **A Connecticut Yankee**. Rodgers/Hart. This revival had Hart's last lyrics in a new song, *To Keep My Love Alive*. Hart was very ill at the time.

Hollywood Chronology

1930 *With a Song in My Heart*. Rodgers/Hart. A year after being staged on Broadway, **Spring Is Here**—with this hit song—was put on film.
You Took Advantage of Me. Rodgers/Hart. From Broadway to Hollywood, used in the movie, **Leathernecking**.
A Ship Without a Sail. Rodgers/Hart. Another Hollywood reprise of a Broadway hit song and show, **Heads Up**, was made into a film.

1932 *Mimi, Lover* and *Isn't it Romantic*. Rodgers/Hart. From, **Love Me Tonight**, starring Jeanette McDonald and Maurice Chevalier.

1933   *You Are Too Beautiful*. Rodgers/Hart. From ***Hallelujah, I'm a Bum***, a film for which Rodgers and Hart wrote rhyming dialogue. *You Are* was really too beautiful for Al Jolson*, who performed it in the movie. Dick Haymes sang this lovely ballad better, later.

1934   *Blue Moon*. Rodgers/Hart. This was one of eleven Rodgers/Hart songs cut from the MGM movie, ***Hollywood Party***. The film was originally Howard Dietz' idea. *The Merry Widow Waltz*. Rodgers/Hart. This was one of five of the duo's songs included in MGM's film version of Lehar's popular operetta, ***The Merry Widow***. The musical movie was produced by the film studio's resident genius, Irving Thalberg.

1935   *Soon, It's Easy to Remember*, and *Down by the River*. Rodgers/Hart. Written for ***Mississippi***, starring Bing Crosby. Herbert Fields (Lou's son and Dorothy's brother) adapted the Booth Tarkington story for the screen.

1938   *Blue Moon*. Rodgers/Hart. Used in Busby Berkeley's movie, ***Hollywood Hotel***.

1939   *There's a Small Hotel*. Rodgers/Hart. Used in the film remake of the fine Broadway musical, ***On Your Toes***. The song's lyrics seem almost more like Hammerstein's romantic type than Hart's cosmopolitan style.
Babes in Arms. Songs by Rodgers/Hart. The title song and *Where or When* were featured in this film version of the stage musical. So was Harpo Marx, strumming *Blue Moon*. Busby Berkeley directed this Arthur Freed screen adaptation, one of his greatest scripts.

1940   ***The Boys from Syracuse***. Songs by Rodgers and Hart. The 1938 Broadway production was a hit; the Hollywood version was not.
You're Nearer and *I Didn't Know What Time It Was*. Rodgers/Hart. Two hits from ***Too Many Girls***.
Girls'. Songs by Rodgers/Hart. A pretty good campus genre movie, starring Eddie Bracken and Cuban heartthrob, Desi Arnaz.

1942   *I Married an Angel* and *Spring Is Here*. Rodgers/Hart. The *I Married* title song and *Spring* were hits reprised from the 1939 Broadway production for this movie musical, the last film Jeanette McDonald and Nelson Eddy made together.

1957   ***Pal Joey***. Rodgers/Hart. This film version was produced with a sanitized script, which Frank Sinatra, Kim Novak, and Rita Hayworth masterfully overcame through their own individual performances. Of course, Rodgers' and Hart's music carried the movie, too, with evergreens from several of their shows: *My Funny Valentine, Bewitched, I Didn't Know What Time It Was, The Lady Is a Tramp, There's a Small Hotel*, and *Zip*.
Mimi. Rodgers/Hart. Sung by Sinatra in his critically acclaimed portrayal of Joe E. Lewis in ***The Joker Is Wild***. The film's other songs were written by James Van Heusen* and Sammy Cahn*.

1962   *Most Beautiful Girl in the World, Falling in Love with Love, Spring Is Here*, and *This Can't Be Love*. Rodgers/Hart. These great songs were included in the not-so-great MGM film remake of the original 1935 stage production of ***Jumbo***.

VICTOR HERBERT, Composer (1859–1944)

Herbert is placed in this chapter rather than in the first one, simply because of the significant influence he, and his music, have had on Golden Age music.

Born in Dublin, Ireland, Herbert was educated in Germany and began his studies as a medical student at age 15, an early ambition he discarded in favor of a musical career—and quite a career it was. Herbert arrived in the United States in 1886, already schooled in classical music. He became the first chair cellist in New York's Metropolitan Opera Orchestra and began writing oratorios. While still enjoying a successful career in orchestra work, including a stint as a bandmaster and as conductor of the Pittsburgh Symphony, Herbert went on to write operas; in 1898, he wrote his first Broadway musical, *The Fortune Teller*. Herbert was also a founding member the American Society of Composers, Authors and Publishers (ASCAP).

Chronology

1898   *Gypsy Love Song*. Herbert/Harry B. Smith (Chapter 4). From *The Fortune Teller*.

1903   *March of the Toys*. Herbert/Glen McDonough. From *Babes in Toyland*.

1905   *Kiss Me Again*. Herbert/Henry Blossom, Jr. From the Broadway operetta, *Mademoiselle Modiste*. Blossom (1866–1919) also wrote *The Red Mill* in 1906.

1910   *I'm Falling in Love with Someone, Italian Street Song*, and *Ah, Sweet Mystery of Life*. Herbert/Rida Johnson Young (Chapter 1). Classics from *Naughty Marietta*.

1913   *Sweethearts*. Herbert/Lyrics, Robert B. Smith. The title song of Herbert's popular operetta. Smith (1875–1951) was Harry B. Smith's brother.

1922   *A Kiss in the Dark*. Herbert/Buddy DeSylva*. Written for *Orange Blossoms* on Broadway.

1939   *Indian Summer*. Herbert/Al Dubin*. Four decades after his first hit, *Indian Summer* was a number 1 chart record for Herbert.

EDWARD HEYMAN, Lyricist (1907–1981)

Heyman was born in New York and grew up in Chicago. He graduated from the University of Michigan and soon after became a staff writer, back in New York, at Radio City Music Hall. His Hollywood career began when he was 22 and his was one of the most successful among show business lyricists. The list of composers Heyman worked with reads like a who's who: Hoagy Carmichael*, Nacio Herb Brown*, Johnny Green*, Vincent Youmans*, and Victor Young*.

Chronology

1929   *I'll Be Reminded of You*. Ken Smith/Heyman. Written for the film, *Vagabond Lover*, and sung by Rudy Vallee.

1930   *Body and Soul*. Johnny Green*/Heyman, Frank Eyton, and Robert Sour (Chapter 4). This is one of the ten most requested songs of all time. The instrumental version by Coleman ''Bean'' Hawkins also must be mentioned.

1931   *Through the Years*. Vincent Youmans/Heyman. Title tune for the Broadway musical, which also included their song, *Drums in My Heart*.
       Out of Nowhere. Green/Heyman. Ask any jazz lover: this is a very popular song.

1932   *My Silent Love*. Dana Suesse/Heyman. A beautiful composition and one of five songs they wrote for the film, **Sweet Surrender**. *My Darling*. Richard Myers/ Heyman. Heard in Earl Carroll's **Vanities** on Broadway.

1933   *I Cover the Waterfront*. Green/Heyman. This is the duo's other top most-requested songs of all times. Listen to Billie Holiday sing it and hear one of the most moving performances of a ballad, ever. *I Cover* was supposed to be used in a Claudette Colbert film of the same title, but did not make the production deadline.

1934   *Blame It on My Youth*. Oscar Levant/Heyman.
I Wanna' Be Loved. Green/Billy Rose and Heyman. For the revue, **Casino de Paris**.
You Oughta' Be in Pictures. Suesse/Heyman. Written for **Ziegfeld's Follies** on Broadway.
After All, You're All I'm After. Arthur Schwartz/Heyman. Bing Crosby sang this ballad in the film, **She Loves Me Not**.

1937   *Boo Hoo, I'll Tell My Mother on You*. Carmen Lombardo and John Jacob Loeb/ Heyman. Lombardo's brother, Guy, and his orchestra played this tune continuously and it became a hit.

1940   *Bluebird of Happiness*. Sandor Harmati/Harry Parr Davies and Heyman. Opera singer Jan Peerce made this one into a hit.

1945   *Love Letters*. Victor Young/Heyman. Young's film title track composition was a chartbuster. Heyman added the words later.

1948   *When I Fall in Love*. Young/Heyman. A fine ballad elegantly recorded by Nat King Cole. It was Heyman's last hit.

BILLY HILL, Composer/Lyricist (1899–1940)

If you switched the first and last names of this songwriter, we might have an apt description for some of his writing; however, the name is actually William J. Hill. Born in Boston, Hill was a serious violin student who moved west to become a cowboy and a surveyor. Hill played violin and piano in dance bands, and supposedly formed the first dance band in the West, in Salt Lake City, Utah. When things went bad, Hill ended up as a doorman at a New York City apartment building.

Chronology

1933   *(I'm Headin' for the) Last Roundup*. Hill (wm).

1934   *Wagon Wheels* and *Rain*. Peter DeRose*/Hill.

1936   *Empty Saddles (in the Old Corral)*. Hill/J. Keirn Brennan (Chapter 1). A Bing Crosby hit from the film, **Rhythm on the Range**.
In the Chapel in the Moonlight. Hill (wm).
Glory of Love. Hill (wm). A number 1 chart song for Benny Goodman.

1938   *On a Little Street in Singapore*. DeRose/Hill.

BOB HILLIARD, Composer/Lyricist (1918–1971)

Hilliard's resume cludes researchers. What is known is that he was a New Yorker who wrote dozens of popular songs.

Chronology

1946   *The Coffee Song (They've Got an Awful Lot . . . In Brazil).* Hilliard and Dick Miles (wm). Written for a Copacabana night club revue. Miles was a composer, born in Dorchester, Massachusetts in 1916 and educated at the New England Conservatory of Music.

1947   *Mention My Name in Sheboygan.* Hilliard, Dick Sanford, and Sammy Mysels (wm). Sanford was born in Gloversville, New York, in 1896; he also wrote the lyrics to *The Singing Hills*. Mysels was born in Pittsburgh, Pennsylvania, in 1906. He was an accomplished painter, sculptor, and graduate of Carnegie Tech. He was also a cabaret entertainer and drummer—and a composer. Mysels wrote *We Three (My Echo, My Shadow and Me)*, an Ink Spots evergreen, in 1940; *Yesterday's Gardenias*, with Nelson Cogane and Dick Robertson, in 1942; and *Bim, Bam Baby*, in 1952.
        Bongo, Bongo, Bongo (I Don't Wanna Leave the Congo). Carl Sigman*/Hilliard.

1949   *I'm Late (for a Very Important Date).* Sammy Fain*/Hilliard. Written for the film, **Alice in Wonderland**.

1950   *Dearie.* Hilliard and Dave Mann (wm). Mann was born in Philadelphia in 1916 and became President Harry Truman's personal pianist. A graduate of the Curtis Institute of Music, Mann was a big band arranger and wrote *No Moon at All*, with Redd Evans, in 1949. Mann, again with Redd Evans (wm), wrote *There I've Said It Again* in 1941 and *No Moon at All* in 1949. In 1954 Evans wrote lyrics to Arthur Kent's *Don't Go to Strangers*.
        Dear Hearts and Gentle People. Fain/Hilliard. Done so well by Dinah Shore.

1953   *Ev'ry Street's a Boulevard in Old New York.* Jule Styne/Hilliard. From **Hazel Flagg** on Broadway.

1955   *In the Wee Small Hours of the Morning.* Mann/Hilliard. A personification of the ''saloon song.''

1960   *My Little Corner of the World.* Lee Pockriss/Hilliard. Pockriss also wrote *Catch a Falling Star*, with Paul J. Vance, a number 1 chart song for Perry Como. Pockriss and Vance hit number 1 again in 1960, with their *Itsy Bitsy Teeny Weenie Yellow Polka Dot Bikini*.

1963   *Our Day Will Come.* Mort Garson/Hilliard. Garson also wrote the music to *Dondi*, with Earl Shuman's lyrics, in 1960.

AL HOFFMAN, Composer/Lyricist (1902–1960)

Hoffman could well be awarded the special prize for the silliest song titles of all time (if he really did write those titles). He was born in Russia and came to the United States as a boy and lived in Seattle. Hoffman was a boy soprano in a synagogue, eventually became a bandleader, and later was a productive writer for Perry Como. He is at least partially responsible for *Mairzy Doats, Chi Baba Chi Baba, Hot Diggity Dog, Bibbidi Bobbidi Boo*, and others.

Chronology

1931 *Heartaches*. Hoffman/John Klenner and Sam Lewis*.
      I Apologize. Hoffman, Ed Nelson, and Al Goodhart (wm). A later hit for Billy Eckstine.

1932 *Auf Wiedersehn, My Dear*. Hoffman, Nelson, Goodhart, and Milton Ager (Chapter 4) (wm).

1934 *Little Man, You've Had a Busy Day*. Hoffman/Maurice Sigler. Sarah Vaughn did this one very well.

1938 *On the Bumpy Road to Love*. Hoffman, Al Lewis, and Murray Mencher (wm). Written for the Judy Garland film, ***Listen Darling***. Mencher co-wrote the lyrics (with Jack Scholl) to *Throw Another Log on the Fire*, composed by Charles Tobias*, in 1934.

1941 *Story of a Starry Night*. Hoffman, Jerry Livingston, and Mann Curtis (lyrics). The music was borrowed from Tchaikovsky's *Pathetique*. Lyricist Curtis wrote, with composer Vic Mizzy, *My Dreams are Getting Better all the Time*, in 1944.

1943 *Mairzy Doats*. Hoffman and Livingston/Drake.
      Close to You. Hoffman, Livingston, and Carl Lampl (wm). This was Frank Sinatra's first recording for the Columbia label.

1948 *Bibbidi Bobbidi Boo* and *Chi Baba Chi Baba*. Hoffman and Livingston/Mack David. Both were used in the cartoon film, ***Cinderella***; both were big hits for Perry Como.
      The trio also wrote *A Dream Is a Wish Your Heart Makes* for the same movie.

1949 *There's No Tomorrow*. Leon Carr, Leo Corday, and Hoffman (wm). Adapted from ***O Sole Mio***. Tony Martin had a big hit with it.

1950 *I'm Gonna Live Til I Die*. Hoffman, Curtis, and Walter Kent (wm). Kent composed *The White Cliffs of Dover* with lyricist Nat Burton in 1941.
      If I Knew You Were Coming I'd Have Baked a Cake. Hoffman, Clem Watts, and Bob Merrill (wm). The first of several cliches set to music by Hoffman et al.

1952 *Takes Two to Tango*. Hoffman and Dick Manning (wm). Two years later, the second of several cliches. Pearl Bailey, accompanied by Don Redman's band, made it into a big hit.

1954 *Papa Loves Mambo*. Hoffman, Manning, and Bix Reichner (wm). Written for Perry Como.

1956 *Hot Diggity Dog (What You Do to Me)*. Hoffman and Manning (lyrics). Another adaptation of a famous melody, this time from Chabrier's *España Rhapsody*. A hit for Perry Como.

HERMAN HUPFELD, Composer/Lyricist (1894–1951)

Born in New Jersey and sent to Germany at an early age to study classical music, Hupfeld turned to popular music. Originally a sax player, he became a bandleader in the U.S. Navy in World War I. In 1931, he contributed a couple of songs to Billy Rose's* 1932 extravaganza, *Everybody's Welcome*. While most of the music was composed by Sammy Fain* for that stage presentation, Hupfeld's song *As Time Goes By* was destined for fame, thanks to the film *Casablanca*, in which it appeared about a decade later.

Chronology

1931   *When Yuba Plays the Rhumba on the Tuba.* Hupfeld (wm). Used on Broadway in *The Third Little Show*.
       As Time Goes By. Hupfeld (wm). Originally performed in the stage musical *Everybody's Welcome* (1932), it was used once again in the Academy Award–winning film classic, *Casablanca*. The song also earned on Oscar and remains a great popular standard.

1932   *Let's Put Out the Lights and Go to Sleep.* Hupfeld (wm). Not quite a smash hit.

HARRY JAMES, Composer/Bandleader/Trumpet Player (1916–1983)

Harry Haag James was born in Albany, Georgia, and educated in Texas and on the road with his father, a bandmaster of the Haag Circus. James learned the trumpet at a very early age; he also was a performing child contortionist with the circus. In high school, James was a champion trumpet soloist, and not too long after, joined the Ben Pollack Band. In the mid-1930s, he was part of the famous trumpet trio with Benny Goodman, alongside Gordon "Chris" Griffin, and Ziggy Elman; his solos on *Sing Sing Sing* and other Goodman classics are some of the most exciting ever recorded. James was one of the technically finest trumpet players of all times, ranked with Doc Severinson and a few others. Some jazz critics were bothered by James' vibrato, but he worked well with the likes of Johnny Hodges, Buster Bailey, the Goodman stars, and other jazz greats.

Leading his own band in 1939, James hired that skinny kid from Hoboken, Frank Sinatra, as his vocalist. And he married a talented and beautiful singer, dancer, and actress, Betty Grable. My recollection is of watching him play baseball in Riverside Park, in New York City—apparently he hired many sidemen when they exhibited a talent for the national pastime as well as for their musical abilities. Sadly, James was also known to consume a bottle of vodka a day.

Chronology

1937   *Peckin'.* James (instr.). He was also the singer on the Pollack band's recording of his song. Later, on the Goodman recording, he was the hot, hot, hot trumpet soloist.

1941   *Music Makers.* James/Don Raye.
       The Mole. James (music). A great instrumental.
       Two O'Clock Jump. Count Basie, Benny Goodman, and James (instr.). A classic from a classic trio.

1944   *I'm Beginning to See the Light.* Duke Ellington, Johnny Hodges, and James/Don George. A fantastic collaboration.

GORDON JENKINS, Composer/Lyricist (1910–1984)

In their musical hearts and minds, Sinatra addicts know and understand the lush beauty of Gordon Jenkin's compositions and arrangements. They also appreciate the great professionalism of the musicians Sinatra and Jenkins worked with over the years. These fans are also probably aware of Jenkins' quirky personality. Nonetheless, this native of Webster Grove, Missouri, contributed much to the superb sounds of Sinatra, Ella Fitzgerald, Nat King Cole, and a host of others who sang—and continue to sing—his beautiful songs.

Jenkins began his musical career as a ukelele and banjo player performing at age 15. He was a brilliant young musician and became the head arranger and conductor at NBC, in New York, at the age of 27. Neither a steady Broadway nor Hollywood songwriter, Jenkins did attempt a score for the musical stage, *Along Fifth Avenue*, in 1949. Although the Sinatra ballads are most memorable, Jenkins wrote and arranged a variety of works, including his underrated *Manhattan Towers*.

Chronology

1933   *Blue Prelude*. Jenkins and Joe Bishop (wm). This was Jenkins' first hit. Bishop also wrote (wm) *Blue Flame* with Leo Corday and Jimmy Noble in 1943.

1934   *When a Woman Loves a Man*. Bernie Hanighen and Jenkins/Johnny Mercer. *P.S., I Love You*. Jenkins/Mercer.

1935   *Goodbye*. Gordon Jenkins (wm). The haunting, closing theme of the Benny Goodman Band.

1939   *Blue Evening*. Jenkins and Bishop (wm).

1943   *San Fernando Valley*. Jenkins (wm). A Bing Crosby hit.

1945   *Homesick, That's All*. Jenkins (wm).

1946   *Married I Can Always Get* and *New York's My Home*. Jenkins (wm). From *Manhattan Towers*. It appears he added the words to *Married* years after he wrote the score.

1963   *This Is All I Ask*. Jenkins (wm). One of the loveliest ballads of any time.

ARTHUR JOHNSTON, Composer (1898–1954)

Arthur James Johnston was for many years the main pianist and chief arranger for Irving Berlin, so it is not surprising that the sound of Johnston's music is very much like the sound of Berlin's. However, none of the rumors about Johnston being a ghost songwriter for Berlin has ever been substantiated. Born in Astoria, Queens, New York, Johnston was playing piano in a silent movie theatre when he was only 15. Soon after he became a vocal arranger and then chief arranger for a Tin Pan Alley publisher. As the music director for Berlin's shows on Broadway, he was a significant member of the Berlin organization. By the late 1920s, he arrived in Hollywood and wrote a number of fine standards.

Chronology

1924 *Mandy, Make Up Your Mind.* Johnston and George W. Meyer (Chapter 1)/Roy Turk and Grant Clarke (Chapter 4). An early example of the similarity with Berlin's melody style.

1931 *Just One More Chance.* Johnston/Sam, Coslow*. A big Bing Crosby hit.

1932 *(Sweet) Moon Song.* Johnston/Coslow. Another Berlinesque song.

1933 *Down the Old Ox Road.* Johnston and Coslow (wm). From the film **College Humor**.
The Day You Came Along. Johnston/Coslow (wm). Written for the movie **Too Much Harmony**.

1934 *Cocktails for Two.* Johnston/Coslow. Originally written for the film **Murder at the Vanities** in slow tempo. Comedic bandleader Spike Jones arranged and recorded this song some years later, up tempo with whacky sounding noise makers, bells, and whistles.
My Old Flame. Johnston/Coslow. This lovely song was written for the Mae West film, **Belle of the Nineties**.

1935 *Thanks a Million.* Johnston/Gus Kahn. Title song for the movie starring Dick Powell.

1936 *Pennies from Heaven.* Johnston/Johnny Burke. Bing Crosby made it a hit.

1937 *The Moon Got in My Eyes* and *It's the Natural Thing to Do.* Johnston/Burke. These two songs were hits from the Crosby movie **Double or Nothing**.

1938 *Between a Kiss and a Sigh.* Johnston/Burke. Another Bing Crosby hit.

AL JOLSON, Songwriter/Entertainer (1886–1950)

Jolson's real name was Asa Yoelson. Much has been written, recorded, and filmed about Jolson's popularity as an entertainer—suffice it to say he was one of the most popular performers of his time. Born in Washington, DC, the son of a Jewish *chazzan* (cantor), Jolson became a star of the stage, film, and radio. We cannot help comparing his contribution to songwriting with that of publisher Irving Mills: a big voice and a big presence, but a big question mark when it comes to actually documenting his songwriting (for an in-depth look at Jolson, please see *The Jazz Singer*).

Chronology

1920 *Avalon.* Jolson and Vincent Rose (wm). Music adapted from a Puccini aria in **Tosca**. Listen to Benny Goodman's recording.

1924 *California, Here I Come.* Joseph Meyer/Buddy DeSylva* and Jolson.

1925 *Keep Smiling at Trouble.* Lewis E. Gensler/DeSylva and Jolson. Gensler and Leo Robin* wrote the popular song, *Love Is Just Around the Corner*.

1927 *Me and My Shadow.* Jolson and Dave Dreyer*/Billy Rose.

1928 *Sonny Boy.* Jolson, DeSylva, Ray Henderson, and Lew Brown (wm). Written for the film **The Singing Fool** starring Al Jolson.
Back in Your Own Back Yard. Dreyer, Billy Rose, and Jolson (wm).

1946   *Anniversary Song* and *There's a Rainbow Round My Shoulder*. Jolson and Saul Chaplin* (wm). Both songs were used in the biographical film, **The Jolson Story**. *Anniversary Song* was composed as *Danube Waves*, by J. Ivanovici.

ISHAM JONES, Composer (1894–1956)

Jones, a multitalented instrumentalist who played piano, saxophone, and violin, was born in Canton, Ohio. He organized his own band when he was 21 and headed for Chicago, where success followed. Jones' band members included Woody Herman and other top sidemen, and years later, Herman took over the musical group's organization. Writing about the Jones sidemen in *The Big Bands*, George Simon called trumpeter Johnny Carlson "magnificent" and listed the band's Saxey Mansfield and Pee Wee Erwin among the best of instrumentalists. Jones' band was a vaudeville headliner in the United States and extended its fame abroad after playing at London's Kit Kat Club. This popular ensemble enjoyed a long tenure of performing until 1936. In the earlier years, Jones had the likes of Gordon Jenkins and Joe Bishop arranging for the band. As a composer, Jones had some fine hits of his own, too.

Chronology

1922   *On the Alamo* and *Broken Hearted Melody*. Jones/Gus Kahn. Kahn was Jones' longtime musical partner.

1923   *Swingin' Down the Lane*. Jones/Khan. An old standard.

1924   *It Had to Be You* and *The One I Love Belongs to Somebody Else*. Jones/Kahn.

1933   *You've Got Me Crying Again*. Jones/Charles Newman (Chapter 4). Joe Williams recorded a beautiful version of this song more than twenty years later.

1936   *There Is No Greater Love*. Jones/Marty Symes (Chapter 4).

SCOTT JOPLIN, Composer (1868–1917)

An enormous influence on jazz and popular song, Scott Joplin—like George M. Cohan*, Victor Herbert*, and Jelly Roll Morton*—was as much a founder of American music as he was a pioneer in it. Joplin was born in Texas, the child of a former slave and a free-born black woman. He studied piano with a German immigrant named Julius Weiss in Texarkana before moving on to Sedalia, Missouri, where he taught music himself, studied the cornet, and played piano at the Maple Leaf Club—thus, the name of his best-known composition.

By 1900, Joplin had two songs, two marches, and a waltz already published by John Stark & Son of Sedalia, the firm that initiated the publication of rags, which combined with the blues, led to jazz. In *Tin Pan Alley*, David Jasen writes, "No ragtime composer had more influence than Joplin. His thirty-eight rags constitute a major achievement in the history of popular music." So, Scott Joplin, the father of ragtime, belongs in the hall of fame in songwriting—and deserves the credit for influencing other giants of songwriting who wrote rags, including Irvin Berlin* and the Gershwins*.

Chronology

1899   *Maple Leaf Rag*. Joplin (instr.).

1902   *The Entertainer*. Joplin (instr.) This song was made popular again seventy-two years later when Marvin Hamlisch arranged and played it for the film, ***The Sting***.

1911   ***Tremonisha***. Songs by Scott Joplin. Joplin wrote this complete opera some time after he arrived in New York City, where he eventually died in poverty.

IRVING KAHAL, Lyricist (1903–1942)

Irving Kahal was a native of Pennsylvania who won an arts scholarship to New York's Cooper Union College. By age 18, he was already singing professionally in Manhattan. He was also a member of Gus Edward's famous kids minstrels. Kahal went on to become a bandleader in his own right. In an all too short career (and life), he wrote many beautiful lyrics for many lovely songs.

Chronology

1927   *Let a Smile Be Your Umbrella*. Sammy Fain*/Francis Wheeler and Kahal. This was Kahal's first published hit. Wheeler composed *The Shiek of Araby* with Harry B. Smith and wrote lyrics for Lehar's *Yours Is My Heart Alone*.

1929   *Wedding Bells Are Breaking Up That Old Gang of Mine*. Fain/Willie Raskin and Kahal. Raskin, Fred Fisher, and Billy Rose wrote *Fifty Million Frenchmen Can't Be Wrong*.

1930   *You Brought a New Kind of Love to Me*. Fain/Pierre Norman Connor and Kahal. This song is a favorite of jazz musicians and was used in the film ***The Big Pond***.

1931   *When I Take My Sugar to Tea*. Fain/Kahal and Connor.

1933   *By a Waterfall*. Fain/Kahal. Used in Hollywood's ***Footlight Parade***.

1935   *Ballad in Blue*. Hoagy Carmichael*/Kahal. Introduced by the Benny Goodman Band.

1936   *The Night Is Young and You're So Beautiful*. Dana Suesse/Kahal and Billy Rose. A delicious ballad.

1937   *I Can Dream, Can't I?* and *I'll Be Seeing You*. Fain/Kahal. Written for what ended up to be only a fifteen-performance Broadway show, ***Right This Way***. But the connoisseurs of popular music speak of *I'll Be* as truly one of the ten greatest love songs of all time.

GUS KAHN, Lyricist (1886–1941)

Kahn, one of the most prolific lyricists of all time, was born in Coblenz, Germany, and came to the United States when he was 5. His family settled in Chicago, and Kahn stayed there—loyal to his American hometown, despite offers from New York to write on Tin Pan Alley and for Broadway—until the lure of golden Hollywood hooked him into the films of the early 1920s and 1930s. Kahn began writing songs at an early age, though his first job was with a hotel supply firm. While he deliberately made the decision to stay in his beloved midwestern city, his special material for vaudeville artists as well as his lyrics ended up on the stages of New York's musical theatres. Kahn wrote hit after hit after hit over a truly amazing forty-year span.

Chronology

1908   *I Wish I Had a Girl*. Kahn (wm). His first hit.

1916   *That Funny Jass Band*. Henry I. Marshall/Kahn. This song was about the Original Dixieland Jazz Band (Chapter 1). "Jass" spelled that way then.
       Pretty Baby. Egbert Van Alstyne (Chapter 1) and Tony Jackson/Kahn. Used on Broadway in *The Passing Show*.

1921   *Ain't We Got Fun?* Richard Whiting*/Kahn and Raymond Egan (Chapter 4).

1922   *Toot, Toot, Tootsie Goodbye*. Ted FioRito (Chapter 4)/Kahn and Ernie Erdman. Al Jolson introduced it on Broadway in *Bombo*, and *Toot* became an American standard.
       Broken Hearted Melody. Isham Jones*/Kahn. Their first collaboration.
       My Buddy and *Carolina in the Morning*. Walter Donaldson*/Kahn.

1923   *On the Alamo*. Jones/Kahn. A solid hit.
       Nobody's Sweetheart. Kahn, Erdman, Billy Meyers, and Elmes Schoebel (wm). For *The Passing Show*. Meyers, Schoebel, and Jack Pettis also wrote *Bugle Call Rag* in 1923.

1924   *It Had to Be You, The One I Love Belongs to Somebody Else*, and *I'll See You in My Dreams*. Jones/Kahn. *It Had* is considered an American popular classic.
       Charlie My Boy. Ted FioRito (Chapter 4)/Kahn. Dan Russo, a member of the FioRito band organization, has also been credited for *Charlie*.

1925   *At Sundown* and *Yes Sir, That's My Baby*. Donaldson/Kahn.

1927   *Chloe*. Neil Moret*/Kahn. Louis Armstrong recorded a great trumpet solo of this song, long before Spike Jones fractured it for comedic effect.

1928   *Love Me or Leave Me* and *Makin' Whoopie*. Donaldson/Kahn.
       Coquette. Johnny Green and Carmen Lombardo/Kahn.

1930   *My Baby Just Cares for Me*. Donaldson/Kahn. For the film version of *Whoopee*, starring Eddie Cantor—another hit for these two songwriters.

1931   *Dream a Little Dream of Me*. Fabian Andre and Wilbur Schwandt/Kahn.
       Guilty. Harry Akst* and Richard Whiting/Kahn.
       I'm Through with Love. Matty Malneck* and Fud Livingston (Chapter 4)/Kahn.

1932   *A Little Street Where Old Friends Meet*. Harry Woods*/Kahn. Lovely Kahn sentiments.
       I'll Never Be the Same. Malneck and Frank Signorelli (Chapter 4)/Kahn. A grand ballad.

1933   *Flying Down to Rio*. Vincent Youmans*/Kahn and Edward Eliscu (Chapter 4). Title song for the film that also featured the tune, *Carioca*.

1934   *One Night of Love*. Victor Schertzinger*/Kahn.

1936   *San Francisco (Open Your Golden Gates)*. Bronislaw Kaper/Kahn. Sung by Jeanette McDonald in the film of the same name. Not to be confused with *I Left My Heart In*.

1937   *All God's Chillun' Got Rhythm*. Kaper and Jurmann/Kahn. From **A Day At the Races**.

1941   *You Stepped Out of a Dream*. Nacio Herb Brown*/Kahn. In Kahn's fourth decade of beautiful hit song writing, he also wrote *Day Dreaming* to the music of Jerome Kern*.

BURT KALMAR, Lyricist (1884–1947) and HARRY RUBY, Composer/Lyricist (1895–1974)

Burt Kalmar and Harry Ruby (Rubenstein) were both born in New York City. Kalmar was a boy musician who ran away from home to join a tent show; he eventually became a Hollywood scenarist and songwriter. Ruby began his career as a song demonstrator at a five-and-dime store, he later contributed to Broadway musical revues, and then became a Hollywood songwriter. A loosely-based biographical movie about the Kalmar and Ruby partnership was produced, called *Three Little Words*—the title of one of the duo's biggest hits.

Chronology

1919   *So Long, Oolong (How Long Ya Gonna Be Gone?)*. Ruby/Kalmar. An engaging novelty used by jazz musicians and Fred Astaire.

1923   *Who's Sorry Now?* Ruby and Ted Snyder (Chapter 4)/Kalmar.

1927   *Thinking of You*. Ruby/Kalmar. Written for the Broadway musical, **Five O'Clock Girl**.

1928   *I Wanna Be Loved by You*. Ruby and Herbert Stothart/Kalmar.

1930   *Three Little Words*. Ruby/Kalmar. For the film **Check and Double Check**, starring Bing Crosby.

1931   *Nevertheless*. Ruby/Kalmar. A fine ballad.

1935   *Give Me a Kiss to Build a Dream On*. Harry Ruby, Oscar Hammerstein*, and Burt Kalmar (wm).

1945   *Give Me the Simple Life*. Rube Bloom*/Ruby. Written for the film, **Wake Up and Live**.

JIMMY KENNEDY, Lyricist (1902–1984)

Kennedy, like Victor Herbert, was from ''the old sod.'' Born in Omagh, Northern Ireland, he was educated at Trinity College and was a schoolteacher for a while. In 1930, he began his career as a songwriter, mostly in comedy. Later, Kennedy did well in Hollywood.

Chronology

1934   *Isle of Capri*. Will Grosz/Kennedy.

1935   *Red Sails in the Sunset*. Hugh Williams/Kennedy. A number 1 chart record for Bing Crosby.

1936   *Did Your Mother Come form Ireland*? Michael Carr/Kennedy.

1938 *Stay in My Arms, Cinderella*. Carr/Kennedy.

1939 *My Prayer*. Georges Boulanger/Kennedy. Another number 1 hit.
South of the Border. Carr/Kennedy. High on the record charts.

1940 *Harbor Lights*. Will Grosz/Kennedy. Background song for the film, **The Long Voyage Home**.

1953 *April in Portugal*. Paul Ferrao/Kennedy (English lyrics).

JEROME KERN, Composer (1885–1945)

Jerome David Kern was a New Yorker and the son of a successful business-man. His father really wanted him to go into business, too, but Kern was de-termined to follow a musical career and finally attended the New York College of Music. Aspiring to be a classical pianist, he studied in Europe as well. How-ever, over time, he gravitated toward the world of popular music and became a staff writer, salesman, and sheet music publisher.

Kern's contributions to the musical theatre actually began in London when he adapted British compositions with producer Charles Frohman from about 1902 through 1904. Later, he achieved the status of the "Dean" of popular songwriting—he was respected and looked up to as a role model by the likes of Gershwin, Rodgers, and the other greats of composition. Jerome Kern was a shrewd, tough, and intense man—and also a financial success. He was an early investor in the Harms music publishing firm and, in 1929, he sold his personal art collection for almost two million dollars.

Kern's music has been described as charming, sophisticated, spontaneous, and melodic. It is mesmerizingly melodic. In *Getting to Know Him*, the biography of Oscar Hammerstein, Hugh Fordin documents the lyricist's feelings about losing Kern, his dear friend and songwriting partner: "After Jerry's death, he had a greater grip on my whole being than anyone else I have ever known." Indeed, it was Kern's firm grasp of what it took to make popular songs great in his own time that still reaches out to us in ours, a grip that keeps us listening again and again and again to his golden music.

Broadway Chronology

1902 *At the Casino*. Kern. A piano piece with no lyrics.

1904 *How'd You Like to Spoon with Me*. Kern/Edward Laska. Kern's first hit.

1907 *I Just Couldn't Do Without You*. Kern/Paul West.

1911 **The Red Petticoat** and **La Belle Paree**. Kern. While there were no Kern hit songs at this time, critics began to take note of his music, featured in these two and other Broadway shows.

1914 *They Didn't Believe Me*. Kern/Herbert Reynolds. Written for **The Girl from Utah** on Broadway. *They Didn't* and other compositions Kern wrote at this time ushered in an era of songwriting based on his preferences for the Vienna and London styles of the day, and his collaborations with lyricists like P. G. Wodehouse (Chapter 4) and Guy Bolton. Many of Kern's songs were what producers called ''interpolations,'' or inserts, and he avoided the genre of segued musical revues. Reynolds (1867–1933) was born in England; his real name was Michael Elder Rourke.

1915 **Very Good Eddie**. Kern (wm). An early Kern show on Broadway.

1917 *Till the Clouds Roll By*. Kern/P. G. Wodehouse and Guy Bolton. Introduced in the musical **Oh! Boy**.

1918 **Oh, Lady**. Kern (wm). Another early Kern show on Broadway.

1920 *Look for the Silver Lining*. Kern/Buddy DeSylva. For the Broadway show **Sally**.

1925 **Sunny**. Kern/Otto Harbach and Oscar Hammerstein. This landmark Broadway production starred Marilyn Miller and featured the first big Kern and Hammerstein hit, *Who*? In the mid-1920s, Charles Dillingham was the major producer of Kern-scored shows, including the not so lucky, **Lucky**, in 1925. But two years later, the face of American musical theatre was changed—and, without a doubt, improved—forever.

1927 **Show Boat**. Kern/Hammerstein. Story by Edna Ferber. This landmark Broadway production, described by many experts as the finest example of what musical theatre should be, was the model for such shows for the next sixteen years. The Kern and Hammerstein songs were fine examples of what music should be: *Ol' Man River, Why Do I Love You?, Can't Help Lovin' Dat Man, Make Believe*, and *You Are Love*. Another great song from this production, *Bill*, was written by Kern and P. G. Wodehouse (Hammerstein is also credited sometimes). *Bill* had been dropped from several other shows, but certainly clicked this time. **Show Boat** has been revived at least four times and continues to delight audiences all around the world.

1929 **Sweet Adeline**. Songs by Kern/Hammerstein. This show introduced two fine songs: *Why Was I Born*? and *Don't Ever Leave Me*. But the best of Kern's music on Broadway was still to come.

1931 *The Night Was Made for Love*. Kern/Otto Harbach. A standout song from **The Cat and the Fiddle**, on Broadway.

1932 **Music in the Air**. Songs by Kern/Hammerstein. This show's great songs included: *I've Told Ev'ry Little Star* and *The Song Is You*, one of Kern's most gorgeous compositions.

1933 **Roberta**. Songs by Kern/Harbach. Max Gordon produced this Broadway musical in which Ray Middleton and British-born Bob Hope debuted. Included the classic songs: *Yesterdays, The Touch of Your Hand, You're Devastating*, and *Smoke Gets in Your Eyes* (which Kern originally wrote as a soft shoe dance tune for **Show Boat**).

1939 *All The Things You Are*. Kern/Hammerstein. One of the finest songs of all time, from their Broadway musical **Very Warm for May**. 1939 was a great year for love songs—one would claim say it was a year when more great American love songs were written than ever before—perhaps a collective emotional response to the growing world-wide war. The next project for Kern and Hammerstein was to have been *Annie Get Your Gun*. But, for reasons centered around Hollywood and money, it did not come off; so, Irving Berlin took that on.

Hollywood Chronology

1929   **Show Boat**. Kern/Hammerstein. Hollywood's first attempt at filming this Broadway triumph was a disappointing first experience and defeat for Kern in California. Most of the great songs were used, but the acting and singing just did not match up in quality.
Sally. The New York musical was adapted for the screen with Marilyn Miller singing Kern and DeSylva's hit, *Look for the Silver Lining*.

1930   **Sunny**. Kern/Harbach and Hammerstein. Another stage-to-screen success for Marilyn Miller singing Kern's music.

1934–35 **The Cat and the Fiddle**. Songs by Kern/Harbach.
Music in the Air. Songs by Kern/Hammerstein.
Roberta. Songs by Kern/Hammerstein, Dorothy Fields, Bernard Dougall.
Sweet Adeline. Songs by Kern/Hammerstein.

1935   **Reckless**. Kern/Hammerstein. Jean Harlow starred in, and sang her interpretation of the title song for, this big MGM movie with a big cast.

1936   **Show Boat**. Kern/Hammerstein. Hollywood's second attempt at filming this Broadway triumph was a great improvement over the first version—thanks to Paul Robeson playing the part of Joe and singing *Ol' Man River*—an American recording triumph.
Swing Time. Scored by Kern and Dorothy Fields. This was Ginger Rogers and Fred Astaire's sixth movie—and the songs were splendid: *Bojangles of Harlem, A Fine Romance, Pick Yourself Up, The Way You Look Tonight* and *Waltz in Swingtime*.

1937   **High, Wide and Handsome**. Kern/Hammerstein. Story by Oscar Hammerstein. A fine western musical featuring the unique story song, *The Folks Who Live on the Hill*.
You Couldn't Be Cuter. Kern/Fields. Written for the film, **Joy of Living**, starring Irene Dunne, who could both act and really put over a song.

1940   *Remind Me*. Kern/Fields. An absolutely superb song used in the movie, **One Night in the Tropics**.

1941   **Sunny**. Kern/Harbach and Hammerstein. A film revival.
Day Dreaming. Kern/Gus Kahn.
The Last Time I Saw Paris. Kern/Hammerstein. Ann Sothern delivered this moving evergreen in the film, **Lady Be Good**.

1942   *Dearly Beloved, I'm Old Fashioned*, and *You Were Never Lovelier*. All Kern/ Johnny Mercer. *Dearly* was the Oscar-nominated song and *You Were* the title tune for this lovely and enjoyable film starring Rita Hayworth and Fred Astaire. The Academy Award winner that year was Irving Berlin's *White Christmas*.

1944   *All the Things You Are*. Kern/Hammerstein. Band vocalist Ginny Sims sang this in the film version of **Very Warm For May**.

1945   *More and More*. Kern/Yip Harburg. Academy Award–nominated song from the movie, **Can't Help Singing**. The Oscar went to Rodgers and Hammerstein for *It Might As Well Be Spring*.

1946   *All Through the Day*. Kern/Hammerstein. Another Oscar nominee from the film, **Centennial Summer**. Kern and Leo Robin had a fine love song in the film, too, *In Love in Vain*.
Till The Clouds Roll By. Hollywood presented this biographical movie of Kern; his great music saved it, along with fine performances by Judy Garland and Frank Sinatra.

TED KOEHLER, Lyricist (1894–1973)

Theodore Koehler was born in Washington, D.C., and trained to be a photoengraver. Luckily, he saw the light and came to New York as a pianist and lyricist where, with Harold Arlen*, he wrote the famous Cotton Club revues.

Chronology

1923   *When Lights Are Low*. Ted FioRito (bandleader)/Koehler. His first published song.

1930   *Get Happy*. Harold Arlen/Koehler. Written for the Broadway musical, **The 9:15 Revue**.

1931   *Between the Devil and the Deep Blue Sea*. Arlen/Koehler. Cab Calloway used this song in the musical revue, **Rhythmania**. Arlen and Koehler wrote *I Love a Parade and Kicking the Gong Around* for the same show.
Wrap Your Troubles in Dreams. Billy Moll and Harry Barris/Koehler.

1932   *I've Got a Right to Sing the Blues*. Arlen/Koehler. Written for Earl Carroll's **Vanities**, on Broadway. A jazz favorite; trombonist Jack Teagarden he made it his theme.
I've Got the World on a String. Arlen/Koehler. Perhaps their biggest and best of all. Cab Calloway introduced it in the Cotton Club revue. Recordings of *I've Got* abound; memorable ones are by Woody Herman, Louis Armstrong, and Frank Sinatra.

1933   *Let's Fall in Love*. Arlen/Koehler. A classic title song for the film starring Ann Sothern.
Stormy Weather. Arlen/Koehler. Introduced by Harold Arlen, himself, along with Leo Reisman's Orchestra. Interestingly, Lena Horne is often credited with the song's introduction, but it was first sung by Ethel Waters.

1934   *As Long As I Live*. Arlen/Koehler. Written for the **Cotton Club Parade**. Jazz lovers adore Benny Goodman's version, which was recorded in 1941.
Ill Wind. Arlen/Koehler. Also written for **Cotton Club Parade**. Listen to Ella Fitzgerald's interpretation of this beautiful song.

1935   *Animal Crackers (In My Soup)*. Ray Henderson/Irving Caesar and Koehler. A tremendous Shirley Temple hit from the movie, **Curly Top**—even if it was a bit offbeat for Koehler.
I'm Shooting High. Jimmy McHugh/Koehler. For Hollywood's **King of Burlesque**.

1939   *Don't Worry 'Bout Me*. Rube Bloom/Koehler. An unforgettable song introduced in the '39 **Cotton Club Parade**. Sinatra performs an excellent version.

1941   *When the Sun Comes Out*. Arlen/Koehler.

1942   *Every Night About This Time*. James Monaco/Koehler. Koehler's last published hit that became an Ink Spots recording and a high chart climber.

ALEX KRAMER, Composer (1903–1998), JOAN WHITNEY, Lyricist (1914–1990), and HY ZARET, Lyricist (1907–   )

Alex Kramer was born in Montreal, Canada, and educated at McGill University before beginning his musical career as a pianist and conductor. In 1938, he went to New York and became a hit songwriter with his wife, Joan Whitney. Born Zoe Parenteau in Pittsburgh, Pennsylvania, Whitney was a dance band singer and radio performer. She and her husband went into song publishing; eventually Whitney founded Southside Records. Hy Zaret, a New Yorker, graduated from West Virginia University and Brooklyn Law School. A practicing attorney, he wrote cantata texts as well as radio scripts.

Chronology

1936   *Dedicated to You*. Saul Chaplin/Sammy Cahn and Zaret. A great song often associated with Billy Eckstine.

1940   *It All Comes Back to Me Now*. Kramer/Whitney and Zaret.

1941   *High on a Windy Hill*. Kramer/Whitney. A number 1 chart record.
       My Sister and I. Kramer/Zaret.

1944   *Candy*. Kramer/Mack David. A big Johnny Mercer hit.
       One Meat Ball. Lou singer/Zaret.

1945   *Money Is the Root of All Evil*. Kramer/Zaret.

1949   *Far Away Places*. Kramer/Whitney. Listen to the beautiful Bing Crosby rendition.
       Comme Ci, Comme Ca. Bruno Coquatrix/Kramer and Whitney.

1955   *Unchained Melody*. Alex North/Zaret. Written for the film, **Unchained**.

BURTON LANE, Composer (1912–1997)

Another born and bred New Yorker, Burton Lane was a 15-year-old student at the High School of Commerce when he wrote marches and worked as a staff composer on Tin Pan Alley. By his late teens, he was contributing material for Broadway shows; in the early 1930s, he was in the company of songwriters Johnny Mercer*, Harold Arlen*, and Yip Harburg* as a composer for Earl Carroll's **Vanities**, the third **Little Show**, and **Americana**.

Broadway Chronology

1940   *There's a Great Day Coming, Manana*. Lane/Yip Harburg. Used in the musical **Hold On to Your Hats** starring Al Jolson and Martha Raye, this was Lane's first Broadway hit.

1944   *Feudin' and Fightin'*. Lane/Al Dubin*. From **Laughing Room Only**.

1947   **Finian's Rainbow**. Lane/Harburg and Fred Saidy. Story by Harburg. New York critics had high praise for this delightful musical and political satire about a fictional character named Billboard Rawkins in a mythical place called

Mississtucky. The memorable Lane melodies included *How Are Things in Glocca Morra?; If This Isn't Love; If I'm Not Near the Girl I Love, I Love the Girl I'm Near; Look to the Rainbow; Something Sort of Grandish*; and *The Begat*.

1965   ***On a Clear Day You Can See Forever***. Songs by Lane/Alan Jay Lerner. The title song and *Come Back to Me* were both big hits from this musical, which ran almost a year on Broadway and was reprised five years later on film. The show, originally titled *I Picked a Daisy*, was to have been written by Lerner and Richard Rodgers, but the lyricist and composer agreed to disagree. So Lerner bought the rights to it and invited Lane to compose the music. *On a Clear Day* turned out to be Lane's last show on Broadway.

Hollywood Chronology

1933   *Everything I Have Is Yours*. Lane/Harold Adamson*. At age 21, Lane had his first Hollywood hit song and it was part of a Warner Brothers biggie, ***Dancing Lady***, starring Joan Crawford, Clark Gable, and Franchot Tone. Lane and Adamson did two other songs for the film; Rodgers and Hart, Freed and Brown, and McHugh and Fields also wrote songs for it. Robert Benchley and the Three Stooges traipsed through ***Dancing Lady***, too.

1934   *Your Head on My Shoulder* and *I Want to Be a Minstrel Man*. Lane/Adamson. Eddie Cantor sang these two songs in the popular Goldwyn film, ***Kid Millions***.

1935   *You're My Thrill*. Lane/Ned Washington. From the film ***Here Comes the Band*** featuring Ted Lewis and his orchestra (and Lewis' familiar greeting, ''Is everybody happy?'').

1938   *Says My Heart*. Lane/Frank Loesser. At hit from the movie ***Cocoanut Grove***. *Moments Like This*. Lane/Loesser. Written for the film ***Collegiate Swing***.

1939   *The Lady's in Love with You*. Lane/Loesser. From the movie ***Some Like It Hot*—** which had the same title as Billy Wilder's later classic film but otherwise had nothing to do with the 1960s Monroe/Lemmon/Curtis comedy.

1940   *I Hear Music* and *Manana*. Lane/Loesser. Two more hits for the songwriting duo, this time from the film, ***Dancing on a Dime***.

1942   *How About You?* Lane/Ralph Freed. One of Lane's loveliest ballads and an Academy Award–nominated song performed beautifully by Judy Garland in ***Babes on Broadway***. It still could not compete with Irving Berlin's* *White Christmas* for the Oscar that year.

1944   *What Are You Doing the Rest of Your Life?* Lane/Ted Koehler. A big hit from the big Warner Brothers' moneymaker, ***Hollywood Canteen***. Lane composed music for five films in 1944, teaming up with lyricists Yip Harburg, Ralph Freed, Lew Brown, and Koehler.

1948   *Feudin' Fussin' and Fightin'*. Lane/Dubin. This screen-adapted title song did very well.

1951   *Too Late Now*. Lane/Alan Jay Lerner. One of their eight songs, a lovely ballad, and an Oscar nominee from the Fred Astaire film, ***Royal Wedding***. But Hoagy Carmichael* and Johnny Mercer's* *In the Cool, Cool, Cool of the Evening* won the Academy Award.

1953   ***Give the Girl a Break***. Songs by Lane/I. Gershwin*.

1955   ***Jupiter's Darling***. Songs by Lane/Adamson. The duo wrote a water ballet, *I Have A Dream*, plus six other songs for this not so swimming MGM movie, starring Esther Williams.

1968   ***Finian's Rainbow***. Lane/Harburg and Saidy. Fred Astaire starred and Francis Ford Coppola directed, but the film critics still panned the movie version of the Broadway musical. The songs? Still wonderful.

1970   ***On a Clear Day You Can See Forever***. Songs by Lane/Lerner. Barbra Streisand starred and sang her heart out, but the critics did not care.

JACK LAWRENCE, Composer/Lyricist (1910–   )

Jack Lawrence was born in Brooklyn, New York. He still writes—even if on anecdotally—about Golden Age music. Lawrence, who attended Long Island University and initially set out to become a podiatrist, began writing songs as a teenager and inevitably chose songwriting as his career. He also sang, fronted his own band, and, in World War II, became a Chief Petty Officer/Bandleader in the United States Coast Guard. Lawrence had a lot of creative collaborators, as documented in his chronology, but it is the nature of his stories that really tell the tale of Jack Lawrence and his music. In a 1997 article in *Sheet Music* magazine, Lawrence writes about his Hollywood collaboration with composer/conductor Johnny Green*. Together, they wrote *The Trembling of a Leaf*, recorded by both Mario Lanza and Lena Horne, but it was never issued or marketed. Recently, media mogul Ted Turner bought the MGM library and along with it, *The Trembling of a Leaf*. According to the exultant 87-year-old Lawrence, "the song will be issued on a CD, soon." What a great "it-ain't-over-till-it's-over" sense of things. By the time this book is published, perhaps *Trembling* will be another Jack Lawrence golden hit.

Chronology

1930   *(By the) Sleepy Lagoon*. Eric Coates/Lawrence.
       With the Wind and the Rain in Your Hair. Lawrence and Clara Edwards (wm).
       These two songs were Lawrence's first two hits.

1932   *Play Fiddle Play*. Arthur Altman and Emery Deutsch/Lawrence. Altman and lyricist Hal David wrote *American Beauty Rose*. Deutsch was born in Hungary in 1907 and, after arriving in the United States, attended Fordham University in New York City, where he achieved success as a track-and-field athlete. Deutsch also composed *When a Gypsy Makes His Violin Play*.

1938   *Sunrise Serenade*. Frankie Carle/Lawrence. 78-record collectors know this one best—it is on the B side of *Moonlight Serenade* (Glenn Miller/Mitchell Parish*).

1939   *Vagabond Dreams*. Hoagy Carmichael*/Lawrence. Glenn Miller had a hit with this one, just like he did with *Sunrise Serenade*.
       In an Eighteenth Century Drawing Room. Raymond Scott/Lawrence. Scott, whose real name was Harry Warnow, (brother of bandleader Mark Warnow), was born in New York in 1909 and got his college degree in electrical engineering. In applying that technical training creatively, he was quite innovative in producing

sounds that may very well have been the forerunner of electronic music. Scott was the popular leader of unique quartets; he collaborated with Lew Pollack (Chapter 4) and Sidney Clare (Chapter 4) on *Toy Trumpet*. Scott also adapted the music for *In an Eighteenth Century Drawing Room* from Mozart's **Piano Sonata in C, K-525**.

If I Didn't Care. Lawrence (wm). A big hit for the Ink Spots.

1940   *All or Nothing at All*. Altman/Lawrence. Used in the film **Doughboys in Ireland**. This classic caught on later, when Harry James and Frank Sinatra recorded it.

       Johnson Rag. Guy Hall and Henry Kleinkauf/Lawrence. The music was written in 1917, the lyrics in 1940.

       Handful of Stars. Ted Shapiro/Lawrence. For the movie **Hullabaloo**.

1941   *Yes My Darling Daughter*. Lawrence (wm). Written for the Broadway production **Crazy with the Heat**.

1944   *Heave Ho My Lads*. Lawrence (wm). Official USMM title song for their wartime film. Lawrence earned his Ensign commission with it.

1945   *Symphony*. Alex Alstone/Lawrence. According to Bill Stern, a 1940s radio commentator known for his exaggerated stories, this song came from a code-word phrase used by the free French in World War II, *C'est Fini*, signalling that capture by the enemy was imminent. Over time, it has somehow become anglicized as "symphony."

1946   **Torch Song**. Scored by Walter Gross and Lawrence. This film starred Joan Crawford (with India Edwards singing her voice-overs) and Michael Wilding (with Walter Gross playing his piano parts). The movie's music included a song that would become a standard, *Tenderly*. Gross (1909–1967), a New Yorker and highly regarded piano soloist, also hosted his own radio show.

1947   *Beyond the Sea*. Charles Trenet/Lawrence. Trenet (Chapter 4) was a French entertainer.

       Linda. Lawrence (wm). Another song, another story: Lawrence wrote this namesake song for the daughter of an American show business attorney and friend. The young woman went on to fame as a musician in her own right, performing with and marrying Paul McCartney.

1950   *Hold My Hand*. Richard Myers/Lawrence. Myers and lyricist Edward Heyman wrote *My Darling* in 1932.

1953   *Ciribiribin*. Alberto Pestalozza/Rudolf Thaler. Lawrence updated this Italian original and it became a big hit for Harry James.

1954   *Poor People of Paris*. Marguerite Monnot/Lawrence.

1959   *Once Upon a Dream*. Sammy Fain*/Lawrence. Used in the Disney film, **Sleeping Beauty**.

PEGGY LEE, Composer/Lyricist/Singer (1920–)

Born Norma Dolores Engstrom (or Egstrom, per the Smithsonian's *American Popular/Music* liner notes) in Jamestown, North Dakota, Peggy Lee is one of the most stylistically unique singers in the whole world—and a fine songwriter, too. Lee began as an actress and then started singing "up front" as "girl vocalist'' with Benny Goodman in the early 1940s. She married guitarist Dave Barbour (Chapter 4) in 1943 and they wrote several popular hit songs together. Although plagued with various illnesses throughout her life, Peggy Lee continues to perform for delighted audiences, who still ''catch the fever'' everytime she sings.

Chronology

1946   *I Don't Know Enough About You*. Lee and Dave Barbour (wm).

1947   *It's a Good Day*. Lee and Barbour (wm).

1948   *Mañana*. Lee and Barbour (wm). One of their biggest hits.

1952   *Where Can I Go Without You?* Victor Young*/Lee.

1954   *Johnny Guitar*. Young/Lee. Lee performed this title song in the film.

CAROLYN LEIGH, Lyricist (1926–1983)

Invoking the criteria for defining and celebrating the timeless music this book covers, Carolyn Paula Leigh belongs among the prominent songwriters of the Golden Age, even though she penned her poetic words in the 1950s and early 1960s. Like a few others in the contemporary category, her sophisticated style and delightful lyrics put her in a class with the best. Had she lived longer and created more of her lovely songs, Leigh's work may have been compared to the voluminous musical material of Dorothy Fields and other top lyricists. Carolyn Leigh was born in New York, graduated from New York University, and after a brief stint as a Manhattan advertising copywriter (while still in her 20s), she began her own successful run on Broadway and elsewhere as a lyricist.

Chronology

1954   *Peter Pan*. Songs by Mark ''Moose'' Charlap/Leigh. Their memorable Broadway score included *I'm Flying, I Won't Grow Up, I've Got to Crow*, and other terrific songs. Hollywood hired Jule Styne*, Betty Comden*, and Adolph Green to implement the film score, but unlike the magical stage material, the movie's music missed making hits.
       Young at Heart. Johnny Richards/Leigh.

1956   *How Little We Know*. Phil Springer/Leigh. Frank Sinatra recorded it, and although it was not as popular as the similarly titled 1940 song by Hoagy Carmichael*, it is lovely nonetheless.

1957   *Witchcraft*. Cy Coleman*/Leigh. Introduced on Broadway in **Walk a Little Faster**.

1958   *Firefly*. Coleman/Leigh. A Tony Bennett top-of-the-chart hit.

1959   *The Best Is Yet to Come*. Coleman/Leigh.

1960   **Wildcat**. Scored by Coleman and Leigh. The duo wrote *Give a Little Whistle, Hey Look Me Over*, and others for this Broadway musical.

1962   **Little Me**. Scored by Coleman and Leigh. The hits from this Broadway show included *I've Got Your Number* and *Real Live Girl*.

Pass Me By. Coleman/Leigh. Written for the film, **Father Goose**, starring Cary Grant.

ALAN JAY LERNER, Lyricist (1918–1986) and FREDERICK LOEWE, Composer (1904–1988)

Lerner, the descendant of a retailing fortune, was born in New York and attended the best prep schools and Harvard, where he wrote for a couple of the Hasty Pudding shows. Back in New York, he became a professional writer: in broadcasting, writing for radio; in advertising, writing for Albert Lasker's famed agency, Lord and Thomas; and on Broadway, and eventually Hollywood, writing for stage and screen. It is interesting to note that before 1954, Lerner was working as a scriptwriter, rather than songwriter, in Hollywood. Among his credits were the screenplay for **An American in Paris** and special dialogue for Fred Astaire in **The Bandwagon**.

Loewe, born in Germany (or Austria, as some books have it), came from a musical family. His father was a Viennese opera singer and Frederick showed early genius as the composer of a musical at age 15. Having graduated from the prestigious Berlin Music Conservatory, at age 19 he wrote his first commercial song, a "shimmy" (a sexy dance well-known in the 1920s and 1930s), with R. Hiner. A year later, Loewe arrived in the United States and had a rough time getting started; he worked as a cowhand, a prospector, and a barroom pianist just to survive. In the 1930s, Loewe worked with lyricist Erle Crooker in a Saint Louis stock company, where his first song was a waltz. In the years that followed he found his real success as a songwriter collaborating with Lerner on Broadway and in Hollywood.

Broadway Chronology

1943 *What's Up?* Loewe/Lerner (libretto and lyrics). This New York show only lasted eight weeks.

1945 *The Day Before Spring*. Loewe/Lerner (libretto and lyrics). Better material, but this show only lasted two weeks.

1947 *Brigadoon*. Loewe/Lerner. Their really fine fantasy musical featured a lovely score, catchy lyrics, and many hits: *The Heather on the Hill; Come to Me, Bend to Me; I'll Go Home with Bonnie Jean; There But for You Go I; Brigadoon;* and the show-stopper, *Almost Like Being in Love*.

1948 *Love Life*. Kurt Weill/Lerner (libretto and lyrics). These two artists must have been disappointed in the reception they got for this musical work (it had a disappointing run of 252 performances at a time when highly popular musicals lasted much longer).

1951 *Paint Your Wagon*. Loewe/Lerner. Their second hit musical in a row, with lovely music, an exciting script, and fine songs, including *I Talk to the Trees* and *They Call the Wind Maria*.

1956 *My Fair Lady*. Loewe/Lerner (story adaptation and lyrics). This prize-winning, record-setting show, based on George Bernard Shaw's *Pygmalion*, delighted audiences for six years with some of the best acting—Rex Harrison and Julie Andrews starred—and best songs, ever, on Broadway: *I Could Have Danced All Night, Get Me to the Church on Time, I've Grown Accustomed to Her Face, The Rain in Spain, On the Street Where You Live, With a Little Bit of Luck, Why Can't the English?, Wouldn't It Be Loverly?* and *Show Me.* Directed by Moss Hart, this brilliant comedy musical was the first Broadway production financially underwritten by a television network, CBS. It obviously paid off, and in the 1980s and 1990s, following CBS' earlier lead, ABC invested in several highly successful Broadway hits. A creative footnote to *My Fair Lady*: Alan Jay Lerner wrote the words and music to a song that was to have been sung by Harrison in the first act. It was titled *Oh, Come to the Ball*, but was deemed too strong (read: sexy) for the actor, and since the show was long, it was cut. There is a recording, however, of Lerner playing and singing the song in an "unplugged" *Lyrics and Lyricists* performance at New York's 92nd Street Y. If you can get the disc, it is worth hearing.

1960   *Camelot*. Loewe/Lerner. A *tour de force* which ran for two years, with Julie Andrews, Richard Burton, and Robert Goulet performing *If Ever I Would Leave You, How to Handle a Woman, I Loved You Once in Silence*, and *Camelot*, the painful, metaphorical anthem for the Kennedy era's "one brief shining moment."

1965   *On A Clear Day You Can See Forever*. Burton Lane*/Lerner. Barbra Streisand starred and sang as only she could—perfectly. It became a fine Hollywood reprise as well, with these great songs supporting the stage-to-screen transition: *Come Back to Me, What Did I Have That I Don't Have Now?*, and the title number.

1969   *Coco*. Andre Previn/Lerner (story and lyrics). This Broadway production only ran one year, despite Katharine Hepburn's performance as Coco Chanel. The title song, by the way, was cut.

1973   *Gigi*. Loewe/Lerner. In a reversal of tradition, this production shined on Broadway after winning acclaim and Oscars in Hollywood.

1976   *1600 Pennsylvania Avenue*. Leonard Bernstein/Lerner (story and lyrics). This Broadway production only ran a week, despite its writers.

1979   *Carmelina*. Loewe/Lerner. Adapted from the more successful film, *Buena Sera, Mrs. Campbell*.

Hollywood Chronology

1954   *Brigadoon*. Loewe/Lerner. Despite MGM and Arthur Freed's production; Vincente Minelli's direction; and Cyd Charisse, Gene Kelly, and Van Johnson's performances, *Brigadoon* did not do well on film.

1958   *Gigi*. Loewe/Lerner. Story adaptation from the French author, Colette, by Lerner This charming and highly successful film won Oscars galore. Vincente Minelli directed fine performances from Leslie Caron, Hermione Gingold, and Maurice Chevalier. The beautiful songs included *The Night They Invented Champagne, Thank Heaven for Little Girls, I Don't Understand the Parisians, I Remember It Well*, and the title song.

1964   *My Fair Lady*. Loewe/Lerner. The Academy Award winner for best Picture; Best Actor (Rex Harrison); Best Supporting Actors (Gladys Cooper and Stanley Holloway); Best Director (George Cukor); Best Costume Design (Cecil Beaton);

Best Musical Score (Andre Previn); and best sound, cinematography, and film editing. The New York Film Critics' Best Picture Award also went to *My Fair Lady*. But there was something missing; and, therein, lies a tale. Movie mogul Jack Warner bought the rights to *My Fair Lady* for his studio. He decided Rex Harrison was wrong for the part of Henry Higgins and asked Cary Grant to do it. Grant supposedly got hysterical with laughter and advised Warner Brothers to stay with Harrison. Then Warner decided he did not want Julie Andrews, either. Thus, Audrey Hepburn got the female lead, which worked out well. (The best of Hollywood's voice-over artists, Marni Nixon, did the singing to Hepburn's lipsyncing.) However, Julie Andrews starred in *Mary Poppins* that year and won the Academy Award for Best Actress for her title role performance.

1970   *On a Clear Day You Can See Forever*. Loewe/Lerner (screenplay and lyrics). Minelli directed Barbra Streisand, Yves Montand, Jack Nicholson, and Bob Newhart in a production that was better than the Broadway version.

1974   *The Little Prince*. Loewe/Lerner (screenplay and lyrics). Choreographed by Bob Fosse. The entire score and title song for this film received Academy Award nominations. Continuing and fitting recognition for Lerner and Loewe—known to be such a talented, but unlikely, team of quirky lyricist and hot tempered composer—who produced such splendid words and music.

EDGAR LESLIE, Composer/Lyricist (1885–1976)

Edgar Leslie was one of the very few writers (Harry Akst was another) who collaborated in creating words and music with Irving Berlin*. Born in Stamford, Connecticut, Leslie grew up in New York City and attended college at Cooper Union in Manhattan. Leslie began his career as a parodist and vaudeville writer, eventually going on to write for the Berlin publishing firm, Phil Spitalny's all-girl band, radio star Arthur Godfrey, and others. He was an ASCAP founding member, as well as a Songwriter's Protective Association founder with Billy Rose* and others.

Chronology

1909   *Sadie Salome Go Home*. Irving Berlin/Leslie.

1915   *America, I Love You*. Leslie and Archie Gottler (wm).

1917   *For Me and My Gal*. George W. Meyer (Chapter 1)/Leslie and E. Ray Goetz. A big standard.

1922   *Rose of the Rio Grande*. Harry Warren* and Ross Gorman/Leslie.
        Blue and Broken Hearted. Leslie/Grant Clarke (Chapter 4).

1927   *Among my Souvenirs*. Horatio Nicholls/Leslie. Another fine standard.

1931   *In a Little Gypsy Tearoom, A Little Bit Independent*, and *Moon Over Miami*. Leslie/Joe Burke*. Fats Waller had *A Little Bit* high up on the charts.

1937   *It Looks Like Rain in Cherry Blossom Lane*. Leslie/Burke.

SAM LEWIS, Lyricist (1885–1959)

Samuel M. Lewis was born in New York and, as a young man, was a Wall Street runner by day and a cafe singer at night. At the beginning of his musical career, he wrote for popular vaudeville entertainers and some of his early songs became standards. Lewis began a long and prosperous partnership with co-lyricist Joe Young* in 1916; more than half of Lewis' writing was a collaborative effort with Young, as can be seen in the chronologies for both lyricists. Sam Lewis also wrote with "hall of fame" composers including Walter Donaldson*, Harry Warren*, Fred Coots*, Con Conrad*, Ray Henderson, and Victor Young*.

Chronology

1914   *When You're a Long, Long Way from Home.* George W. Meyer (Chapter 1)/ Lewis. Possibly his first hit.

1916   *Where Did Robinson Crusoe Go with Friday on Saturday Night?* Meyer and Joe Young/Lewis. A novelty song written for Al Jolson and the show, **Robinson Crusoe, Jr.**

1918   *Just a Baby's Prayer at Twilight.* M. K. Jerome/Lewis and Young.
Rock-a-Bye Your Baby with a Dixie Melody and *Hello Central, Give Me No-Man's Land.* Jean Schwartz (Chapter 1)/Lewis and Young.
My Mammy. Walter Donaldson/Lewis and Young. *Rock-a-Bye, Central, Give Me, and My Mammy* were all written for the Broadway musical **Sinbad**, which was composed for the most part by Sigmund Romberg*. Al Jolson starred and had hits with all three of these numbers.

1919   *How Ya Gonna Keep 'em Down on the Farm After They've Seen Broadway?* Donaldson/Lewis and Young. Long titles were in when this wartime classic was composed.

1920   *I'd Love to Fall Asleep in My Mammy's Arms.* Fred Ahlert*/Lewis and Young.
Singin' the Blues. Con Conrad*/Lewis and Young.

1921   *Tuck Me to Sleep in My Old 'Tucky Home.* George W. Meyer (Chapter 1)/Lewis and Young. Al Jolson introduced it, as he did for so many of this genre.

1925   *Dinah.* Harry Askt*/Lewis and Young. For the Broadway show, **Plantation Revue**.

1926   *In a Little Spanish Town.* Mabel Wayne*/Lewis and Young.

1928   *Laugh, Clown, Laugh.* Ted FioRito (Chapter 4)/Lewis and Young.

1929   *I Kiss Your Hand, Madame.* Ralph Erwin/Lewis and Young. Used in the film **Emperor Waltz**, starring Bing Crosby.
Absence Makes the Heart Grow Fonder. Harry Warren/Lewis and Young.
Old Man Sunshine. Akst/Lewis and Young. The trio wrote this song and two others for the George Jessel movie, **Lucky Boy**. Jessel was a friend—and some say, imitator—of Al Jolson; over time, he became popular as the "Toastmaster of the United States."

1930   *Cryin' for the Carolines.* Warren/Lewis and Young. This song and three others by these songwriters were included in the film, **Spring Is Here**, a re-write of the Broadway show by Rodgers/Hart and Owen Davis.

1931   *Just Friends* and *Heartaches.* John Klenner/Lewis. Absolutely lovely ballads.

1932   *Street of Dreams.* Victor Young/Lewis.

1933   *One Minute to One*. Fred Coots/Lewis. Film title song introduced by vaudeville crooner Harry Richman.

1935   *For All We Know*. J. Fred Coots/Lewis. A really beautiful ballad.
I Believe in Miracles. Meyer and Pete Wendling/Lewis.
Beautiful Lady in Blue. Coots/Lewis.
Then You've Never Been Blue. Coots and FioRito/Young. For the 1935 film, **Every Night at Eight**.

1936   *Gloomy Sunday*. Renzso Seress/Lewis (English lyrics). Billie Holiday made a beautiful recording of this lovely Italian composition.
Close to Me. Peter DeRose*/Lewis.

HARRY LINK, Composer (1896–1957), HOLT MARVELL, Lyricist (1901–1969), and JACK STRACHEY, Composer/Lyricist (1894–1972)

Link was a Philadelphian who graduated from the University of Pennsylvania's Wharton School and became a music publishing executive. Marvell's real name was Eric Maschwitz and he came from Birmingham, England. A Cambridge graduate and author of books and musical plays, he worked for MGM as a Hollywood scriptwriter and lyricist. Marvell was a light colonel in the British army in World War II. Strachey, "to the manor born," was an Oxford graduate who started as a performing pianist and went on to become a songwriter.

Chronology

1926   *I'm Just Wild About Animal Crackers*. Sam Coslow*, Link, and Freddie Rich (wm).

1929   *I've Got a Feeling I'm Falling*. Fats Waller*/Link and Billy Rose*.

1935   *These Foolish Things (Remind Me of You)*. Link and Strachey/Marvell. One of the great popular ballads of the Golden Age and all time. Introduced in London in 1935, the classic American recordings are by Billie Holiday and Benny Goodman*—and there are many more.
The World Is Mine Tonight. George Posford/Marvell.

1939   *At the Balalaika*. Posford and Herbert Stothart/Marvell, Chet Forrest*, and Robert Wright. For the movie, **Balalaika**.

1940   *A Nightingale Sang in Berkeley Square*. Manning Sherman/Marvell. For the London revue, **New Faces**.

1948   *No Orchids for My Lady*. Alan Stranks/Strachey.

JERRY LIVINGSTON, Composer/Lyricist (1909–1987)

Born in Denver, Colorado, Livingston attended the University of Arizona. He was a pianist and bandleader who, in 1932, went east to begin his career in New York, and later moved back out west to Hollywood. Like many of his songwriting peers, Livingston eventually became a music publisher. As far as is known, he was not related to Jay Livingston nor Fud Livingston (Chapter 4)—who were not related either.

Chronology

1933　*It's the Talk of the Town* and *Under a Blanket Blue*. Livingston/Al Neiburg and Marty Symes (Chapter 4). Neiburg was born in 1902, and in 1930 collaborated on the evergreen, *I'm Confessin'*, with Doc Daugherty and Ellis Reynolds (Chapter 4).

1939　*Blue and Sentimental*. Count Basie and Livingston (wm).

1940　*(This Is the) Story of a Starry Night*. Adaptation by Livingston, Al Hoffman*, and Mann Curtis. From an original Tchaikovsky composition.

1943　*Mairzy Doats*. Livingston, Hoffman, and Milton Drake (wm). The complete story of the creation of this enormously popular song is included under Hoffman and Drake in Chapter Four.

1948　*Bibidi Bobbidi Boo* and *A Dream Is a Wish Your Heart Makes*. Livingston, Mack David, and Hoffman (wm). Both songs were used in Disney's original **Cinderella**.

1955　*Wake the Town and Tell the People*. Livingston/Sammy Gallop.

1960　*Surfside Six*. Livingston/David. Title track written for the popular television series.
　　　Chi Baba Chi Baba. Livingston, David, and Hoffman (wm).

FRANK LOESSER, Composer/Lyricist (1910–1969)

If an overall ranking of songwriters were ever compiled, Frank Loesser would surely be very high on that list. Born in New York City, the son of a musician (the elder Loesser had been a well-known accompanist back in Germany), Frank was already composing at age 6. Loesser hated to practice on the piano and did not like school very much, either, dropping out of City College at age 15. From then on, for a very long time, he moved from job to job: he was a journalist for suburban newspapers, a writer for *Women's Wear Daily* and a lyricist for William Schuman before Schuman started composing symphonic orchestrations. In the early 1930s, the Leo Feist publishing company actually published Loesser's first song, *In Love with a Memory of You*, after they had fired him for writing flop after flop. That song was picked up by Republic Pictures and got Loesser his first Hollywood job; that did not last either. In 1936, on the verge of poverty, Loesser was trying to become a nightclub performer, so he went back to New York and ended up writing for **The Illustrator Show**, which closed after only four performances. Undaunted, he landed another job in Hollywood with Universal Studios—and a short time later moved over to Paramount, where, finally, his songwriting stardom was born.

Broadway Chronology

1936　*Bang, the Bell Rang*. Loesser (wm). His first song for Broadway was written for **The Illustrator Show**, which was thought to be way too risque by the proper New York critics—and bang, the bell tolled—and the show closed.

1948　**Where's Charley?** Songs by Loesser. On Broadway again, following his

Hollywood successes before and during the World War II years, Loesser wrote this musical version of *Charley's Aunt*. *My Darling* and *Once in Love With Amy* were both hits from the show. Ray Bolger was a hit too, his singing and dancing were highly applauded by critics and theatregoers alike. Music buffs still enjoy listening to Bolger's lilting recording of *Once in Love With Amy*.

1950   *Guys and Dolls*. Songs by Loesser. Book by Abe Burrows (Borowitz) and Jo Swerling. Somewhat Runyonesque themselves, Burrows and Loesser created characters based on Damon Runyon's Broadway stories. The production's marvelous cast sang *Luck Be a Lady Tonight; A Bushel and a Peck; I've Never Been in Love Before; If I Were a Bell; Take Back Your Mink; Sit Down, You're Rockin' the Boat; I'll Know; More I Cannot Wish You*, and *Sue Me*. Gerald Bordman, the guru of all theatrical anthologists, called *Guys and Dolls* ''one of the master-works of the musical theatre.'' Four decades later, revival audiences agreed: the 1992 reprise of *Guys and Dolls* set a record for the most performances of a revived musical.

1956   *Most Happy Fella*. Adaptation and Songs by Loesser. Story by Sidney Howard. This musical version of *They Knew What They Wanted* featured several memorable hit songs, including *Standing on the Corner, Big D*, and the title tune.

1960   *Greenwillow*. Songs by Loesser. Despite the songwriter's music and Anthony Perkins and Cecil Kellaway's fine acting, this production closed after three months.

1961   *How to Succeed in Business Without Really Trying*. Songs by Loesser. Story by Shepherd Mead. This very funny musical satire was produced by Cy Feur and Ernest Martin and starred the irrepressible Robert Morse and the funky Rudy Vallee. The comedy, words, and music garnered a Pulitzer Prize and a run of more than 1,400 performances. The standard, *I Believe in You*, was written for this show. Once again, Frank Loesser showed everybody how to succeed in show business.

Hollywood Chronology

1934   *Moon of Manakoora*. Alfred Newman/Loesser. Heard in the film, *Hurricane*.

1937   *Lovely One*. Manning Sherman/Loesser. This song was written for the movie *Vogues of '38*, and was Loesser's first lyricist film credit.

1938   *Says My Heart*. Burton Lane*/Loesser. Used in the movie musical *Coconut Grove*, it became a hit ballad.
       Small Fry. Hoagy Carmichael*/Loesser. Bing Crosby performed it in the film, *Sing You Sinners*.
       Two Sleepy People. Carmichael/Loesser. Bob Hope and Shirley Ross sang this one in the movie, *Thanks for the Memory* (title song by Robin and Rainger*).

1939   *The Lady's in Love With You*. Lane/Loesser. Written for *Some Like It Hot*, a very different film from the later Billy Wilder classic of the 1960s.
       Heart and Soul. Carmichael/Loesser. An American standard, originally written for the short subject film, *A Song Is Born*.

1940   *I Hear Music*. Lane/Loesser. From the movie, *Dancing on a Dime*. Ella Fitzgerald recorded a truly thrilling rendition of this hit.
       Say It (Over and Over Again). James McHugh*/Loesser. From *Buck Benny Rides Again*.

1941   *Dolores*. Louis Alter/Loesser. An Academy Award–nominated song from the film, **Las Vegas Nights**. It was performed in the movie by Frank Sinatra, singing on screen for the first time, up front with Tommy Dorsey's band. *The Last Time I Saw Paris* won the Oscar that year.

Kiss the Boys Goodbye. Scored by Victor Schertzinger and Loesser. The title song was sung by Mary Martin, *Sand in My Shoes* was sung by Connee Boswell, and *I'll Never Let a Day Pass By* was another hit from this movie, which Schertzinger also directed.

1942   *I Don't Want to Walk Without You*. Jule Styne*/Loesser. Betty Jane Rhodes sang this ballad in the film, **Sweater Girl**. Harry James and vocalist Helen Forrest made it a hit on the charts.

Jingle, Jangle, Jingle. Joseph J. Lilley/Loesser.

Can't Get Out of This Mood and *I Get the Neck of the Chicken*. Jimmy McHugh/Loesser. Written for the movie, **Seven Days Leave.**

Praise the Lord and Pass the Ammunition. Frank Loesser (wm). Not for a film; not for a play. This one was for the men and women in uniform—purely patriotic.

1943   *They're Either Too Young or Too Old* and *The Dreamer*. Arthur Schwartz*/Loesser. Both written for **Thank Your Lucky Stars**. Despite her inexperience in concert, Bette Davis delightfully delivered *They're Either* in the film. It was an Oscar nominee, but lost to *You'll Never Know*.

1944   *Spring Will Be a Little Late This Year*. Frank Loesser (wm). An absolutely lovely song written for the film, **Christmas Holiday**.

I Don't Want to Walk Without You. Styne/Loesser. Used again, this time in the movie, **You Can't Ration Love**.

Murder, He Says. McHugh/Loesser. Betty Hutton belted this one out in **Jam Session**.

1945   *Leave Us Face It* and *We're in Love*. Loesser/Abe Burrows. These two songs were written for the movie, **Duffy's Tavern**, which was a spin-off from a popular radio show of the time.

1947   *I Wish I Didn't Love You So* and *Papa Don't Preach to Me*. Loesser (wm). Both songs were written for the film, **The Perils of Pauline**. *I Wish* was nominated for an Oscar (losing to *Zip-a-Dee-Doo-Dah*) and was sung in the movie by Betty Hutton, whose sister Marion was then the ''girl singer'' for Glenn Miller.

What Are You Doing New Years Eve? Loesser (wm).

Tallahassee. Loesser (wm). Used in the Rosemary Clooney and Bing Crosby movie, **Variety Girl**.

1948   *On a Slow Boat to China*. Loesser (wm).

1949   *Baby It's Cold Outside*. Loesser (wm). The Oscar went that year to *Baby It's Cold Outside*, from **Neptune's Daughter**. Musicians have praised another song by Loesser (wm) from that film which did not make the charts or the hit parades, *My Heart Beats Faster*.

1950   *Hoop De Doo*. Milton DeLugg/Loesser. This was the theme song of a popular nighttime television variety program. DeLugg was the show's musical director and bandleader.

1952   **Hans Christian Anderson**. Songs by Frank Loesser. This award-winning Samuel

Goldwyn extravaganza featured Loesser's words and music in *Wonderful Copenhagen, Anywhere I Wander, No Two People, Thumbelina*—all great hits and *Thumbelina* an Academy Award nominee. But the Oscar that year went to Tiomkin and Washington's title track music for **High Noon**.

1955 **Guys and Dolls**. Songs by Frank Loesser. This musical score was considered the songwriter's crowning achievement—on stage and in this screen version starring Marlon Brando and Frank Sinatra and an excellent ensemble cast. Loesser added one more song for the movie, *Adelaide's Lament*.

1967 **How to Succeed in Business Without Really Trying**. Songs by Loesser. To its eternal credit, Mirisch-United Artists presented the film version as an intact replication of the Pulitzer Prize–winning Broadway show. It surely did succeed.

CARMEN LOMBARDO, Composer/Lyricist (1903–1971)

There were several related Lombardos in the famous Royal Canadians, the orchestra led for so many years by Guy Lombardo. Carmen and brothers Lebert and Victor were sidemen in the band. Carmen Lombardo was born in London, Ontario, Canada, and joined his big brother's band at the age of 14 as a saxophone player and a ''boy singer.'' An early entertainer on radio, Carmen had hits of his own as a songwriter.

Chronology

1928 *Sweethearts on Parade*. Lombardo/Charles Newman.
     Coquette. Lombardo and Johnny Green*/Gus Kahn*.

1933 *Ooh Look There (Ain't She Pretty?)*. Lombardo and Clarence Todd (wm).

1937 *Sailboat in the Moonlight and Boo Hoo*. Lombardo and John Jacob Loeb/Edward Heyman. *Boo Hoo* was a big hit with Guy Lombardo's orchestra. Loeb also wrote *Rosie The Riveter* in 1942 with lyrics by Redd Evans.

1964 *Seems Like Old Times*. Lombardo and John Jacob Loeb (wm). Another hit for the Lombardo band. Of course, the biggest of all Guy Lombardo hits was *Auld Lang Syne* (1711 Music, Unknown Composer; Added Lyrics, Robert Burns). It is still a New Year's Eve tradition, shared by young and old alike, to listen and dance to—and even watch old movies and tapes of—Lombardo's version of this wistful musical poem.

BALLARD MACDONALD, Lyricist (1882–1935)

George Gershwin only had a few collaborators other than his brother, Ira, but Portland, Oregon, born Ballard MacDonald was one of the lyricists on one of Gershwin's very best, *Somebody Loves Me*. A Princeton graduate, playwright, and author of special material for Broadway and Hollywood, MacDonald wrote some great standards.

Chronology

1913 *On the Trail of the Lonesome Pine*. Harry Carroll (Chapter 1)/MacDonald.

1917 *Back Home Again in Indiana*. James F. Hanley (Chapter 4) MacDonald.

1918   *Beautiful Ohio*. Robert A. King/MacDonald. It was the best-selling song of that year. King also wrote under the pseudonym, Mary Earl.

1920   *Rose of Washington Square*. Hanley/MacDonald. Fanny Brice introduced this song in the **Ziegfeld Follies**.
       Somebody Else, Not Me. Hanley/MacDonald.

1921   *Second Hand Rose*. Grant Clarke (Chapter 4)/MacDonald. A Brice favorite in the **Follies**. About forty years later Barbra Streisand did it again, brilliantly, in **Funny Girl** on Broadway and on the screen.

1922   *Parade of the Wooden Soldiers*. Leon Jessel/MacDonald (English lyrics).

1924   *Somebody Loves Me*. George Gerswhin*/MacDonald and Buddy DeSylva*.

1925   *Clap Hands, Here Comes Charlie*. Joseph Meyer*/MacDonald and Billy Rose*. Written for vaudeville's **Salt and Pepper**, this was also a big song for the Chick Webb Band and the theme song of Charlie Barnet's Band.

JAMES MCHUGH, Composer (1894–1969)

A native of Boston, James McHugh had musical parents, studied piano as a young man, and later turned down a scholarship to the Boston Conservatory of Music in favor of a Tin Pan Alley songplugging job. In New York, he went to work for Irving Berlin's music publishing firm. Like Harold Arlen*, McHugh wrote Cotton Club revues music in Harlem and in 1924, had his first big hit. He eventually became a music publisher himself and one of the finest popular composers of all time.

Broadway Chronology

1924   *When My Sugar Walks Down the Street*. McHugh/Gene Austin (and Irving Mills?). This was his first big one.

1927   *I Can't Believe That You're in Love With Me*. McHugh and Clarence Gaskill (wm). For the Broadway revue, **Gay Paree**.

1928   **Blackbirds of 1928**. Songs by McHugh and Dorothy Fields*. This was McHugh's first Broadway hit musical and the beginning of his highly successful collaboration with lyricist Fields. For this show they wrote: *Diga Diga Doo, I Can't Give You Anything But Love*, and *I Must Have That Man*. The 518-performance production starred the great tap dancer Bill "Bojanles" Robinson. A story in a 1978 *Playbill* for the musical, **Ain't Misbehavin'**, reprised the legend that Fats Waller and Andy Razaf had sold *I Can't Give* and *Sunny Side* (below) to McHugh and Fields. Threatened law suits? Out of court settlements? The songs' real writers? More questions than answers; but both sides of this Broadway legend linger on.

1930   *Exactly Like You* and *On the Sunny Side of the Street*. McHugh/Fields. Two jazz classics written for **The International Revue**. Politically correct critics planned the show. In 1930 and 1931, McHugh and Fields wrote songs for three other musicals: **The Vanderbilt Revue**, which was Lew Fields' last show; **Rhapsody in Black**, a ten-week production with Ethel Waters; and **Singin' the Blues**, which featured only incidental songs from the two writers.

1939   *South American Way*. McHugh/Al Dubin*. After being in Hollywood for a while, McHugh returned to New York and worked with Dubin for Ole Olsen and Chick Johnson's fun-filled Broadway musical, **Streets of Paris**. Carmen Miranda, Abbott and Costello, Bobby Clark, and Gower Champion sang and danced their way through this romp. The McHugh/Dubin song for this show should not be confused with Harold Rome's *South America, Take It Away*.

1940   **Keep Off the Grass**. Songs by McHugh and Dubin. *Clear Out of This World* may have been the best song from this show produced by the Schuberts. It should not be mixed up with the Arlen/Mercer 1945 standard, *Out of This World*, from the Bing Crosby film of the same name.

1948   **As the Girls Go**. McHugh/Adamson. A bright musical produced by Mike Todd, featuring nice songs, but no chart busters.

Hollywood Chronology

1929   *What Has Become of Hinky Dinky Parlay Vous?* McHugh, Irwin Dash, Irving Mills, and Dubin. This was McHugh's first big hit from a movie, **This Cockeyed World**, which was a Fox sequel to Maxwell Anderson and Lawrence Stallings' **What Price Glory**?

1930   **Love in the Rough**. McHugh/Fields. They wrote five songs for this film; unfortunately, none of them are remembered.

1931   *You're in the Army Now*. McHugh/Fields. Written for the movie, **Cuban Love Song**.

1935   *I Feel a Song Coming On*. McHugh/Fields. After several years of writing less than memorable songs for movies, including **The Big Broadcast** and **Dancing Lady**, McHugh and Fields certainly followed through on their feelings in writing this evergreen, for **Every Night at Eight**.
       Lovely to Look At. McHugh and Jerome Kern*/Fields. Up for an Oscar, it lost to Warren/Dubin's *Lullaby of Broadway*. Berlin's *Cheek to Cheek* lost, too.

1935/36   *Hooray for Love*. McHugh/Fields. Film title song.
       I'm Shooting High. McHugh/Ted Koehler. They wrote this one and several more for the 20th Century Fox movie, **King of Burlesque**.
       Let's Sing Again. McHugh/Gus Kahn*. Another title song for a film.

1937   *Where Are You?* McHugh/Harold Adamson*. A very pretty ballad written for the movie, **Top of the Town**. *You're a Sweetheart*. McHugh/Adamson. Written for the Universal film of the same name.

1938   *My Own*. McHugh/Adamson. This ballad was written for **That Certain Age**, and received an Academy Award nomination. Rainger and Robin's *Thanks for the Memory* won the Oscar.
       I Love to Whistle. McHugh/Adamson. They wrote this one and three other for the film, **Mad about Music**, starring Deanna Durbin.

1940   *I'd Know You Anywhere* and *You've Got Me This Way*. McHugh/Johnny Mercer*. *I'd Know* was an Oscar nominee, but lost to Harline/Washington's *When You Wish Upon a Star*.
       Say It (Over and Over Again). McHugh/Frank Loesser*. Written for the movie **Buck Benny Rides Again** starring Jack Benny.

1941   *My Resistance Is Low*. McHugh/Mercer. Written for **You're the One**; it got an Oscar nomination, but lost to Kern and Hammerstein's *The Last Time I Saw Paris*.

1942   *Can't Get Out of This Mood* and *I Get the Neck of the Chicken*. McHugh/Loesser. This duo wrote five more songs for the movie **Seven Days Leave**.

1943   *Say a Pray'r for the Boys Over There*. McHugh/Herb Magidson. An Academy Award-nominee from the film, **Hers to Hold**. But Warren and Gordon's *You'll Never Know* won that year.
    Comin' In on a Wing and a Prayer. McHugh/Adamson. A big Air Corps patriotic tune, and a number 1 chart record.
    Let's Get Lost and *Murder, He Says*. McHugh/Loesser. Written for the musical movie **Happy Go Lucky**, starring Mary Martin and Dick Powell. Betty Hutton exuberantly belted out *Murder*.
    Around the World. Scored by McHugh and Adamson. They wrote seven songs for this film, including *Don't Believe Everything You Dream*.

1944   *I Couldn't Sleep a Wink Last Night, A Lovely Way to Spend an Evening*, and *The Music Stopped*. McHugh/Adamson. Written for the film **Higher and Higher**, all three were showcase songs for Frank Sinatra. *I Couldn't* was nominated for an Oscar along with eleven other songs that year; Van Heusen and Burke's *Swinging on a Star* came out the winner.
    I Feel a Song Coming On. McHugh/Fields. This 1935 hit was reprised for the 1944 star-filled musical movie, **Follow the Boys**.

1946   *Dig You Later*. McHugh/Adamson. Sung by Perry Como, this was one of five tunes the songwriters penned for the film, **Doll Face.**
    I Didn't Mean a Word I Said. McHugh/Adamson. Written for another movie full of music, **Do You Love Me?**

1948   *It's a Most Unusual Day*. McHugh/Adamson. From the film, **A Date With Judy**.

HERB MAGIDSON, Lyricist (1906–1986)

Born in Braddock, Pennsylvania, Herb Magidson was a journalism student at the University of Pittsburgh. He began writing songs in high school and musically he just kept going and going and going. Magidson went on to become a songwriting pioneer in Hollywood and he is honored among the top composer and lyricists for winning the first Academy Award for a film song—and for writing so many fine lyrics for a variety of films and hit parade songs.

Chronology

1934   *The Continental*. Con Conrad*/Magidson. Written for **The Gay Divorcee**, this was the very first song to win an Academy Award.

1937   *Gone with the Wind*. Allie Wrubel/Magidson. This song had absolutely no connection to the famous novel and film of the same name, but it was number 1 on the charts.

1938   *Music, Maestro Please*. Wrubel/Magidson. Another chart topper. Benny Goodman
and other big bands of the era had very successful recordings.
I'm Afraid the Masquerade Is Over. Wrubel/Magidson.

1940   *I'm Stepping Out with a Memory Tonight*. Wrubel/Magidson.

1943   *Say a Pray'r for the Boys Over There*. James McHugh*/Magidson. Written for
the film, **Hers to Hold**.

1945   *I'll Buy That Dream*. Wrubel/Magidson. From the movie, **Sing Your Way Home**.

1948   *I'll Dance at Your Wedding*. Ben Oakland/Magidson.

1950   *Enjoy Yourself (It's Later Than You Think)*. Carl Sigman/Magidson.

MATTY MALNECK, Composer (1904–1981)

Malneck was born in Newark, New Jersey, and was raised in Colorado. He
began as a professional violinist, playing with dance bands at the age of only
16. After a stint as an arranger with Paul Whiteman, he formed his own orchestra
and enjoyed considerable popularity in the Big Band era.

Chronology

1931   *I'm Through with Love*. Matty Malneck and Fud Livingston (Chapter 4)/Gus
Kahn*.

1932   *I'll Never Be the Same*. Malneck and Frank Signorelli (Chapter 4)/Kahn.

1935   *If You Were Mine*. Malneck/Johnny Mercer*. A fine standard introduced in the
film, **Beat the Band**.

1936   *Goody, Goody*. Malneck/Mercer.

1939   *Stairway to the Stars*. Malneck and Signorelli/Mitchell Parish. This evergreen's
music was written in 1936; the lyrics in 1939.

1946   *Shangri-la*. Malneck and Robert Maxwell/Carl Sigman*.

JOHNNY MERCER, Lyricist/Composer (1909–1976)

John Herndon Mercer, of Savannah, Georgia, was more than a great lyricist
and composer. He was a bandleader, a singer, a co-founder of Capitol Records,
a founding member and president of the Songwriters Hall of Fame, and a most
personable man who wrote more than a thousand songs—many of them popular
standards. All this from a son of southern wealth, who after prep school in
Virginia tried his hand at selling real estate, and later on went to New York
aspiring to be an actor. Fortunately for the music world, neither of those ventures
worked out for Mercer. Instead he wrote lyrics for the great composers: Harold
Arlen*, Jerome Kern*, Hoogy Carmichael*, James McHugh*, Arthur
Schwartz*, Harry Warren*, Henry Mancini*, and Richard Whiting.

Mercer's songs were heard in at least three dozen films from 1933 to 1973.
Mercer was also busy writing for Broadway show people and for musicians and
music lovers elsewhere—it seemed like everywhere—during this same period
of time. From 1958 to 1960 Mercer wrote for a Danny Kaye film, but had no

real hits. His *L'il Abner* Broadway score, with Gene DePaul, was made into a film, but again no real hits. And Sammy Davis, Jr., sang Whiting and Mercer's *Hooray for Hollywood* in **Pepe**, a show that never really had much pep, despite cameos by major entertainers. The last three years of Mercer's contributions to the film industry included another Academy Award nominee, *Darling Lili*, the movie title song written with Henry Mancini. The very last song Johnny Mercer wrote for Hollywood was *The Phony King of England*, for Disney's cartoon, **Robin Hood**.

Alone, Mercer wrote the music and lyrics to a number of classics. For more thorough information about the ubiquitous and versatile Johnny Mercer, the biography written by his wife, *My Huckleberry Friend*, is recommended.

Broadway and Tin Pan Alley Chronology

1930   *Out of Breath and Scared to Death of You*. Mercer (wm). Written for **Garrick Gaities**, the production featuring some of Rodgers and Hart's triumphs. There is a fine recording of Mercer singing *Out of Breath*, live, at the 92nd Street Y in New York City years and years later.

1933   *Lazybones*. Hoagy Carmichael/Mercer.

1934   *P.S., I Love You*. Gordon Jenkins/Mercer.

1937   *Bob White*. Mercer and Bernie Hanighen (wm).
       Hooray for Hollywood. Richard Whiting*/Mercer. For the film *Hollywood Hotel*.

1939   *Blue Rain* and *I Thought About You*. James Van Heusen/Mercer. *Day In, Day Out* and *Fools Rush In*. Rube Bloom/Mercer. All four of these songs were hits.

1940   *Mister Meadowlark*. Walter Donaldson/Mercer. *Ooh What You Said*. Carmichael/Mercer.

1942   *Skylark*. Carmichael/Mercer.
       Strip Polka. Johnny Mercer (wm).

1943   *Trav'lin' Light*. Trummy Young and Jimmy Mundy/Mercer. One of Billie Holiday's greatest songs.

1947   *Midnight Sun*. Lionel Hampton and Sonny Burke/Mercer. Listen to Ella Fitzgerald interpret some of Mercer's most beautiful lyrics as she sings this song.

1948   *Early Autumn*. Woody Herman and Ralph Burns/Mercer. A big band classic.

1950   *Autumn Leaves*. Joseph Kozma/Mercer. Those haunting, drifting words of his.

1951   *Here's to My Lady*. Rube Bloom/Mercer.
       When the World Was Young. M. Phillipe Gerard/Mercer. More lovely lyrics.

1952   *Glow Worm*. Paul Lincke (Chapter 1)/Mercer. This old German song—with Mercer's lyrics—was a huge hit for the Mills Brothers.

1958   *Satin Doll*. Duke Ellington* and Billy Strayhorn*/Mercer.

1959   *I Wanna Be Around*. Mercer (wm). Sadie Vimmerstedt wrote to Mercer with an idea for a song; apparently she sent him the title and a couple of lines. He wrote the rest of *I Wanna* and shared royalties—equally—with Vimmerstedt, which he did not have to do.

1966   *The Summer Wind*. Henry Mayer/Mercer (English lyrics).

Hollywood Chronology

1933   *What Will I Do Without You?* Hilda Gottleib/Mercer. His first film song was for **College Coach**.

1934   *If I Had a Million Dollars*. Matty Malneck/Mercer. Written for the movie **Transatlantic Merry-Go-Round**, starring Jack Benny and Hopalong Cassidy. The next year, Mercer wrote lyrics for six songs composed by Lewis Gensler, for a film in which Mercer acted in a part as a musician, **Old Man Rhythm**.

1935   *If You Were Mine*. Malneck/Mercer. Up to that time, this was Mercer's best and biggest hit. It was written for the movie **The California Collegians**, a film in which Mercer led a band.

1936   *I'm an Old Cowhand*. Johnny Mercer (wm). Bing Crosby sang it in **Rhythm on the Range** and the song became a Western standard.

1937   *Have You Got Any Castles, Baby?* Richard Whiting/Mercer. One of the eight songs this duo wrote for the film, **Varsity Show**. Busby Berkeley, bandleader Fred Waring, and B-movie queens the Lane sisters, all made their debuts in this motion picture.
       Too Marvelous for Words. Whiting/Mercer. A classic song from a non-classic college campus movie, **Ready, Willing and Able**.

1938   *Jeepers Creepers*. Harry Warren/Mercer. Written for the film, **Going Places**, and nominated for an Oscar. *Thanks for the Memory* won that year, but *Jeepers Creepers* is still very popular.
       Girlfriend of the Whirling Dervish. Warren/Mercer. The hit song from the hit movie **Garden of the Moon**, starring Pat O'Brien, Dick Powell, and John Payne. Sometimes Al Dubin* is credited with the lyrics.

1940   *I'd Know You Anywhere* and *You've Got Me This Way*. James McHugh/Mercer. From the film **You'll Find Out**, *I'd Know* was Mercer's second Academy Award-nominated song. *When You Wish Upon a Star* won the Oscar that year.

1941   *Blues in the Night*. Arlen/Mercer. This title song was another Oscar nominee, but lost to *The Last Time I Saw Paris*. *This Time the Dream's on Me* was the other beautiful song in *Blues*. Richard Whorf starred and the Lunceford orchestra shined.
       Poor Mr. Chisholm. Bernie Hanighen/Mercer. A funny song written for the film **Second Chorus**, with Fred Astaire acting on screen and Bobby Hackett playing trumpet off screen—great music.
       Birth of the Blues. A Victor Schertzinger directed film about jazz musicians and their music. Harry Lillis Crosby, Mary Martin, and Jack Teagarden (accompanied on screen by his band) sang *Birth* and Mercer's *The Waiter and the Porter and the Upstairs Maid*. The song *Birth of the Blues* was written in 1926 by Ray Henderson*/Buddy DeSylva* and Lew Brown*.

1942   *Dearly Beloved* and *I'm Old Fashioned*. Jerome Kern/Mercer. Written, along with the title song, for the film **You Were Never Lovelier**. *Dearly* was an Oscar nominee but lost to *White Christmas*. As for the movie, Astaire and Hayworth looked great and danced better; Cugat's orchestra played magnificently; and Nan Wynn voiced over Hayworth's lip-syncing. An excellent screen musical.

The Fleet's In. Songs by Victor Schertzinger/Mercer. This was the second remake of the original 1930 film starring Clara Bow. Schertzinger also directed this version, which lyrically overflowed with Mercer's words in *Tangerine, Build a Better Mousetrap, I Remember You*, and *Arthur Murray Taught Me Dancing in a Hurry*.

That Old Black Magic and *Hit the Road to Dreamland*. Harold Arlen/Mercer. Just two of the great songs by these two writers for the film **Star Spangled Rhythm**. The movie was loaded with Paramount stars, including Goddard, Holden, Lake, Crosby, and Hope. George Balanchine choreographed it.

1943   *One for My Baby* and *My Shining Hour*. Arlen/Mercer. Used in the movie **The Sky's the Limit**, starring Fred Astaire.

1944   *How Little We Know*. Hoagy Carmichael/Mercer. Written for the classic Bogart and Bacall film, **To Have and To Have Not**, based on Ernest Hemingway's novel. Carmichael appeared in the movie.

Here Come the Waves. Songs by Arlen/Mercer. Bing Crosby's big hit movie had big hit songs, including Oscar-nominee *Accentuate the Positive* and *Let's Take the Long Way Home*. The Academy Award went to *It Might as Well Be Spring*.

1945   *Laura*. David Raskin/Mercer. This is one of the most beautiful and haunting musical compositions ever, and the title song of a haunting film. Dick Haymes' soundtrack arrangement is recommended by some; others prefer the Woody Herman version with Bill Harris on trombone, embracing each lingering memorable note.

June Comes Around Every Year. Arlen/Mercer. This hit and the title song were written for the movie **Out of This World**, with Eddie Bracken. The voice behind the screen was Bing Crosby's.

1946   *On the Atchison, Topeka and the Santa Fe*. Warren/Mercer. One of ten songs the duo wrote for the Judy Garland hit film, **Harvey Girls**, and the winner of the Academy Award for Best Song that year.

1950   *Too Marvelous for Words*. Whiting/Mercer. The 1937 hit was used again in **Young Man with a Horn**, a fictional film composite loosely based on the lives of Bunny Berigan and Bix Beiderbecke. Kirk Douglas and Laureen Bacall were superb in their roles; so was Harry James on trumpet behind the scenes. The on-screen story was musically woven together with about a dozen evergreen songs.

1951   *In the Cool, Cool, Cool of the Evening*. Carmichael/Mercer. From the Frank Capra directed film, **Here Comes the Groom**, starring Bing Crosby. Another Oscar for Mercer.

1952   *Derry Down Dilly*. Burton Lane*/Mercer. A most enjoyable song written for the movie **Everything I Have Is Yours**, featuring the most enjoyable dancing of Marge and Gower Champion.

1955   *Something's Gotta Give*. Mercer (wm). Written for the third remake of **Daddy Long Legs**, following the 1919 and 1931 versions. Fred Astaire starred in this production, and insisted that Mercer had to be the movie's lyricist. Mercer repaid the compliment and then some with *Something's Gotta, Slue Foot*, the film's title song, and, I think, his greatest song of all, *Dream*, which was actually written

ten years earlier. *Something's Gotta Give* sounded like a sure Academy Award winner, but *Love Is a Many Splendored Thing* got the Oscar.

1956   *And the Angels Sing*. Ziggy Elman/Mercer. This quintessentially Yiddish composition was included in the music for a film biography of Benny Goodman, **The Benny Goodman Story**. Mercer graciously assimilated into the song's rhythms with rhymes even Irving Berlin could love. The song was written in 1939.

1961   *Moon River*. Henry Mancini/Mercer. This was Mercer's third Academy Award–winning song, a beautiful composition written for the film **Breakfast at Tiffany's**. Truman Capote wrote the screenplay and Audrey Hepburn starred in this truly classic motion picture. Mercer's wife adopted her husband's lovely *Moon River* lyrics for the title of her biography about him, *My Huckleberry Friend*.

1962   *Days of Wine and Roses*. Mancini/Mercer. On an Oscar roll for the second year in a row, this song earned an Academy Award for these two wonderful writers for this poignant film title song. Jack Lemmon gave a riveting performance in *Days*.

JOSEPH MEYER, Composer (1894–1987)

Born in Modesto, California, Meyer worked in Hollywood toward the end of the pioneer days of musical scoring.

Chronology

1922   *My Honey's Lovin' Arms*. Meyer/Herman Ruby. His first hit, with lyricist Ruby (1891–1959).

1924   *California, Here I Come*. Meyer/Buddy DeSylva* and Al Jolson*.

1925   *If You Knew Susie (Like I Know Susie)*. Meyer/DeSylva. For Jolson's Broadway show, **Big Boy**.
       Clap Hands, Here Comes Charlie. Meyer/Ballard MacDonald* and Billy Rose*.

1926   *Crazy Rhythm*. Meyer/Gus Kahn* and Irving Caesar*.

IRVING MILLS, Songwriter (1894–1985)

Russian-born Irving Mills came to the United States and became a dance band singer. His first great success came through establishing himself as the personnel manager for such major musical figures as Duke Ellington*, Cab Calloway, and Jimmie Lunceford. Mills attained even more when he and his brother, Jack, built one of Tin Pan Alley's top publishing companies. He was known as a very tough contract negotiator and not only became quite a financial success on his own, but helped make his clients financially successful, too. The ASCAP directory lists Irving Mills as a composer, author, and publisher. He is also credited as co-writer of some major songs, all of which are listed in the chronology. However, the following quotes about Mills from *The Guiness Encyclopedia of Popular Music* (Colin Larkin, Editor) may be instructive: ''unscrupulousness suggested by his binding contracts. . . . dubious practice of appending his name to certain ventures. . . . as co-composer with Ellington on

many songs . . . (these) are accreditations which can hardly be taken seriously.''
Thus, readers of the chronology can believe the credits, or not. Incidently, recordings titled with ''Irving Mills and His Hotsy Totsy Gang'' were really led
by Benny Goodman. It is also known that the eminent lyricist, Mitchell Parish*,
who was a Mills employee, was prohibited from being credited for his words
on Duke Ellington and Albany Bigard's *Mood Indigo*; which so incensed Parish
that he quit writing lyrics for several years before he returned to his musical
craft.

Chronology

1924   *When My Sugar Walks Down the Street*. James McHugh, Gene Austin, and Mills
         (wm).
         Riverboat Shuffle. Hoagy Carmichael*, Dick Voynow, Mitchell Parish, and Mills
         (wm).

1925   *Lonesomest Girl in Town*. McHugh/Al Dubin* and Mills.

1926   *Henderson Stomp*. Fletcher Henderson and Mills (instr.).

1929   *The Mooche*. Duke Ellington/Mills.

1930   *Ring Dem Bells*. Ellington/Mills.

1931   *Rockin' in Rhythm*. Ellington and Harry Carney/Mills.
         Mood Indigo. Ellington and Albany Bigard/Parish and Mills.
         Minnie the Moocher. Cab Calloway/Clarence Gaskill and Mills.

1932   *It Don't Mean a Thing If It Ain't Got That Swing*. Ellington/Mills.

1933   *Sophisticated Lady*. Ellington/Parish and Mills. One of the most beautiful of all
         American love songs.

1934   *Solitude*. Ellington/Edward DeLange and Mills.
         Stompin' at the Savoy. Benny Goodman and Edgar Sampson (Chapter 4)/Andy
         Razaf* and Mills.
         Moonglow. Will Hudson and DeLange/Mills.
         If Dreams Come True. Goodman and Sampson/Mills.

1935   *Blue Lou*. Sampson and Mills (wm).
         Down South Camp Meetin'. Fletcher Henderson/Mills.

1936   *Organ Grinder's Swing*. Hudson/Parish and Mills.

1937   *Caravan*. Juan Tizol/Mills. Probably the most memorable recording was done by
         Duke Ellington's band.

1938   *I Let a Song Go Out of My Heart*. Ellington/John Redmond, Henry Nemo
         (Chapter 4), and Mills.
         Prelude to a Kiss. Ellington/Irving Gordon (Chapter 4), and Mills.

1943   *Straighten Up and Fly Right*. Nat King Cole and Mills (wm).

JAMES V. MONACO, Composer (1885–1945)

Born in Italy, James Monaco came to the United States when he was 6 years
old, and soon became a schoolboy pianist; by 17, he was a Coney Island ''pro-

fessional." Monaco's chronology of musical works for Hollywood is chock full of hits.

Chronology

1913 *You Made Me Love You*. Monaco/Joe McCarthy, Sr. Introduced on Broadway in **Honeymoon Express**.

1938 *My Heart Is Taking Lessons*. Monaco/Johnny Burke. Written for the film **Dr. Rhythm**, and sung by Bing Crosby.
      I've Got a Pocketful of Dreams. Monaco/Burke. For the movie **Sing You Sinners**, also with Bing Crosby.
      An Apple for the Teacher. Monaco/Burke. Used in **Star Maker**, another Crosby film that year.

1939 *Six Lessons from Madam La Zonga*. Monaco/Charles Newman.

1940 *Only Forever*. Monaco/Burke. From the movie **Rhythm on the River**, with Bing Crosby singing.
      April Played the Fiddle. Monaco/Burke. Written for the film **If I Had My Way**.
      Too Romantic. Monaco/Burke. Crosby again, this time in the film **Road to Singapore**.

1942 *Every Night About This Time*. Monaco/Ted Koehler.

1944 *I'm Making Believe*. Monaco/Mack Gordon*. For the movie **Sweet and Lowdown**.

1945 *I Can't Begin to Tell You*. Monaco/Gordon. Written for the film **The Dolly Sisters**.

NEIL MORET, Composer/Lyricist (1878–1943)

Charles Neil Daniels was born in Leavenworth, Kansas, and became a songwriter at the age of 17. His first hit was performed by the John Philiip Sousa Band before it was published in 1904. Daniels changed his name to Moret for some unknown reason; and he might well have been placed in Chapter 1, however, most of his hit songs were written after World War I. Moret eventually became a Tin Pan Alley publishing executive with the Remick organization in New York.

Chronology

1904 *Margery*. Moret (wm). His first published song.

1908 *I Had a Dream Dear*. Moret/Seymour A. Rice and Al H. Brown.

1925 *Moonlight and Roses*. Moret/Ben Black.

1927 *Chloe*. Moret/Gus Kahn*. Spike Jones had a ruinous comedic rendition of this years later.

1928 *She's Funny That Way*. Moret and Richard Whiting* (wm). Sometimes the gender is changed to *He's Funny That Way*.
      You Tell Me Your Dreams (And I'll Tell You Mine). Moret, A. H. Brown, Seymour Rice (Chapter 1) (wm).

1931   *Put Your Arms Around Me, Honey (Hold Me Tight)*. Moret, Gus Arnheim, and
Charles Tobias (wm).

JELLY ROLL MORTON, Composer (1890–1941)

Ferdinand Joseph Lementhe (Morton) was born in New Orleans—and he
claimed to have, personally, invented jazz in 1902. Such an outlandish statement,
a proclamation he never wavered from, was part of his personality and the stuff
Jelly Roll legends are made of. He was a marvelous left-handed pianist with a
style that influenced piano players for generations. Morton composed ragtime
and jazz piano solos that remain premier examples of American music. His
recordings document the amazing talent that made this special man such a superb
musician.

Jelly Roll Morton clearly paid his dues, too: he composed, arranged, sang,
and performed in vaudeville. In the early 1920s he played "jass" in Chicago,
recording with the Red Hot Peppers, a band he organized and fronted—and for
whom he selected the best jazz players (Creole musicians who emigrated to
Chicago in those halcyon days). In 1928, Morton left the Midwest for the North-
east, completing the same New Orleans-to-Chicago-to-New York route that
Louis Armstrong*, Earl Hines, and others had taken before him.

One of the most important musical documentaries of all time, the history of
jazz in Morton's word, was recorded by the United States Library of Congress.
Over a six-week period in 1938, jazz historian Alex Lomax conducted taped
interviews with Jelly Roll, in which the composer told his stories and played
his music. These taped performances are notable and precious among all American musical archives. So are Morton's compositions which, quite simply, guar-
antee him a place among the songwriting icons of Golden Music.

Chronology

1915   *Jelly Roll Blues*. Morton (instr.). His first published work.

1923   *Wolverine Blues*. Morton (instr.). This song was so popular that a group of
Midwestern musicians, including Bix Beiderbecke, named their band "The
Wolverines."

1923/24   *King Porter Stomp*. Morton (instr.). This was the first of sixteen solo piano
pieces that Morton wrote and performed to be recorded by Gennett Records
and published by Walter Melrose (Chapter 4). In his book, *Tin Pan Alley*,
David Jasen wrote about the composer and his seminal arrangements of these
solos: "Morton created a style of arranging which encompassed other
jazzmen's styles and yet retained his own conceptions." An exceptional
interpretation and playing of *King Porter* can be heard in the 1935 Fletcher
Henderson arrangement performed by Benny Goodman. Like Morton, it is
legendary.

1925   *Milenberg Joys*. Morton (instr.). The last of his "hits," if that is the word for this truly joyful work. Jelly Roll Morton continued to compose blues, stomps, and other music, with the Red Hot Peppers, until the end of the decade.

JOSEF MYROW, Composer (1910–1987)

Born in Russia, Josef Myrow came to the United States at age 2. His family settled in Philadelphia, where young Myrow won scholarships to the Philadelphia Conservatory of Music and the Curtis Institute. As did forty or so other songwriters, Myrow attended the University of Pennsylvania, and as a student of piano and classical composition, soloed with the Philadelphia and Cleveland symphony orchestras. He then conducted musical comedy in Canada; wrote songs for New York and Florida nightclub revues; worked as a program and music director for a radio station; and finally went to Hollywood, where he became a major composer of motion picture scores.

Chronology

1940   *Fable of the Rose.* Myrow/Bix Reichner. Reichner wrote *You Better Go Now* to music by Irvin Graham in 1936.
       Five O'Clock Whistle. Myrow, Kim Gannon, Gene Irwin and Henry Nemo (Chapter 4) (wm).

1941   *Autumn Nocturne.* Myrow/Gannon. Bandleader Claude Thornhill made this one a big hit.

1946   *If I'm Lucky.* Myrow/Eddie DeLange. Film title song.
       On the Boardwalk in Atlantic City and *You Make Me Feel So Young.* Myrow/Mack Gordon*. Written for the movie ***Three Little Girls in Blue***, which Gordon also produced. Years later, Frank Sinatra made *You Make Me* most popular.

1947   *Kokomo, Indiana* and *You Do.* Myrow/Gordon. These two songs were written for the film ***Mother Wore Tights***. *You Do* got an Academy Award nomination, but *Zip-a-Dee-Doo-Dah* won that year.

1949   *It Happens Every Spring.* Myrow/Gordon. Another film title song.

1950   *Wilhelmina.* Myrow/Gordon. An Oscar nominee from the movie, ***Wabash Avenue***. *Mona Lisa* won the Academy Award.

RAY NOBLE, Composer/Lyricist (1903–1978)

Raymond Stanley Noble was born in Brighton, England. He started out to be a classical pianist but ended up being a bandleader, a comedian, an actor, and a fine songwriter. Prior to his Hollywood career, he was the successful conductor of the Mayfair Dance Orchestra in London, which featured the vocalist Al Bowlly. From 1934 to 1937, Noble's band played in the United States with notable sidemen including trombonist Glenn Miller, trumpeter Pee Wee Irwin, pianist/arranger Claude Thornhill, and saxophonist Bud Freeman. Noble's most successful film scores were for ***Damsel in Distress*** and ***The Big Broadcast of 1936***.

Chronology

1931 *Goodnight Sweetheart*. Noble, Reg Connelly, Jimmy Campbell (Chapter 4), and Rudy Vallee (Chapter 5) (wm). In 1929 Vallee and Charles Henderson wrote *Deep Night* (wm). Also in 1929 Vallee and Leon Zimmerman wrote *I'm Just a Vagabond Lover* (wm). In 1930 Vallee and J. Paul Fogarty wrote *Betty-Co-ed* (wm). Vallee was a bandleader, singer, and actor as well.

1932 *By the Fireside*. Noble, Connelly and Campbell (wm).

1934 *The Very Thought of You*. Noble (wm). A beautiful classic ballad.

1936 *The Touch of Your Lips*. Noble (wm).

1938 *I Hadn't Anyone, Till You*. Noble (wm).
       Cherokee. Noble (music). Charlie Barnet made this instrumental popular.

BEN OAKLAND, Composer (1907–1979)

Ben Oakland was a Brooklynite and self-taught pianist who, at age 9, made his debut in Carnegie Hall. He later was accompanist to stage stars Helen Morgan, George Jessel, and others. In the early days of film, Oakland was a staff songwriter at major Hollywood studios; during World War II he entertained the troops in stage shows overseas.

Chronology

1932 *If I Love Again*. Oakland/Jack Murray. Performed in the Broadway musical, **Americana**. Murray (1906–1984) was a partner of Oakland's on the 1931 Ziegfeld **Follies**.

1934 *Champagne Waltz*. Oakland/Milton Drake and Con Conrad.

1937 *I'll Take Romance*. Oakland/Oscar Hammerstein*.

1940 *Java Jive*. Oakland/Drake.

1948 *I'll Dance at Your Wedding*. Oakland/Herb Magidson*.

SY OLIVER, Composer/Lyricist (1910–1988)

Melvin James Oliver, of Battle Creek, Michigan, was the son of two music teachers. He became a trumpet player in the early 1930s, and submitted his own arrangements of songs he was playing to bandleader Jimmie Lunceford, who hired him. Oliver arranged for a number of star musicians, including Louis Armstrong*, Tommy Dorsey, Ella Fizgerald, and Frank Sinatra*. Oliver, who led his own band for a time, ranks with the best of the Big Band arrangers—and he wrote some swinging compositions, too.

Chronology

1937 *For Dancers Only*. Oliver/Don Raye and Vic Schoen. This one became known as a Lunceford song.

1939 *Tain't What You Do, It's the Way That You Do It*. Oliver and Trummy Young (wm). A big Lunceford hit.

1942   *Well Git It.* Oliver (music). Tommy Dorsey had a resounding swing hit with this instrumental.

1943   *Yes, Indeed.* Oliver (music). Another Dorsey instrumental hit.

1945   *Opus One.* Oliver/Sid Garris. Another Dorsey swing classic, with Oliver playing trumpet in the band when these hits were being made.

MITCHELL PARISH, Lyricist (1900–1993)

Born in Shreveport, Louisiana, Mitchell Parish went to Columbia University and earned his BA degree in pre-medical studies. While working as a clerk in a Manhattan hospital, he showed some of his lyrices to one of the doctors who, in turn, showed them to a music publisher (quite possibly Jack or Irving Mills*), and Parish was on his way. As early as 1919, Parish was a staff writer for Mills Music. Very few of his songs were written for Broadway or for Hollywood, his work was Tin Pan Alley all the way. He did contribute to **Blackbirds**, on Broadway in 1938, and did write for a few films, as listed in the chronology. Parish's disturbing employment situation with Mills led to his interrupting his musical career for a period to become a court stenographer (for more on this incident, see the Duke Ellington and Mills enteries).

Chronology

1925   *Riverboat Shuffle.* Hoagy Carmichael*/Parish. The lyricist's first hit.

1928   *Sweet Lorraine.* Cliff Burwell/Parish. An evergreen and jazz favorite. Burwell was born in New Haven, Connecticut, in 1898 and was a pianist as well as composer.

1929   *Star Dust.* Carmichael/Parish. Parish wrote his marvelous lyrics two years after Carmichael composed his memorable music. The truly superb aesthetic quality of *Star Dust's* free verse and rhyming poetry is rare in popular music, matching the finest lyrical writing of Porter, Hammerstein, Hart, and Harburg.

1931   *Emaline.* Frank Perkins/Parish. Some musical chronologists date this collaboration in 1934.
       Mood Indigo. Duke Ellington and Albany Bigard/Parish and Mills. Although credited, this legendary composition's lyrics were probably penned by Parish without Mills' collaboration.

1932   *Take Me in Your Arms.* Fred Markush and Fritz Rotter/Parish (English lyrics). A fine song written by European composers and used in the Hollywood film, *Hi Buddy*.
       Sentimental Gentleman from Georgia. Perkins/Parish.

1933   *One Morning in May.* Carmichael/Parish.
       Sophisticated Lady. Ellington/Parish and Mills.

1934   *Stars Fell on Alabama.* Frank Perkins (Chapter 4)/Parish. *Deep Purple* and *Lilacs in the Rain.* Peter DeRose/Parish. *Stars Fell* and *Deep Purple* are two really big standards.

1936   *Organ Grinder Swing.* Will Hudson, Parish, and Mills (wm).

1938   *Don't Be That Way*. Benny Goodman and Edgar Sampson/Parish. A Goodman classic.

1939   *Stairway to the Stars*. Matty Malneck* and Frank Signorelli (Chapter 4)/Parish.
Let Me Love You Tonight. Rene Touzet/Parish.
The Lamp Is Low. DeRose, Touzet and Bert Shefter (music adaptation)/Parish. An original Ravel composition turned into a popular hit.

1940   *Starlit Hour*. DeRose/Parish.

1942   *All I Need Is You*. DeRose, Benny Davis, and Parish (wm).

1950   *Tzena, Tzena, Tzena*. Julius Grossman and Isaachaar Miron/Parish (English lyrics). This number from **Songs of Israel** became a hit.

1951   *Blue Tango*. Leroy Anderson/Parish.

1953   *Ruby*. Heinz Roehm/Parish. Written for the film **Ruby Gentry**.

1958   *Volare*. Domenico Modugno/Parish (English lyrics). This Italian composition is also known as *Ni'l Blu*.

LEW POLLACK, Composer/Lyricist (1895–1946)

Lew Pollack was born in New York City and played as the solo pianist in the Damrosch Chorale at the age of 14. He was also a violinist and before emigrating to Hollywood he was a movie theatre pianist. In movieland he was one of the pioneer songwriters.

Chronology

1913   *Charmaine*. Erno Rapee/Pollack. Rapee (1891–1945), the long-time conductor of the Radio City Music Hall orchestra, was born in Budapest and became a foremost composer of movie themes in the 1920s and 1930s. *Charmaine* was later used in the film, **What Price Glory?**

1925   *Cheatin' On Me*. Pollack and Yellen* (wm).

1927   *Diane*. Rapee/Pollack. For the film **Seventh Heaven**.

1934   *Two Cigarettes in the Dark*. Pollack/Paul Francis Webster*. The song was heard on Broadway in **Kill That Story**.

1937   *The Toy Trumpet*. Raymond Scott/Sidney Mitchell and Pollack. It was performed in the film **Rebecca of Sunnybrook Farm**.

COLE PORTER, Composer/Lyricist (1891–1964)

Cole Porter, one of the giants among popular songwriters, was born into a rich family in Peru, Indiana. The wealth actually came from his mother's father; Cole's father, Samuel Fenwick Porter, was a pharmicist. But rich inheritances can come in a variety of forms; it was Samuel Porter who read Browning to his son, and that poetic influence did not go unnoticed in Cole's later lyrics. His father's literary gift may have had an even more immediate impact on the young Porter, who, at age 11, had his first work published, entitled *The Bobolink Waltz*.

After prepping at the prestigious Worcester Academy, Porter went on to Yale, where his musical career actually began. He was a most popular entertainer among his classmates, as well as a cheerleader, actor, and all-around personality. He wrote several songs for a 1910 college revue and for varsity shows each year he was in attendance there. Graduating from Yale in 1913, Porter started his graduate studies in the renowned law school at Harvard. But that was short-lived and Porter made a life-changing move across the Cambridge campus to study music—and from there to produce years and years of joyful melodies and brilliant lyrics for Broadway, Hollywood, and everybody everywhere who loves music.

A world traveler, Porter enlisted as an ambulance driver in World War I. Soon after the war, he married Linda Thomas, to whom he remained married until her death, just of few years before his own. All through his life, Porter was all too often thought of as a snob, a highbrow, and a dilettante; the truth is, he was an intense, serious, and hardworking artist. In his biographical essay, *Cole*, Brendan Gill observed ''at every turn, unfailingly, Cole Porter furnished the world with far more joy than he got back.''

Chronology

1910   *Bull Dog (Eli Yale)*. Porter (wm). His first varsity show produced one classic: the Yale fight song. Biographer Gill calls the songs from that show, ''Porter's earliest surviving (works).''

1911   *Cora*. Songs by Porter. His first musical comedy.

1912   *And the Villian Pursued Her*. Songs by Porter. His second musical comedy, in which Monty Wooley, who became Porter's lifelong friend, starred.

1915   *See America First*. Songs by Porter. In New York, Porter had sold songs to Lew Fields for shows. *See* was the first all-Porter lyrics production.

1919   *Hitchy Koo*. Songs by Porter. Story by Lawrason Riggs. This was Porter's first post–World War I show—it had no real hits. Riggs was a Yale man, who later became a priest. By 1926, Porter had almost given up writing songs and shows because, despite his clever and even brilliantly funny songs, he had no hits.

1928   *Let's Do It (Lets Follow Love)* and *Let's Misbehave*. Porter (wm). He kept writing and, finally, had a hit with this *Let's Do It* for the show *Paris*.

1929   *What Is This Thing Called Love?* Porter (wm). From Broadway's *Wake Up and Dream*.
       You Do Something to Me. Porter (wm). From his second Broadway musical of that season, *Fifty Million Frenchmen*.

1930   *Love for Sale* and *Let's Fly Away*. Porter (wm). From *The New Yorkers*, from which someone decided to remove the song *Just One of Those Things*.

1932   *Night and Day*. Porter (wm). From *The Gay Divorce*. According to Porter, this song was inspired by a Mohammedan call to worship he had heard in his extensive travels. He completed *Night and Day* on the beach at Newport.
       Miss Otis Regrets. Porter (wm). He dedicated this sardonic song to socialite and partygiver Elsa Maxwell.

1934   *Anything Goes*. Songs by Porter. A big Broadway hit for Ethel Merman, William Gaxton, and Victor Moore. *All Through the Night; I Get a Kick Out of You; You're the Top; Blow, Gabriel, Blow*; and the title song were even bigger hits for Porter, and still are. Another song which was not used was *Kate the Great*, the first of four songs Porter wrote using his mother's first name.
Don't Fence Me In. Porter (wm). He wrote this most un-Porter-like song for the Hollywood film **Adios Argentina**, but the movie was never produced.

1935   *Jubilee*. Songs by Porter. Script by Moss Hart. This show was written on an extended cruise to far off places, including the Fiji Islands. Porter and his wife, Linda, were accompanied by Moss Hart, Yalie friend Monty Wooley, and an entourage. Thanks to Hart's story, *Jubilee* ran 169 performances, quite a success for the depressed 1930s. Wooley was the musical's director; among the leading players in this Sam H. Harris and Max Gordon production was a young man by the name of Montgomery Clift. The three (in this case, on-the-way-to-becoming) hit songs from *Jubilee* were *Why Shouldn't I?, Just One of Those Things*, and *Begin the Beguine. Beguine* did not really begin to hit for some time. Artie Shaw, who recorded it a few years later, was credited with giving it the great popularity it deserved. Porter was grateful, Shaw was delighted, both were happy with their royalties.

1936   *Red, Hot and Blue*. Songs by Porter. Book by Lindsay Crouse. An Ethel Merman tour de force, also starring Jimmy Durante and Bob Hope. The songs that made the hit lists were *Ridin' High, It's Delovely*, and *Down in the Depths on the 19th Floor*.
Born to Dance. Songs by Porter. MGM made a deal with Porter to come back out to Hollywood to score this film; he did—and thrived—his wife, Linda, hated it. He wrote *Goodbye, Little Dream, Goodbye* for Frances Langford to sing in the movie and the Hollywood producers were so enthusiastic about it that they offered him a raise (from $75,000 to $100,000) if he would come back the following year. But *Goodbye* was dropped from the film—and practically forgotten. Virginia Bruce introduced Porter's classic, *I've Got You Under My Skin*, in the film and Jimmy Stewart managed to sing *Easy to Love*. Porter had originally written *Easy* for the Broadway musical **Anything Goes**—William Gaxton was to have performed it, but the notes were too high for him, so the song was cut. The notes were too high for Stewart, too, but like the lyrics say (in Hollywood), anything goes. Interestingly, Porter is the one who recommended Jimmy Stewart for the **Born to Dance** lead, opposite Eleanor Powell.

1937   *In the Still of the Night*. Porter (wm). This beautiful ballad and the title song were introduced in the movie **Rosalie**, starring Nelson Eddy.

1938   *At Long Last Love*. Porter (wm). Back on Broadway, this song was written for the show **You Never Know**, and was sung by Clifton Webb, another Porter friend. *My Heart Belongs to Daddy* and *Get Out of Town*. Porter (wm). Written for the stage musical **Leave It to Me**. Mary Martin sang *My Heart* in one of her earlier Broadway performances.

1939   *DuBarry Was a Lady*. Songs by Porter. Another opening, another Ethel Merman showcase. *Do I Love You (Do I)?* was the big hit, along with two other fine Porter songs which would be reprised in the film *High Society* several decades later, *Did You Evah?* and *It Was Written in the Stars*. *DuBarry* also featured the hit, *Friendship*, and another tune, *Katie Went to Haiti*.

1940 *Let's Be Buddies*. Porter (wm). Written for *Panama Hattie*, on Broadway.
      I Concentrate on You. Porter (wm). Written for the Holywood film *Broadway Melody*.

1941 *Let's Not Talk About Love* and *Everything I Love*. Porter (wm). From Broadway's *Let's Face It*.

1943 *By the Mississinewah*. Porter (wm). A musical elegy to a boyhood memory of a beloved river in Ohio, performed on Broadway in *Something for the Boys*.
      You'd Be So Nice to Come Home To. Porter (wm). Don Ameche sang this song to former Les Brown ''girl vocalist'' Janet Blair in the movie *Something to Shout About*.

1944 *I Love You*. Porter (wm). Perhaps Porter's most beautiful ballad, this song was introduced in the Broadway musical *Mexican Hayride*, which was produced by Mike Todd and written by Herbert and Dorothy Fields*. Gypsy Rose Lee revealed her act, Bobby Clark delivered his comedy, and Cole Porter scored his fine music—a great trip all around.
      Ev'ry Time We Say Goodbye. Porter (wm). A Porter hit song from Billy Rose's* stage presentation, *The Seven Lively Arts*. The extravaganza revue was written by Moss Hart, George S. Kaufman, Ben Hecht, and others. It starred Bea Lillie and Bert Lahr, and had the Benny Goodman band as well. The show was really not a universal hit, but passionate jazz fans who enjoyed Goodman and his sidemen, especially Red Norvo and Teddy Wilson, loved it.

1948 *Be a Clown*. Porter (wm). The big Porter number in the fine MGM and Arthur Freed film *The Pirate*. It starred Judy Garland and Gene Kelly in one of his masterful screen performances.
      Kiss Me Kate. Songs by Porter. Story by Sam and Bella Spewack. Outside, Porter had his mother's name on the Broadway theatre marquee; inside, the smash musical was about Shakespeare's *Taming of the Shrew*, to Porter's lyrics and melodies. The songs were irresistible: *Another Opening, Another Show; Why Can't You Behave?; Wunderbar; So in Love; We Open in Venice; Were Thine That Special Face; Too Darn Hot; Where Is the Life That Late I Led?; Always True to You in My Fashion; Brush Up Your Shakespeare*; and *Bianca*. After forty-odd years of writing songs, this was Porter at his peak.

1949 *Farewell Amanda*. Porter (wm). David Wayne sang this song in *Adam's Rib*, one of the best Spencer Tracy and Katharine Hepburn films produced. The quirky screenplay was written by Garson Kanin and Ruth Gordon.

1950 *From This Moment On*. Porter (wm). Written for the Broadway musical *Out of this World*, which had a 157-performance run without the song—it was dropped before the show debuted. Fortunately, this fine ballad was added to the film version of *Kiss Me Kate*, and *From This Moment On* has been a timeless standard ever since.

1953 *Can Can*. Songs by Porter. Story by Abe Burrows. A most successful musical on Broadway and on film, with Shirley MacLaine and Frank Sinatra. Given the story by the raspy-voiced humorist and the songs like *C'est Magnifique*, *It's All Right With Me*, *I Love Paris*, and *I Am in Love*, it could not go wrong.

1955 *All of You*. Porter (wm). This was the only hit song from Porter's last Broadway musical, **Silk Stockings**. But a typically clever, typically Porter number must be mentioned: *It's a Chemical Reaction*.

1956 **High Society**. Songs by Porter. This was the movie musical version of Philip Barry's stage play and Katharine Hepburn's early film, **The Philadelphia Story**. Porter's wonderful songs, *True Love*, *I Love You Samantha*, *You're Sensational*, and a couple of his funny oldies were sung by Bing Crosby, Frank Sinatra, and Grace Kelly, just before she became the Princess of Monaco. And Louis Armstrong delighted the movie's audiences with *And There You Has Jazz*.

1957 *Ca C'est L'Amour*. Porter (wm). Written for the Hollywood film **Les Girls**, this was the only song that made it as a hit. This was true, despite Porter's score and Mitzi Gaynor and Gene Kelly's performances.

1958 **Alladin**. Songs by Porter. Porter wrote this music for humorist S. J. Perleman's version of the famous story, produced for the CBS television network.

RALPH RAINGER, Composer (1901–1942)

Rainger, whose real name was Ralph Reichenthal, was born in New York City and studied music there at the Damrosch Institute. He also attended Brown University and went on to law school. In 1926, he became a Broadway theatre pianist and later toured in vaudeville as an accompanist and arranger. Rainger had a fine career in Hollywood, writing for fifty films from 1938 to the year of his death. A great deal of his composing was done in collaboration with lyricist Leo Robin. In 1942, Ralph Rainger's life was tragically cut short by a plane crash.

Chronology

1929 *Moanin' Low*. Rainger/Howard Dietz*. For **The Little Show**, by Arthur Schwartz. Rainger played piano duos in this Broadway musical.

1934 *Love in Bloom*. Rainger and Leo Robin (wm). Written for the movie **She Loves Me Not**, starring Kitty Carlisle and Bing Crosby.
Here Is My Heart and *June in January*. Rainger and Robin (wm). For the Carlisle and Crosby film, **Here Is My Heart**.

1936 *I Wished on the Moon*. Rainger/Dorothy Parker. Introduced by Crosby in the movie **The Big Broadcast of 1936**. Billie Holiday turned it into one of her classics. The lyricist was the trendy and talented writer of charm and cynicism, Dorothy Parker—the wittiest of the wisecracking intellectuals in New York's famous literary luncheon and party group, at the Algonquin Hotel's famed "Round Table."

1937 *Blue Hawaii*. Rainger/Robin. Written for **Waikiki Wedding**, starring Bing Crosby. *Sweet Leilani*, Harry Owens' song from the same film, won the Academy Award that year.

1938   *Thanks for the Memory*. Rainger/Robin. The Oscar-winning song from that year's **Big Broadcast** film. It became Bob Hope's theme song.

1939   *I Have Eyes*. Rainger/Robin. Written for the cartoon movie **Gulliver's Travels**. *You're a Sweet Little Headache* and *Faithful Forever*. Rainger/Robin. For the film **Paris Honeymoon**.

DAVID RAKSIN, Composer (1912–   )

While he wrote only one popular hit song, David Raksin is recognized as one of the most prominent composers (primarily film scores) of the Golden Age. A Philadelphian who attended the University of Pennsylvania, he studied concert piano with his father, Isadore, and with Arnold Schoenberg. Raksin left the serious side of the music business to become a singer, radio entertainer, and bandleader. For a time, he even worked as a magician, and at one point used the name John Sartrain, Jr. Most important musically, Raksin worked in Hollywood for forty years and composed more than one hundred film scores, including one for Charlie Chaplin's classic, **Modern Times**, and a memorable one for **The Bad and the Beautiful**. And of course, Raksin wrote the haunting theme for the film, **Laura**.

Chronology

1945   *Laura*. Raksin/Johnny Mercer*. Raksin's one big hit. Our vote for the best recording goes to Woody Herman, with the fine trombone solo by Bill Harris, circa 1945.

ANDY RAZAF, Lyricist (1895–1973)

Grand Duke Andreamenentania Razafinkeriefo was the grandson of John Waller, the U.S. Consul to Madagascar, and no relation to Thomas "Fats" Waller, with whom Razaf wrote some fine songs. Razaf's mother married a Madagascan prince and nephew of the queen of that country; but sadly, Razaf was not an heir to any monarchical fortune. He was born in Washington, DC, where it appears his father abandoned the family. Razaf and his mother then moved to New York City and, at age 16, he dropped out of school and worked as an elevator operator. At age 18, he wrote his first song, *Baltimo*, but it was not until a decade later that Razaf had his first song published. He went on to write lyrics for more than fifty shows and revues in New York and Chicago and elsewhere; much of his well-known work was as Fats Waller's lyrical collaborator, although he also teamed up with Eubie Blake, Don Redman, Edgar Sampson, and Chick Webb.

Sadly, Razaf was known to have been somewhat of a rogue, involved in troublesome relationships and heavy drinking. He claimed that he and Waller sold Dorothy Fields* and James McHugh* the songs *I Can't Give You Anything But Love* and *On the Sunny Side of the Street*—cheap—but nothing ever came of any legal actions on behalf of Razaf and Waller. For all of that, Razaf was still honored by the U.S. government for his work as a World War II savings bond promoter and salesperson, having written several songs for that effort.

Chronology

1928   *Louisiana.* J. C. Johnson and Bob Schaefer/Razaf.

1929   *Gee Baby, Ain't I Good to You?* Don Redman/Razaf.
Ain't Misbehavin'. Fats Waller and Harry Brooks/Razaf. Probably Razaf's biggest hit—Waller made it famous.
Honeysuckle Rose. Waller/Razaf and Brooks. An enormous chart buster that remains a jazz classic.
S'posin. Paul Denniker/Razaf. One of the prettiest songs Bing Crosby ever sang.

1930   *Blue Turning Grey Over You.* Waller/Razaf.
Memories of You. Eubie Blake (Chapter 1)/Razaf. First heard on Broadway, in Lew Leslie's **Blackbirds**.

1932   *Keepin' Out of Mischief Now.* Waller/Razaf.

1933   *What Did I Do to Be So Black and Blue.* Harry Brooks and Waller/Razaf. A sad, serious song with moving lyrics by Razaf.

1936   *Milkman's Matinee.* Razaf, Denniker, and Joe Davis (wm). Identifying theme and name of the old WNEW-AM radio program, in New York City.
Stompin' at the Savoy. Edgar Sampson, Chick Webb, and Benny Goodman*/ Razaf.

1937   *That's What I Like About the South.* Razaf (wm). This one became bandleader and comedian Phil Harris' theme song.

1938   *In the Mood.* Joe Garland/Razaf. A number 1 chart record for Glenn Miller and still the quintessential classic song for swing dancing. Garland was a highly regarded saxophonist-arranger who worked with Louis Armstrong, Earl Hines, and others. In 1932, another saxophonist-arranger, Don Redman, wrote and recorded an instrumental named *Hot and Anxious. In the Mood* sounds amazingly like Redman's composition.

1942   *Knock Me a Kiss.* Mike Jackson/Razaf. This was Razaf's last hit song.

HARRY REVEL, Composer (1905–1958)

Born in London, England, Harry Revel performed as a pianist all over the world; in the United States he wrote for the **Ziegfeld Follies of 1931**. Revel arrived in Hollywood in 1933 to write music for the silver screen, and had a number of hits, all with lyricist Mack Gordon*.

Chronology

1933   *Did You Ever See a Dream Walking?* Revel/Gordon. Written for the film **Sitting Pretty**.

1934   *Stay as Sweet as You Are and Wake Up and Live.* Revel/Gordon. Both written for the film **College Rhythm.**
Love Thy Neighbor. Revel/Gordon. For **We're Not Dressing.**
With My Eyes Wide Open. Revel/Gordon. From the movie **Shoot the Works**.

1935   *Without a Word of Warning* and *From the Top of Your Head to the Tip of Your Toes*. Revel/Gordon. Both songs written for the film ***Two for Tonight***.

1936   *Goodnight, My Love*. Revel/Gordon. Possibly their prettiest song, written for the film ***Stowaway.***
       I Feel Like a Feather in the Breeze. Revel/Gordon. From ***Collegiate***.

1937   *There's a Lull in My Life and Never in a Million Years*. Revel/Gordon. Written for the movie ***Wake Up and Live***, which had the same title as their 1934 song.

LEO ROBIN, Lyricist (1900–1984)

Born in Pittsburgh, Leo Robin's parents were both writers; after graduation from the University of Pittsburgh, Robin became a newspaperman. He was also a publicist, but his greatest success came as one of Hollywood's pioneer—and mainstay—songwriters. Prior to his movie career, Robin wrote lyrics for a musical written and produced by Vincent Youmans* on Broadway. That was in 1927, and Robin did not return to the Great White Way until twenty-two years later to write lyrics for ***Gentlemen Prefer Blondes***, with music composed by Jule Styne*. Carol Channing starred in that smash hit which featured Styne/Robin gems like: *Diamonds Are a Girl's Best Friend* and *The Little Girl from Little Rock*. Robin's next Broadway show was in 1955, the musical version of ***My Sister Eileen***, which featured songs with his lyrics including *Give Me a Band and My Baby*. In 1929, Leo Robin debuted as a motion picture songwriter. And the rest, as they say, is history.

Chronology

1927   *Hallelujah* and *Sometimes I'm Happy*. Vincent Youmans/Robin and Clifford Grey. From Youmans' Broadway musical, ***Hit the Deck***.

1929   *Louise*. Richard Whiting*/Robin. Written for the film ***Innocents of Paris***, with Maurice Chevalier.

1930   *Beyond the Blue Horizon*. Whiting/Robin. For the movie ***Monte Carlo***.

1931   *Prisoner of Love*. Clarence Gaskill/Robin. This song was not specifically written for a film, but it did become a hit recording for the first "crooner," Russ Columbo, who also has been credited as co-songwriter.

1932   *Please*. Ralph Rainger*/Robin. The first of many of Robin's collaborations with Rainger, this one was written for the most popular crooner of them all, Bing Crosby, singing in the motion picture ***The Big Broadcast***.

1934   *Love in Bloom*. Rainger/Robin. For the film ***She Loves Me Not***, with Crosby and Kitty Carlisle.
       Love is Just Around the Corner. Lewis Gensler/Robin.
       June in January. Rainger and Robin (wm). Written for the movie ***Here Is My Heart***, again with Kitty Carlisle and Bing Crosby.
       With Every Breath I Take. Rainger/Robin.

1935   *Miss Brown to You*. Whiting/Robin. Written for that year's version of the film ***The Big Broadcast***; it was perfect for Billie Holiday, who made it into one of her own jazz classics.

1936   *If I Should Lose You*. Rainger/Robin. Written for the movie ***Rose of the Rancho.***
       Moonlight and Shadows. Frederick Hollander/Robin.

1937   *Blue Hawaii*. Rainger/Robin. Written for another Bing Crosby film, ***Waikiki***
       Wedding.

1939   *You're a Sweet Little Headache* and *Faithful Forever*. Rainger/Robin. For the
       movie ***Paris Honeymoon.***
       I Have Eyes. Rainger/Robin. Written for ***Gulliver's Travel***, a cartoon film.

1941   *You Started Something*. Rainger/Robin.

1946   *In Love in Vain*. Jerome Kern*/Robin. A beautiful song written for the film
       Centennial Summer.
       Gal in Callico. Arthur Schwartz/Robin. From the movie ***The Time, The Place***
       and The Girl.

1948   *For Every Man There's a Woman*. Harold Arlen*/Robin. This song was used in
       the movie ***Casbah***.

1951   *My Ideal*. Whiting and Newell Chase/Robin. Written for the film ***Playboy of***
       Paris, this was Robin's last hit and surely a standard.

RICHARD RODGERS, Composer (1902–1979)

A native New Yorker and graduate of Columbia University, Richard Rodgers
came from a well-to-do family; his father was a physician and his mother a fine
pianist. Rodgers began to play the piano at the age of 6. As a young man, his
hero was Jerome Kern*. At college, he met Lorenz Hart* and they actually
submitted a song to a Broadway revue in 1919. A year later, they co-wrote the
varsity show at Columbia, *Fly with Me*, and the songs from that production
were reprised on Broadway in *Poor Little Ritz Girl*. In 1943, Lorenz Hart died
at the age of 47. Although their partnership had often been a stormy one, Rodgers was left without the brilliant collaborator with whom he had worked since
their college days in the 1920s.

It was Rodgers' second partnership that was to become the most successful
one in the history of American popular music: with Oscar Hammerstein II*,
formerly the lyricist and librettist for Jerome Kern*, Otto Harbach*, and Sigmund Romberg*. This was more than a great musical collaboration—this was
a milestone, often referred to as the personification of "The New American
Musical Theatre." In 1960, Oscar Hammerstein died of cancer and Richard
Rodgers lost his second partner—and beloved friend.

Many of the fine Broadway scores by Rodgers were reprised on film: ***Babes***
in Arms, The Boys from Syracuse, Too Many Girls, A Connecticut Yankee,
South Pacific, Oklahoma, The Sound of Music, and others. In 1945, Rodgers
and Hammerstein went to Hollywood to write songs for a musical film, which
had been originally produced by Fox in 1933 as a straight drama, with no music
or singing. The movie was ***State Fair***—with Hammerstein's libretto and Rodgers' music. Thus, the only musical written especially for film by Rodgers and
Hammerstein became one of Hollywood's finest. Among the film's hit songs:

That's for Me and *It Might as Well Be Spring*—the much deserved Academy Award winner that year—another classic standard from Richard Rodgers. Rather than get caught up in cliches, such as ''he was enormously productive,'' suffice it to say that no composer in history—from Wolfgang Amadeus Mozart to John Lennon—has been played more than Richard Rodgers. His prolific works and their performances illustrate his singular influence on all of our music.

Chronology

1919 *Any Old Place with You*. Rodgers/Hart. Their first published song was performed in **Lonely Romeo**, on Broadway.

1920 **Poor Little Ritz Girl**. Scored by Rodgers and Hart. From the Columbia campus to the Broadway stage.

1925 *Manhattan* and *Sentimental Me*. Rodgers/Hart. First written for **Greenwich Village Follies**; eventually used in the Theatre Guild's **Garrick Gaieties**.

1926 *Mountain Greenery*. Rodgers/Hart. Used in that year's **Garrick Gaities.**
      Blue Room. Rodgers/Hart. Heard in the Broadway production, **The Girl Friend**.

1927 *Thou Swell*. Rodgers/Hart. Used in **A Connecticut Yankee**.

1928 *You Took Advantage of Me*. Rodgers/Hart. Featured in the Broadway revue **Present Arms**.

1929 *With a Song in My Heart* and *Why Can't I?* Rodgers/Hart Written for **Spring Is Here**, on Broadway.

1930 *Ten Cents a Dance*. Rodgers/Hart. This one brought the Broadway house down.
      A Ship Without a Sail. Rodgers/Hart. Written for the Broadway show **Heads Up**.

1931 *I've Got Five Dollars*. Rodgers/Hart. From **America's Sweetheart**, again on Broadway.

1932 *Isn't It Romantic? Lover*, and *Mimi*. Rodgers/Hart. From the film **Love Me Tonight**.

1933 *You Are Too Beautiful*. Rodgers/Hart. Written for the Al Jolson movie, **Hallelujah, I'm a Bum**.

1935 *It's Easy to Remember* and *Blue Moon*. Rodgers/Hart. From **Mississippi**, a number 1 chart record for the film's star, Bing Crosby. *Blue Moon* had been dropped from a 1932 Jimmy Durante movie.
      Little Girl Blue. Rodgers/Hart. Written for **Jumbo** on Broadway, back where the songwriters preferred to be. Sometimes sung *Little Boy Blue*.

1936 *Glad to Be Unhappy* and *There's a Small Hotel*. Rodgers/Hart. Written for the Broadway production **On Your Toes**. The show also included Rodger's ballet, *Slaughter on Tenth Avenue*, which was choreographed by Gyorgi Balnchivadze (who later changed his name to George Balanchine). Billie Holiday probably did the best interpretation of *Glad*.

1937 *Johnny One-Note* and *I Wish I Were in Love Again*. Rodgers/Hart. From the hit show on Broadway, **Babes in Arms**—later to become a major motion picture.
      Have You Met Miss Jones? Rodgers/Hart. From **I'd Rather be Right**.

1938 *I Married an Angel*. Rodgers/Hart. The title song from the Broadway show. The big bands picked up on this one and played it again and again.

Falling in Love With Love and *This Can't Be Love*. Rodgers/Hart. The duality of emotions written for the Broadway musical, *The Boys from Syracuse*.
Blue Moon. Rodgers/Hart. Reprised in a second film, *Hollywood Hotel*.

1939   *I Didn't Know What Time It Was* and *Give It Back to the Indians*. Rodgers/Hart. Completing a great decade of creativity, the duo wrote these two songs and other fine tunes for *Too Many Girls* on Broadway.

1940   *Pal Joey*. Songs by Rodgers/Hart. This Broadway musical play was based on John O'Hara's fine short story writing, and featured the hit song, *Bewitched, Bothered and Bewildered*—as well as the young dancer from Pittsburgh who made his debut in the role of Joey, Gene Kelly.

1941   *It Never Entered My Mind*. Rodgers/Hart. From Broadway's *Higher and Higher*.

1943   *Oklahoma!* Script and Songs by Rodgers/Hammerstein. When Irving Berlin* declined it, the new partners accepted the project of adapting Lynn Riggs' novel, *Green Grow the Lilacs*, into a Broadway musical which they originally titled *Away We Go*. With the great director Rueben Mamoulian and legendary choreographer Agnes DeMille guiding the production, *Oklahoma!* changed the face of the musical. The Broadway production ran 2,200 performances; it continues to be staged all around the world, keeping the music in our hearts and the words on our lips. It has served as a great debut for several singers and actors, including John Raitt and Celeste Holm—and the State of Oklahoma got an official state song. But most important of all are Rodgers and Hammerstein's great songs: *Surrey with the Fringe on Top, (Everything's Up to Date in) Kansas City, I Cain't Say No, Many a New Day, People Will Say We're in Love, Out of My Dreams, Poor Jud Is Dead*, and the title song. It was thrilling musical theatre (as well as a fine film) and it was only the beginning for Rodgers and Hammerstein.

1945   *Carousel*. Book and Songs by Rodgers/Hammerstein. Years earlier, Giacomo Puccini had declined composing an opera—and then George Gershwin* had turned down writing a musical—based on Ferenc Molnar's serious play, *Liliom*. Rodgers and Hammerstein accepted this adaptation project and it became their second epic. Librettist Hammerstein changed the locale of the play from Hungary to New England; Agnes DeMille arranged a stunning ballet; and Rodgers wrote a tender, deep, and memorable musical score (calling it the most satisfying music he had ever written). And the songs that carried the production to popularity were magnificent: *June Is Busting Out All Over, Soliloquoy, You'll Never Walk Alone, The Carousel Waltz*, and *If I Loved You*. All musical theatre standards.

1946   *Annie Get Your Gun*. Scored by Irving Berlin. Produced by Rodgers and Hammerstein. A hit musical for Berlin—a financial success for the new impresarios.

1947   *Allegro*. Songs by Rodgers/Hammerstein. Oscar Hammerstein wrote the original story for this musical and Agnes DeMille choreographed another stunning ballet. It had memorable songs, too, including *A Fellow Needs a Girl* and *The Gentleman Is a Dope*; *Allegro* did not make it through a year.

1949   *South Pacific*. Songs by Rodgers/Hammerstein. Adaptation by Hammerstein and Josh Logan. Based on James A. Michener's Pulitzer Prize-winning book, *Tales of the South Pacific*, the play had a score which can be compared, in quality and memorability, to any of the partners' previous musicals. The public certainly thought so: *South Pacific* had the largest advance ticket sales in the history of musical theatre. It also had Mary Martin, Ezio Pinza, and a superb cast. It also had a message, lots of fun, and lots of great hits from the score: *Some Enchanted Evening, There Is Nothing Like a Dame, I'm Gonna Wash That Man Right Out of My Hair, Bali Ha'i, I'm in Love With a Wonderful Guy, Younger Than Springtime, You've Got to Be Carefully Taught, This Nearly Was Mine,* and *Bloody Mary Is the Girl I Love.* Another sensational Rodgers and Hammerstein musical; another multi-award winner; and another classic which continues to be produced and played the world over.

1951   *The King and I*. Songs by Rodgers/Hammerstein. Adapted from the book and movie, **Anna and the King of Siam**, this musical was written for the stage—and especially for superstar Gertrude Lawrence. The role of the king made Yul Brunner a new superstar; the songs made up a galaxy of hits that audiences have repeatedly enjoyed, originally on stage, in the fine movie version that followed, and in popular revivals since: *Hello, Young Lovers; Something Wonderful; I Whistle a Happy Tune; Getting to Know You, I Have Dreamed,* and more.

1953   *Me and Juliet*. Songs by Rodgers/Hammerstein. This was the least popular of the of the duo's musicals and only ran about a year. Some critics accused Hammerstein of writing a "contrived and exaggerated" story. But a great Rodgers composition was introduced, *No Other Love,* which was used later in the award-winning film documentary, **Victory at Sea**. Rodgers' original title for *No Other Love* was *Beneath the Southern Cross.*

1955   *Pipe Dream*. Songs by Rodgers/Hammerstein. Based on John Steinbeck's story, *Sweet Thursday,* this stage musical featured opera diva Helen Traubel. Unfortunately, the production was unsuccessful and there were no memorable songs.

1958   *Flower Drum Song*. Songs by Rodgers/Hammerstein. Undaunted, the composer and lyricist wrote this delightful little musical and it was a big success. *Love, Look Away* and *You Are Beautiful* were fine ballads. *I Enjoy Being a Girl* was the showstopper.

1959   *The Sound of Music*. Songs by Rodgers/Hammerstein. Rodgers composed and Hammerstein wrote this giant Broadway musical. Based on the real life experiences of the Von Trapp family, the story by Howard Lindsay and Russell Crouse was delightful, G-rated, family fare. The music and lyrics of the title song, *My Favorite Things, Do Re Me, Climb Every Mountain,* and *Edelweiss* were even more delightful. On stage, Mary Martin was marvelous in her leading performance; four years later, Julie Andrews was superb in her starring role on film. *The Sound of Music* broke audience attendance records for the theatre and the screen, and garnered the acclaims of music and movie critics—and the Academy Awards.

1962   *No Strings*. Songs by Rodgers (wm). This musical about interracial romances had one lasting ballad, *The Sweetest Sounds.*

1965   *Do I Hear a Waltz*? Songs by Rodgers/Stephen Sondheim. This not so successful Broadway musical was based on Arthur Laurents' *Time of the Cuckoo.* The title song was the most memorable. Sondheim had been a protégé of Oscar Hammerstein.

1970   ***Two by Two***. Songs by Rodgers/Martin Chanin. This was Rodgers' last Broadway musical; and Danny Kaye starred in the role of Noah (from the Bible) in the production's interesting story. Rodgers and Kaye did not see eye to eye on ***Two By Two***, and the show did not survive their stormy clashes.

SIGMUND ROMBERG, Composer (1887–1951)

Born in Hungary, Sigmund Romberg arrived in the United States in 1909 and worked in a pencil factory for a while, moonlighting as a pianist in Hungarian cafes. He was a student of the viola, trumpet, and drums, and at 14, Romberg was the conductor of his own school orchestra and band. At 16, he composed his first march, dedicated to the Grand Duchess Clotide. After a couple of years in the army, Romberg decided to become an engineer, but any success in that career was short-lived. He eventually went on to become an accomplished composer and popular conductor on the radio; in World War II, he organized tours overseas to entertain the troops.

Chronology

1915   *Auf Wiedersehn*. Romberg/Herbert Reynolds. His first composition written for Broadway, it was used in the musical ***Blue Paradise***.

1924   *The Drinking Song*. Romberg/Dorothy Donnelly. His first hit song, written for the operetta ***The Student Prince of Heidelberg***.

1926   *The Desert Song*. Romberg/Oscar Hammerstein* and Otto Harbach*. The big hit title song of the operetta.

1928   ***New Moon***. Romberg/Hammerstein and Harbach. The trio wrote a number of songs for this Broadway show, including: *One Alone, One Kiss, Softly as in a Morning Sunrise*, and *Lover Come Back to Me*, the latter adapted from Pyotr Ilyich Tchaikovsky's *June Barcarolle*.

1935   *When I Grow Too Old to Dream*. Romberg/Hammerstein. Used in the film, ***The Night Is Young***.

1945   *Close as Pages in a Book*. Romberg/Dorothy Fields*. Arguably one of the prettiest of all Romberg songs, it was featured in ***Up in Central Park***.

BILLY ROSE, Lyricist (1899–1966)

Billy Rose (Rosenberg) is a legend in show business. He was born in New York City and attended a commercial high school where he became a whiz stenographer. After winning a championship with that non-musical skill, he went to work for the famous Bernard Baruch at the War Industries Board during World War I. Later, on Broadway, Rose wrote lyrics for a number of composers, produced highly successful revues, wrote a newspaper column, and earned the reputation of being the flashiest of all nightclub impresarios. His Diamond Horseshoe was the place where stars of the day entertained and where who's who were seen in the audience. Rose, who married the entertainer Fannie Brice and the swimmer Eleanor Holm, and who kept company with some of the most beautiful women in town, was also a very wise investor. Over the years, he accumulated a large estate and produced an impressive list of lyrical credits.

Chronology

1923   *That Old Gang of Mine*. Ray Henderson* Rose and Mort Dixon*.
       Barney Google (With the Goo Goo Google-y Eyes). Con Conrad*/Rose. Written for an Olsen and Johnson vaudeville revue.
       You've Got to See Mama Every Night or You Won't See Mama at All. Conrad*/ Rose. For Sophie Tucker's vaudeville act.

1924   *Follow the Swallow*. Henderson/Rose and Dixon. From the **Greenwich Village Follies**.

1925   *A Cup of Coffee, a Sandwich and You*. Joseph Meyer*/Rose, Jack Buchanan, and Al Dubin*.
       Clap Hands, Here Comes Charlie. Meyer/Rose and Ballard MacDonald*. Originally written for **Salt and Pepper**, a vaudeville show, it eventually became the theme song of the Charlie Barnet Band.

1926   *I Found a Million Dollar Baby (in a Five and Ten Cent Store)*. Fred Fisher (Chapter 1) and Harry Warren*/Rose and Dixon.

1927   *Me and My Shadow*. Dave Dreyer*/Rose. This was the theme song of bandleader and singer Ted Lewis.
       Here Comes the Showboat. Maceo Pinkard (Chapter 4)/Rose. Originally used in **Americana**, on Broadway, it was added to the film version of the classic stage musical, **Show Boat**. *Here Comes* was also used as the theme song of a popular radio show.

1928   *Back in Your Own Back Yard*. Dreyer/Rose.

1929   *Great Day, Without a Song*, and *More Than You Know*. Vincent Youmans*/ Edward Eliscu (Chapter 4) and Rose. Three fine hit songs from Broodway's **Great Day**.
       I've Got a Feeling I'm Falling. Harry Link* and Fats Waller*/Rose.

1930   *Cheerful Little Earful*. Warren/I. Gershwin* and Rose. Intriguing lyrical credits on this one.
       Would You Like to Take a Walk? Warren/Rose and Dixon. Both *Cheerful Little* and *Would You* were used in the Broadway production **Sweet and Low**.

1933   *It's Only a Paper Moon*. Harold Arlen*/E. Y. Harburg* and Rose. Fascinating lyrical credits on this one, too.

BOB RUSSELL, Composer/Lyricist (1914–1970)

Sidney Keith Russell was born in Passaic, New Jersey. He wrote words to the music of Duke Ellington*, Carl Sigman, and several Latin American composers, including Ernesto Lecuona. Russell also composed several Hollywood film scores.

Chronology

1939   *Brazil*. Ary Barroso/Russell.

1941   *Frenesi*. Alberto Dominguez/Russell and Ray Charles. This was a tremendous hit

for Artie Shaw. And this was the "other" Ray Charles. Dominguez also composed *Perfidia* in 1941 with Milton Leeds' lyrics.
Maria Elena. Lorenzo Barcelata/Russell.
Time Was. Miguel Prado/Russell. This composition was originally titled *Duerme.*

1942   *At the Crossroads.* Lecuona/Russell. This is the English title for *Malaguena.*
Don't Get Around Much Anymore. Duke Ellington*/Russell. Probably Russell's biggest lyrical hit.
Babalu. Margarita Lecuona/Russell.

1944   *I Didn't Know About You.* Ellington/Russell.

1947   *Miserlou.* N. Roubanis/Russell, Milton Leeds, and Fred Wise.

1948   *Ballerina.* Carl Sigman* and Russell (wm). Nat King Cole had a number 1 chart record with this song.
Matinee. Sigman/Russell.
You Came a Long Way from Saint Louis. Ray McKinley and John B. Brooks/Russell.

1949   *Crazy, He Calls Me.* Sigman/Russell. A fine ballad.

1953   *Blue Gardenia.* Lester Lee and Russell (wm). In 1942 Lee and Zeke Manners wrote *Pennsylvania Polka* (wm), a big Andrews Sisters' hit.

1967   *Eyes of Love.* Quincy Jones/Russell. Written for the film ***Banning***.

VICTOR SCHERTZINGER, Composer (1890–1941)

One of the most brilliant of the Hollywood creatives, Victor Schertzinger was a child prodigy. He was born in Mahanoy City, Pennsylvania; by age 8, he had played music with Victor Herbert*. Following his musical studies in Brussels, he performed as a concert violinist. Schertzinger arrived in Hollywood in 1916 and became a composer and a director of films.

Chronology

1916   ***Civilization***. Scored by Schertzinger. This film score composition was his first published work; he went on to write dozens of others.

1941   *I'll Never Let a Day Pass By, Sand in My Shoes,* and *Kiss the Boys Goodbye.* Schertzinger/Frank Loesser*. The third song, *Kiss,* was the title song of a film Schertzinger also directed.
Not Mine. Schertzinger/Johnny Mercer*.

1942   ***The Fleet's In***. Songs by Schertzinger/Mercer. Schertzinger also directed this film. The film's songs include *I Remember You, Tangerine, If You Build a Better Mousetrap,* and more.

ARTHUR SCHWARTZ, Composer (1900–1984)

The praises of the Gershwins*, Richard Rodgers*, Cole Porter*, and Irving Berlin* are consistently sung by music experts who often neglect to include Arthur Schwartz among these all-time masters of the art of popular composition. This brilliant, Brooklyn-born composer and producer made Phi Beta Kappa at

Columbia University, taught school and, passing up a law career, created some of the loveliest melodies of Golden Age music—many of which were written with lyricist Howard Dietz*.

From 1926 to 1930, Schwartz' compositions were heard in a number of Broadway shows and revues, including **The Grand Street Follies, The New Yorkers**, Ned Wayburn's **Gambles, Ripples**, and **The Little Show**. To truly appreciate his tremendous contribution to Hollywood filmmaking, take another look at the super motion picture musical, **That's Entertainment**. Seeing (and listening) is believing—Arthur Schwartz is, indeed, among the songwriting superstars.

Broadway Chronology

1929   *I Guess I'll Have to Change My Plan*. Schwartz/Howard Dietz. Schwartz and Lorenz Hart* originally wrote this as a campy summer camp song entitled, *I Love to Lie Awake in Bed* or *The Pajama Song*. Dietz rewrote the words and *I Guess* became a big hit in **The Little Show**. Schwartz' son, Jonathan (a musicologist and radio personality), has been heard to sing quite an enjoyable version of his dad's song.

1930   *Something to Remember You By*. Schwartz/Dietz. From **Three's a Crowd**.

1931   **The Band Wagon**. Songs by Schwartz Dietz. The hits from one of Broadway's finest revues include: *I Love Louisa, New Sun in the Sky, High and Low*, and the classic, *Dancing in the Dark*. These were reprised in the 1953 film version of **The Band Wagon**, which featured more Schwartz/Dietz songs.

1932   *Louisiana Hayride, Alone Together*, and *A Shine on Your Shoes*. Schwartz/Dietz. From their Broadway score for **Flying Colors**.

1934   *You and the Night and the Music* and *If There Is Someone Lovelier Than You*. Schwartz/Dietz. Two wonderful melodies written for **Revenge with Music**. *Then I'll Be Tired of You*. Schwartz/E. Y. Harburg*.

1935   *Love Is a Dancing Thing*. Schwartz/Dietz. From **At Home Abroad**.

1937   **Virginia**. Songs by Schwartz and Albert Stillman. This production was commissioned by the Rockefellers to promote the restoration of Williamsburg. *Triplets* and *I See Your Face Before Me*. Schwartz/Dietz. Written for the show **Between the Devil**. *I See* is a gorgeous ballad.

1939   **Stars**. Songs by Schwartz/Dorothy Fields*. One of lyricist Fields' many Broadway shows in the late 1930s.

1946   **Park Avenue**. Songs by Schwartz/I. Gershwin. This superb songwriting team contributed several songs to this Broadway show.

1948   *Haunted Heart* and *Rhode Island Is Famous for You*. Schwartz/Dietz. Two delightful tunes introduced in the show, **Inside U.S.A**.

1951   *Make the Man Love Me*. Schwartz/Fields. A highly praised song from the writing duo's highly praised **A Tree Grows in Brooklyn**.

1954   **By the Beautiful Sea**. Songs by Schwartz and Fields. Despite their combined craft, no hits by these two beautiful songwriters.

1963   *Jennie*. Songs by Schwartz/Dietz. This show starred Mary Martin and had fine music, but it did not succeed on Broadway.

Hollywood Chronology

1930   *Queen High*. Songs by Schwartz and Ralph Rainger*/Edward Eliscu. This was Schwartz' first Hollywood assignment.
Brother Just Laugh It Off. Schwartz and Rainger/Harburg. A highly praised song written for the film *Follow the Leader*, which was Ethel Merman's first movie.

1934   *She Loves Me Not*. Schwartz/Edward Heyman*. The duo had one song featured in this film. In 1936 and 1937, Schwartz wrote a number of songs with Dietz and Heyman, but had no memorable hits from his single collaborations with them.

1941   *When Are We Going to Land Abroad?* Schwartz/Mercer. Several big bands popularized this double entendre novelty song, introduced in the movie *Navy Blues*.

1942   *Cairo*. Songs by Schwartz/Harburg. The composer and lyricist wrote three songs, including the title tune, for the stars of this film, Jeanette McDonald and Ethel Waters.

1943   *They're Either Too Young or Too Old*. Schwartz/Loesser. *Thank Your Lucky Stars*, a Warner Brothers extravaganza film full of stars and songs, included Bette Davis introducing this one.

1944   *Cover Girl*. Songs by Jerome Kern* and Ira Gershwin. Produced by Schwartz. An excellent Hollywood musical and certainly a good indication of the producer's good taste.

1946   *A Rainy Night in Rio, Oh, But I Do*, and *A Gal in Calico*. Schwartz/Leo Robin*. The songwriters penned these and three more tunes for the film, *The Time, The Place and The Girl*. *A Gal* was an Academy Award nominee, but lost to *Zip-a-Dee-Doo-Dah*.

1951   *Excuse My Dust*. Songs by Schwartz/Fields. The old Broadway partners wrote six songs for this film. Two years later, Schwartz and Johnny Mercer wrote five songs for one of Esther Williams' many swimming movies.

CARL SIGMAN, Composer/Lyricist (1909–   )

In addition to being a native New Yorker, a graduate of the New York University Law School, and a song-writer, Carl Sigman was a World War II paratrooper hero who earned six combat stars and the Bronze Star. Sigman's first published song was *Please Come Out of Your Dream*; in Hollywood, he wrote the words and music for a number of films.

Chronology

1940   *All Too Soon*. Duke Ellington*/Sigman.
Pennsylvania-6–5000. Jerry Gray/Sigman. This became a huge Glenn Miller novelty hit. The song's title was taken from the telephone number of the Pennsylvania Hotel in Manhattan, where the Miller band played at the time.

1946   *Shangri-la*. Matty Malneck* and Robert Maxwell/Sigman.

1947 *Bongo, Bongo, Bongo (I Don't Want to Leave the Congo)*. Sigman and Bob Hilliard (wm). Written for **Angels in the Wings**, on Broadway.
Ballerina. Sigman and Bob Russell* (wm).

1948 *Matinee*. Sigman/Russell.

1949 *Crazy, He Calls Me*. Sigman/Russell.

1950 *Enjoy Yourself (It's Later Than You Think)*. Sigman/Herb Magidson*.

1951 *It's All in the Game*. Charles G. Dawes/Sigman. Sigman added the lyrics after Dawes, a general and vice president of the United States, had composed the music in 1912.

1953 *Ebb Tide*. Robert Maxwell/Sigman.

1955 *Dream Along with Me*. Sigman (wm). This became Perry Como's hit theme.

1957 *Arrivederci Roma*. Renato Rascel/Sigman (English lyrics). Mario Lanza introduced this song in the film **Seven Hills of Rome**.

1962 *What Now My Love?* Gilbert Becaud/Sigman (English lyrics). A very popular song in the 1960s—Sinatra had a hit with it.

1966 *A Day in the Life of a Fool*. Luis Bonfa/Sigman (English lyrics). Another extremely popular song in the 1960s and another hit for Sinatra. The original title was *Manha De Carnaval*.

1970 *Love Story (Where Do I Begin?)*. Francis Lai/Sigman. This film title song was a huge hit.

FRANK SINATRA, Composer/Lyricist (1915–1998)

Thousands of accolades and millions of words have been written about the man who was called the world's greatest entertainer. "Ol' Blue Eyes," "The Chairman of the Board," and other complimentary titles (such as "The Voice") were given to Sinatra. Like Crosby, or perhaps even more so, he contributed more to the popular song genre than any singer. According to many of the experts, he lifted the popular song to an art form.

Chronology

1941 *This Love of Mine*. Henry Sanicola, Sol Parker/Sinatra.

1951 *I'm a Fool to Want You*. Joel Herron, Jack Wolf, Sinatra (wm).

SUNNY SKYLAR, Composer/Lyricist (1913–   )

His real name is Selig Sidney Sheftel, and he was born and raised in Brooklyn, New York. Skylar became a vocalist and bandleader of some renown wrote lyrics to quite a few Latin American songs.

Chronology

1940 *Fifteen Minute Intermission*. Skylar and Bette Cannon (wm).

1941 *Just a Little Bit South of North Carolina*. Skylar, Cannon, and Arthur Sheftel (wm).

1942   *It Must Be Jelly ('Cause Jam Don't Shake Like That)*. Music, Chummy McGregor (pianist) and George Williams; Lyrics, Sunny Skylar. McGregor played piano with Glenn Miller.

1943   *Amor*. Music, Gabriel Ruiz; (English) Lyrics, Skylar. This song was a big hit from the film, **Broadway Rhythm**.

1944   *Besame Mucho*. Music, Consuelo Vasquez; Lyrics, Skylar. A number 1 chart record for Jimmy Dorsey and crooner Bob Eberly.
Gotta be This or That. Skylar (wm). A Benny Goodman hit.

1945   *Waitin' for the Train to Come in*. Skylar/Martin Block (wm). Block, a popular disc jockey, also wrote *I Guess I'll Have to Dream The Rest* with Harold Green and Mickey Stoner (wm). Peggy Lee's blues version is highly recommended.

1949   *You're Breaking My Heart*. Adapted by Skylar and Pat Genaro. This song was based on Leoncavallo's *Lamatinata*; and Vic Damone's recording is most memorable.

1963   *Don't Wait Too Long*. wm, Sunny Skylar. A lovely ballad made lovelier by Francis Albert Sinatra.

STEPHEN SONDHEIM, Composer/Lyricist (1930–   )

A New Yorker and Williams College graduate, Stephen Joshua Sondheim is a contemporary songwriter—yet he is placed here, among the most prominent, for his incomparable contributions to the American musical theatre. A protégé of Oscar Hammerstein* (Sondheim's family had a home in Bucks County, Pennsylvania, near the Hammersteins'), he is reclusive and seemingly mysterious; nonetheless, Stephen Sondheim is an enormously talented man who continues to produce fine work. Given his creative accomplishments on Broadway and beyond, if he has not already done so, Stephen Sondheim is surely destined to become one of songwriting's musical legends.

Chronology

1957   **West Side Story**. Songs by Leonard Bernstein*/Sondheim. This award-winning Broadway production is filled with evergreens including: *I Feel Pretty, Something's Coming, Somewhere, Tonight*, and many more.

1959   **Gypsy**. Songs by Jule Styne*/Sondheim. Another smash Broadway musical featuring hit after hit—*All I Need Is a Girl, Everything's Coming Up Roses, Let Me Entertain You, Small World, Together Wherever We Go, You Gotta Have a Gimmick*, and more.

1962   **A Funny Thing Happened on the Way to the Forum**. Songs by Sondheim. A riotous comedy with a number of very funny songs. *Comedy Tonight* and *Lovely* were just two of the hits from this Broadway success.

1964   *Anyone Can Whistle*. Sondheim (wm). In the dark, when the lights went out on this title song and Broadway show after only nine performances.

1965   **Do I Hear a Waltz?** Songs by Rodgers*/Sondheim. Based on Arthur Laurents' Pulitzer Prize–winning play, *The Time of the Cuckoo*, this Broadway musical had a 220-performance run, not exactly up to Rodgers' standards. The title song, though, has survived beautifully.

1970   *Company*. Songs by Sondheim. This Broadway musical produced some bright hit songs, including *Being Alive, The Ladies Who Lunch*, and *Side By Side By Side*. Critics favorably compared Sondheim's lyrics to Alan Lerner's*—at their best.

1971   *Follies*. Songs by Sondheim. His lyrics were praised again, but Broadway wags said nobody could remember his music and hum it or whistle it after leaving the theatre.

1973   *A Little Night Music*. Songs by Sondheim. The words and music for this Broadway musical earned Sondheim his third consecutive Tony award; the show-stopping *Send in the Clowns* can not only be remembered, sung, and whistled, it can be considered an American standard. It is Sondheim's best ballad—delivered magnificently by Sarah Vaughn.

1976   *Pacific Overtures*. Songs by Sondheim/John Weidman. It closed quickly.

1979   *Sweeney Todd*. Songs by Sondheim. An all-around winning Broadway musical. *Pretty Women* and *Not While I'm Around* are classic Sondheim.

1981   *Old Friends*. Sondheim (wm). From *Merrily We Roll Along*, on Broadway.

1984   *Putting It Together*. Sondheim (wm). Barbra Streisand made a great recording of this one, from Sondheim's *Sunday in the Park with George*.

SAM H. STEPT, Composer/Lyricist (1897–1964)

Stept was born in Odessa, Russia, and came to the United States when he was 3; his family settled in Pittsburgh, Pennsylvania. He began his musical career as a classical pianist and conductor, and later formed his own dance band. In 1928, Sam Stept went to New York as a singer in musical revues. Like so many of their songwriting peers, he and lyricist Bud Green formed a publishing company on Tin Pan Alley.

Chronology

1928   *That's My Weakness Now*. Stept/Green*. His first hit song.
        I'll Always Be in Love With You. Stept/Green, and Herman Ruby. A jazz favorite, first used in the film *Syncopation*.

1930   *Please Don't Talk About Me When I'm Gone*. Stept/Sidney Clare (Chapter 4). A fine standard.

1936   *All My Life*. Stept/Sidney Mitchell (Chapter 4). Written for the movie *Laughing Irish Eyes*. Fats Waller* made one of the classic recordings of this song.

1937   *It Seems Like Old Times*. Stept and Charles Tobias* (wm). Famed radio and television personality Arthur Godfrey used this as his theme song.

1939   *Comes Love*. Stept, Tobias, and Lew Brown (wm). A lovely ballad from the film *Yokel Boy*.

AL STILLMAN, Lyricist (1906–1979)

A New York University graduate and former newspaper man, native New Yorker Al Stillman contributed verse to newspaper columns, a practice seldom seen any more. After a stint at Radio Music Hall as a staff writer, he composed a Hollywood score and went on to a successful career as a lyric writer.

Chronology

1938   *Room with a View.* Einar Swan (Chapter 4)/Stillman.

1939   *One, Two, Three, Kick.* Xavier Cugat/Stillman. This was the Cugat orchestra's anthem during the conga craze.

1940   *Say, Si Si.* Ernesto Lecuona/Stillman (English lyrics).
       The Breeze and I. Lecuona and Toots Camarata/Stillman. A chartbuster for Tommy Dorsey's band and vocalist Bob Eberle.

1941   *Bless 'Em All.* Jimmy Hughes and Frank Lake/Stillman. The composers of this popular World War II song were both Australians.

1942   *Juke Box Saturday Night.* Paul McGrane/Stillman. This number 1 chart hit is still played on the radio.

1950   *Don'cha Go Way Mad.* Jimmy Mundy (Chapter 4) and Illinois Jacquet/Stillman. Both Ella Fitzgerald and Mel Torme had hit recordings with this song.

1953   *I Believe.* Stillman, Ervin Drake, Irvin Graham, and Jimmy Shirl (wm).

1955   *Home for the Holidays* and *Moments to Remember.* Robert Allen/Stillman.
       It's Not for Me to Say. Allen/Stillman. Written for the film **Lizzie**, this song was a big hit for Johnny Mathis.
       Chances Are. Allen/Stillman. Mathis took this one all the way to number 1 on the charts. Allen also composed *A Very Special Love.*

BILLY STRAYHORN, Composer/Lyricist (1915–1967)

Brilliant and beloved, William Strayhorn was known in the music world as "Swee' Pea," a nickname given to him by his friend Lena Horne. Sidemen in Duke Ellington's orchestra also called him "Strays." Born in Pittsburgh and trained in classical music, Strayhorn met Ellington* in 1938, and the next year he began working with the Duke as an arranger and composer and sometimes pianist. Ellington may well have called Strayhorn his right arm—for the decades of collaboration and friendship. Swee' Pea surely fit the culture of that special music called "Ellingtonia." A major force in jazz and popular music for thirty years, Billy Strayhorn left us too soon.

Chronology

1938   *I'm Checking Out, Goodbye.* Ellington and Strayhorn (wm). Or, as Rosemary Clooney pronounced it when she sang it, *Goom Bye.*
       Lush Life. Strayhorn (wm). Simply his greatest music.

1939   *Something to Live For.* Ellington and Strayhorn (wm).

1941   *Take the "A" Train.* Ellington and Strayhorn (wm). Their classic together.

Day Dream. Ellington and Strayhorn/John LaTouche (Chapter 4). *Just a Sittin' and a Rockin'.* Ellington and Strayhorn/Lee Gaines.

1952   *Chelsea Bridge.* Strayhorn (Instr.). A great instrumental.

1958   *Satin Doll.* Ellington and Strayhorn/Johnny Mercer*. Arguably the most popular composition by the Duke and Strays.

JULE STYNE, Composer (1905–1994)

Julius Kerwin Stein was born into a musical family in London, England, and came to the United States as a child—and a prodigy. At age 9, he was playing concert piano solos, and as a teenager, he was leading bands. Styne's lyricist partners included Stephen Sondheim*, Sammy Cahn*, Betty Comden* and Adolph Green, Leo Robin*, Frank Loesser*, Yip Harburg*, and Erroll Garner. Styne and Cahn wrote together beginning in 1933, and their first collaboration was for a Monogram film release, *Sweetheart of Sigma Chi.* Although it was not a hit for another thirteen years, a song from the movie eventually became a classic, *Five Minutes More.* The film was remade in 1946 and Frank Sinatra recorded *Five* and made it a very popular song. In addition to writing hits for Hollywood, Styne and Cahn wrote three other big songs in 1945 and 46 that became—and remain—popular through audio recordings and live performances by a variety of artists: *Can't You Read Between The Lines?; Let It Snow, Let It Snow, Let It Snow;* and *The Things We Did Last Summer.*

During his first decade in Hollywood, Jule Styne worked for Columbia, MGM, Universal, Republic, Fox, Paramount and RKO, and other smaller studios like Monogram. He was building quite a portfolio and reputation for himself. (A footnote of names: sometimes Jule Styne has been mistaken for Jules Stein, the founder of MCA—an eye doctor turned show business mogul. The two men were not related.)

A composer of great talent and productivity—and a Tin Pan Alley, Broadway and Hollywood legend—Jule Styne wrote about 1,400 popular songs.

Broadway Chronology

1944   *Guess I'll Hang My Tears Out to Dry.* Styne/Sammy Cahn*. From **Glad to See Ya** on Broadway.

1947/48   *Papa Won't You Dance with Me?* and *I Still Get Jealous.* Styne/Sammy Cahn. His first songs for musical theatre were for the season's biggest Broadway hit, **High Button Shoes**.

1949   *Diamonds Are a Girl's Best Friend, Bye Bye Baby*, and *Little Girl from Little Rock.* Styne/Leo Robin. Written for the smash hit **Gentlemen Prefer Blondes**, another major triumph thanks to the music—and comedienne star Carol Channing.

1953   *Ev'ry Street's a Boulevard in Old New York.* Styne/Bob Hilliard*. From the show **Hazel Flagg**.

1956   ***Bells Are Ringing***. Songs by Styne/Betty Comden and Adolph Green. The fine Judy Holliday starred in this hit that ran two years in New York. The great songs from the show include *Just in Time, The Party's Over, Drop That Name*, and *It's a Perfect Relationship*.

1959   ***Gypsy***. Songs by Styne and Stephen Sondheim. Produced by David Merrick and Leland Hayward. This big musical winner about Gypsy Rose Lee and her family was originally staged by Jerome Robbins, and starred Ethel Merman. The classic hit songs include *Small World, Together, Everything's Coming Up Roses, All I Need Is the Girl, Let Me Entertain You*, and *Some People*.

1960   *Make Someone Happy*. Styne/Comden and Green. Styne's big hit from ***Do Re Mi***.

1961   *Comes Once in a Lifetime*. Styne/Comden and Green. From the David Merrick-produced show, ***Subway's Are for Sleeping***.

1964   ***Funny Girl***. Songs by Styne/Bob Merrill. The magnificent Barbra Streisand starred as vaudeville singer and comedienne Fanny Brice in the biggest hit of 1964. The magnificent songs included *Sadie, Sadie; Don't Rain on My Parade; People; Before the Parade Passes Me By; I Am Woman*; and many more.
       Fade Out, Fade In. Songs by Styne. A Broadway musical that ran for 271 performances, starring a very funny Carol Burnett.

1967   ***Hallelujah, Baby***. Songs by Styne/Comden and Green (libretto and lyrics). Based on Arthur Laurents fine story, this Broadway show ran nine months with a fine lead performance from Leslie Uggams.

Hollywood Chronology

1940   *Who Am I?* Styne/Walter Bullock. This Academy Award–nominated song was written for the movie ***The Hit Parade of 1941***.

1942   *It Seems to Me I've Heard That Song Before*. Styne/Cahn. Written for the film ***Youth on Parade***, this song was nominated for an Oscar, along with nine others, including Irving Berlin's *White Christmas*, which won. Styne also wrote a number of other songs with Frank Loesser and Herb Magidson*, but had no real hits with them that year.

1943   *Change of Heart* and *Take a Chance*. Styne/Harold Adamson. These were two of Styne's best songs in 1943. He did a lot of writing, collaborating throughout the year with: Adamson, Cahn, Loesser, Eddie Cherkose, Sol Meyer, George A. Brown, and Kim Gannon—but no classics emerged from these efforts.

1944   *I'll Walk Alone*. Styne/Cahn. Written for the movie ***Follow the Boys***, it was an Oscar nominee. Van Heusen and Burke's *Swinging on a Star* got the award.
       I Don't Want to Walk Without You. Styne/Loesser. From the film ***You Can't Ration Love***.
       Anchors Away. Songs by Styne/Cahn. A great musical starring Gene Kelly and Frank Sinatra and these hit songs: *I Fall in Love Too Easily, I Begged Her, What Makes the Sunset*, and *The Charm of You*. *I Fall* was an Academy Award nominee and *I Begged* was a big hit recording for Sinatra.
       One More Smile. Styne/Cahn. One of the best songs they wrote for the film version of ***Knickerbocker Holiday***, the Broadway classic by Kurt Weill and Maxwell Anderson.

Saturday Night Is the Loneliest Night of the Week. Styne/Cahn.

Victory Polka. Styne/Cahn. Their contribution to the World War II patriotic genre, used in the movie ***Jam Session.***

Step Lively. Songs by Styne and Cahn. Frank Sinatra did four songs from this film, but none made the *Hit Parade* or *Billboard* charts.

Poor Little Rhode Island and *There Goes That Song Again.* Styne/Cahn. The partners wrote these two popular songs for the Columbia studio to use in films.

1945 *Anywhere.* Styne/Cahn. From the film ***Tonight and Every Night.*** With World War II winding down, big songs were the order of the day—by the order of the studio moguls. This song missed winning the Academy Award because it was the year Rodgers and Hammerstein won with their classic, *It Might as Well Be Spring. Anywhere* was used again two years later in the film ***Glamour Girl***, which featured famous drummer Gene Krupa.

1947 ***It Happened in Brooklyn.*** Songs by Styne/Cahn. The duo wrote for several studios in '47, but really clicked with this film starring Jimmy Durante and Frank Sinatra, who was then 22 years old (the accompanying pianist in the movie was Andre Previn, who was then 17 years old). Styne and Cahn's hit songs included *Time After Time, Brooklyn Bridge, It's the Same Old Dream,* and *I Believe.*

1948 *It's Magic.* Styne/Cahn. This Oscar-nominated song was introduced by Doris Day in the film ***Romance on the High Seas***. It was Day's first hit of many in her long and distinguished singing and acting career. Like Janet Blair just ahead of her, Doris Day had sung with Les Brown's Band of Renown right before breaking into movies. *It's Magic* lost out on the Academy Award to Evans and Livingston's *Buttons and Bows.* Nonetheless, the film featured several other popular songs, including *It's You or No One* and *Put 'Em in a Box, Tie 'Em with a Ribbon and Throw 'Em in the Deep Blue Sea.*

1949 *It's a Great Feeling.* Styne/Cahn. The title song and Academy Award nominee from a film that featured seven Styne/Cahn songs. Doris Day starred and sang in this movie, too. Loesser's *Baby It's Cold Outside* won the Oscar.

1950 *It's Been a Long, Long Time.* Styne/Cahn. From the movie ***I'll Get By***, a remake of ***Tin Pan Alley***. Harry James and singer Helen Forrest turned this song into a chart buster.

1951 *Bettin' on a Man.* Styne/Leo Robin. Written for the film ***Meet Me After the Show***, starring Betty Grable.

1952 *I'll Walk Alone.* Styne/Cahn. Among the literally dozens of popular songs used in the movie ***With a Song in My Heart***, a biographical film about singer Jane Froman. Susan Hayward starred and was responsible for the big increase in tissue sales during the run of this emotional motion picture.

Gentlemen Prefer Blondes. Songs by Styne/Robin. Adapted for the silver screen, starring Carol Channing and Marilyn Monroe. Good film; great songs.

1954 *Three Coins in a Fountain.* Styne/Cahn. This film title song won the Academy Award that year.

How Do I Speak to an Angel? Styne/Hilliard. Written for Jerry Lewis and Dean Martin's funny film, ***Living It Up***, which was a remake of Selznick's ***Nothing Sacred***. On the Broadway stage, ***Living It Up*** was titled ***Hazel Flagg***.

1960 **Bells Are Ringing**. Songs by Styne/Comden and Green. Adapted from stage to screen, this movie version was another musical hit for Judy Holliday, this time starring with Dean Martin—and her real true love, jazz legend Gerry Mulligan. Andre Previn won the Academy Award for his film score of *Bells*.

1962 **Gypsy**. Songs by Styne and Sondheim. The film adaptation featured old songs from their Broadway show and some new ones for the movie. The best tunes were still *Everything's Coming Up Roses, Some People, You Gotta Have a Gimmick, Let Me Entertain You, All I Need Is the Girl*, and *Small World*.

1968 **Funny Girl**. Songs by Styne/Bob Merrill (Chapter 3). Styne had a capstone Hollywood musical—an award winner in several categories. Barbra Streisand (reprising her Fanny Brice role from the stage production) tied with Katherine Hepburn for the Oscar for Best Actress.

DANA SUESSE, Composer (1911–1987)

Dana Suesse was born in Kansas City, Missouri, and attended Sacred Heart convents in the South and the West. A piano prodigy who studied with prominent teachers, she made her debut with Paul Whiteman's orchestra as a pianist and songwriter. A serious composer, one of Suesse's major songs was taken from a jazz concerto she wrote. In the 1930s, she worked and recorded her music in Hollywood.

Chronology

1931 *Ho Hum*. Suesse/Edward Heyman*.
      Whistling in the Dark. Suesse/Alan Boretz. These were Suesse's first published songs. *Whistling* was used in a Marx Brothers film.

1932 *My Silent Love*. Suesse/Heyman. Her biggest hit song.

1934 *You Oughta' Be in Pictures*. Suesse/Heyman. Written for the **Ziegfeld Follies**.

1936 *The Night Is Young and You're So Beautiful*. Suesse/Irving Kahal* and Billy Rose*. A lovely standard ballad.

1939 *Yours for a Song*. Suesse/Ted Fetter and Rose. Written for the New York World's Fair *Aquacade*, a swimming extravaganza produced by Billy Rose.

CHARLES TOBIAS, Composer/Lyricist (1898–1970)

New York-born Charles Tobias was a successful songwriter whose career began on Tin Pan Alley when he was still a teenager. Beginning as a song demonstrator, he rose to staff composer and was an on-air performer in the early days of radio. In the 1930s, Tobias composed for Broadway revues and Hollywood films. He also published songs with his brother, Harry (1896–1985), and songwriter Sam Stept*. Harry Tobias and Charles Kisco wrote *It's A Lonesome Old Town When You're Not Around* (wm) in 1930.

Chronology

1929 *Miss You (Since You Went Away Dear)*. Tobias/Harry Tobias. Harry was also the lyricist for the song *Sweet and Lovely*, composed by Gus Arnheim and Jules Lemare.

1934 *Seems Like Old Times*. Tobias and Sam Stept. (wm).

1939 *Comes Love*. Tobias/Stept and Lew Brown. A lovely ballad written for the film musical **Yokel Boy**.

1940 *Little Curly Chair in a High Chair*. Nat Simon/Tobias. From the film **Forty Little Mothers**.

1941 *We Did It Before and We Can Do It Again*. Tobias/Cliff Friend*. A World War II patriotic song introduced on Broadway by Eddie Cantor in **Banjo Eyes**.
      Rose O'Day. Tobias and Al Lewis (wm).

1942 *Don't Sit Under the Apple Tree with Anyone Else But Me*. Tobias, Stept, and Brown (wm). Used in the film **Private Buckaroo**, this song became a huge hit for the Andrew Sisters.
      I Came Here to Talk for Joe. Tobias, Stept, and Brown (wm).

1944 *Time Waits for No One*. Tobias/Friend. Written for the movie **Shine on Harvest Moon**.

1946 *The Little Old Lamplighter*. Simon/Tobias. A number 1 chart record.

1964 *Those Lazy, Hazy, Crazy Day of Summer*. Hans Carste/Tobias. Thirty-five years after composing his first hit, Tobias wrote the words to this song, which Nat King Cole turned into an annual, seasonal hit.

ROY TURK, Lyricist (1892–1934)

Within his all-too-short life, Roy Turk became an accomplished lyricist in only one decade of songwriting. Born in New York City, Turk attended City College of New York and studied architecture, which he gave up for the music business. After serving in the U.S. Navy during World War I, he joined a Tin Pan Alley publishing firm and wrote special material for vaudeville. Turk worked in New York and in Hollywood, contributing to a number of outstanding standards.

Chronology

1922 *Aggravatin' Papa*. J. Russel Robinson (Chapter 1)/Turk. Originally composed as a fox trot, legendary Bessie Smith recorded it as a blues number.

1923 *Beale Street Mama*. Robinson/Turk.

1924 *Mandy, Make Up Your Mind*. Arthur Johnston and Grant Clarke (Chapter 4)/Turk and George W. Meyer (Chapter 1). This song has an Irving Berlinesque quality about it, which may be explained by the fact that Johnston was Berlin's pianist.

1926 *Are You Lonesome Tonight?* Lou Handman/Turk. This was a big hit for Turk and Handman (a vaudevillian, pianist, and composer).

Gimme a Little Kiss (Will Ya' Huh?). Turk, ''Whispering Jack'' Smith, and Maceo Pinkard (Chapter 4) (wm).

1928   *I'll Get By*. Fred Ahlert*/Turk. One of the best of all popular ballads. *Mean to Me*. Ahlert/Turk. Same year and team; another evergreen.

1929   *Walkin' My Baby Back Home*. Alhert/Turk.

1931   *I Don't Know Why (I Just Do)* and *Where the Blue of the Night Meets the Gold of the Day*. Ahlert/Turk. Two more evergreens. *Where the Blue* was introduced in the film **The Big Broadcast**; Bing Crosby made it his theme song.

1932   *Love You Funny Thing* and *I'll Follow You*. Ahlert/Turk. The songwriting duo's last two hits. Turk died two years later.

JAMES VAN HEUSEN, Composer (1913–1990)

Edward Chester Babcock took a famous men's shirt brand name and made it his own new last name to go along with his newly adopted first name: James Van Heusen. It has been said that this distinguished and mneumonic change was suggested by fellow songwriter Harold Arlen*, who, like Van Heusen, was from upstate New York and had changed his own last name from the original and less euphonic Arluck. Van Heusen was born in Syracuse, and for a while, was a music student at Syracuse University before he quit college to join a Manhattan music publishing firm, where he worked as a pianist and song demonstrator. Leaving New York for California while still only in his 20s, Van Heusen began a three-decade career as one of Hollywood's most successful composers—as well as an occasional collaborator for Broadway productions back in Manhattan. He was also a creator of great musical notions (songs not written for film or stage).

Broadway Chronology

1946   **Nellie Bly**. Songs by Van Heusen/Johnny Burke*. In *The American Musical Theatre*, Gerald Bordman called Van Heusen's first work for the Broadway stage ''a competent job.'' There were no real hit songs from the Eddie Cantor-produced musical.

1953   *Here's That Rainy Day*. Van Heusen/Burke. This marvelous ballad may have been the best song these two writers ever created—it certainly is a classic. The song was written for the stage version of a 1936 Flemish movie, **Carnival in Flanders**, presented on Broadway by the brilliant film director Preston Sturges. The play only lasted one week.

1965   *Everybody Has a Right to Be Wrong*. Van Heusen/Sammy Cahn*. A memorable song from **Skyscraper**, another forgotten show on Broadway which was based on Elmer Rice's non-musical, **Dream Girls**.

1966   *Walking Happy*. Van Heusen/Cahn. The title song from the musical, which was based on **Hobson's Choice**.

Hollywood Chronology

1939   *Oh You Crazy Moon*. Van Heusen/Burke.
       All This And Heaven Too; Heaven Can Wait and *Darn That Dream*. Van Heusen/
       Eddie DeLange*. *All This* was a promotional song for the movie of the same
       name.
       Blue Rain and *I Thought About You*. Van Heusen/Johnny Mercer*.

1940   *Do You Know Why?* Van Heusen/Burke. Written for the film **Love Thy Neighbor**,
       starring Jack Benny.
       Polka Dots and Moonbeams and *Imagination*. Van Heusen/Burke.
       Shake Down the Stars. Van Heusen/DeLange.

1941   *It's Always You*. Van Heusen/Burke. Written for the movie **Road to Zanzibar**,
       and the ubiquitous comedy team of Crosby and Hope.
       Humpty Dumpty Heart. Van Heusen/Burke. Written for **Playmates**, which turned
       out to be John Barrymore's last film.

1942   *Moonlight Becomes You*. Van Heusen/Burke. A fine ballad sung by Bing Crosby
       in **Road to Morocco**.

1944   *Sunday, Monday or Always*. Van Heusen/Burke. One of seven songs they wrote
       for **Dixie**, the film biography of Daniel Decatur Emmett.
       Going My Way. Van Heusen/Burke. This title song was just one of the Academy
       Award–winning categories for the fine film.
       Suddenly It's Spring. Van Heusen/Burke. Written for the movie **Lady in the Dark**.
       It Could Happen to You. Van Heusen/Burke. Written for the film **And the Angels
       Sing**, starring Betty Hutton. Ziggy Elman and Johnny Mercer wrote the title song.

1945   *Sleighride in July*. Van Heusen/Burke. This was an Oscar-nominated song from
       the film **Belle of the Yukon**, with Dinah Shore. Rodgers and Hammerstein's
       classic, *It Might as Well Be Spring* won the Academy Award.
       It's Anybody's Spring. Van Heusen/Burke. Spring must have been in the air and
       on songwriters' minds. This spring song was written for Crosby and Hope in
       Road to Utopia, along with *Personality; Put It There, Pal; Would You?; Good
       Time Charley*, and *Welcome to My Dream*.
       Nancy. Van Heusen/Phil Silvers. Written especially for Nancy Sinatra.

1947   *My Heart Is a Hobo* and *Smile Right Back at the Sun*. Van Heusen/Burke. The
       two hit songs from **Welcome Stranger**, the sequel film to **Going My Way**. Crosby
       and company were all back for this reunion movie.
       Harmony. Van Heusen/Burke. This song was actually more successful than the
       film in which it was featured, **Variety Girl**, starring Crosby and Hope.

1948   *But Beautiful, You Don't Have to Know the Language*, and *Apalachacola, F.L.A.*
       Van Heusen/Burke. From the ongoing Bing Crosby and Bog Hope film journey—
       this time **The Road to Rio**.

1955   *You My Love*. Van Heusen/Mack Gordon*. Sung by Frank Sinatra* in the film
       Young at Heart.

1957   *All the Way*. Van Heusen/Cahn. The Academy Award-winning song from the fine
       film about comedian Joe E. Lewis, **The Joker Is Wild**. The beginning of a

rewarding writing relationship between Van Heusen and Cahn, and Sinatra
singing their songs.

1959   *When No One Cares*. Van Heusen/Cahn.

1960   *The Second Time Around*. Van Heusen/Cahn. A lovely ballad and Oscar nominee
from the film **High Time**, starring Bing Crosby.
High Hopes. Van Heusen/Cahn. From the Frank Sinatra film, **Hole in the Head**,
this song won the Academy Award. John F. Kennedy also adopted *High Hopes*
as the theme song for his 1960 presidential campaign.

1961   *Pocketful of Miracles*. Van Heusen/Cahn. This film title song was another Sinatra
hit.

1963   *Call Me Irresponsible*. Van Heusen/Cahn. This lovely composition was part of
the non-musical movie, **Poppa's Delicate Condition**, and won the Oscar for best
film song that year.

1964   *My Kind of Town (Chicago Is)*. Van Heusen/Cahn. From the film **Robin and the
Seven Hoods**, starring Sinatra and a number of his so-called Rat Pack buddies.
My Kind was a giant hit for Sinatra, but lost to *Chim Chim Cher-ee*, from the
movie **Mary Poppins**, in the Oscar competition that year.

1965   *Love and Marriage*. Van Heusen/Cahn. A big hit and an evergreen, originally
written for the award-winning television special presentation of **Our Town**.

1967   *Thoroughly Modern Millie*. Van Heusen/Cahn. This movie title song was
nominated for an Academy Award, but lost to Bricusse's (Chapter 3) *Talk to the
Animals* from **Dr. Doolittle**.

1968   *Star*. Van Heusen/Cahn. The title song and an Oscar nominee from the film
biography of Gertrude Lawrence, starring Julie Andrews. Frank Sinatra recorded
a moving interpretation of this underrated ballad.

THOMAS "FATS" WALLER, Composer/Lyricist (1904–1943)

Fats Waller was a great entertainer, singer, pianist, and organist—and was
supposedly the first American invited to play one of the grandest organs in the
world, inside the Cathedral of Notre Dame in Paris. Waller studied music with
James P. Johnson, and, according to a 1952 *ASCAP Directory*, he gave piano
lessons to Count Basie. Waller's joy of life—lived on the edge—may have led
to his early demise; but in his short stay here he accomplished much as a
composer and performer. This Harlem-born son of a preacher had his first hit
in 1925, *Squeeze Me*, the words and music co-written with Clarence Williams.

Chronology

1929   *Honeysuckle Rose*. Waller and Andy Razaf* (wm). This great jazz standard was
originally written for a dance routine in a revue called **Load of Coal**.
Ain't Misbehavin'. Waller and Harry Brooks/Razaf. First used in the revue,
Connie's Hot Chocolates.
I've Got a Feeling I'm Falling. Waller and Harry Link*/Billy Rose*. This was
the year of the big stock market crash.

1930   *Blue Turning Grey Over You*. Waller/Razaf. Louis Armstrong had a hit with this
one.

1931   *I'm Crazy 'Bout My Baby (And My Baby's Crazy 'Bout Me)*. Waller and Alexander Hill (wm).

1932   *Keeping Out of Mischief Now*. Waller/Razaf.

1933   *What Did I Do to Be So Black and Blue?* Waller, Razaf, and Brooks (wm). A moving and significant musical message about being African American.

1936   *Stealin' Apples*. Waller/Razaf.

1937   *The Joint Is Jumpin'*. Waller and J. C. Johnson/Razaf. Typical Waller—swinging and whimsical.

1941   *All That Meat and No Potatoes*. Waller and Ed Kirkeby (wm). A popular novelty song.

1942   *Jitterbug Waltz*. Waller (instr.). His famed piano instrumental.

HARRY WARREN, Composer (1893–1981)

Using his real name, Salvatore Guaragna, would have been difficult for mainstream people to remember, pronounce, or spell, so this most productive of Hollywood composers used the simpler Harry Warren. Born in Brooklyn and originally a brass band drummer, Warren worked the carnival circuit, labored as a stagehand and actor, and eventually rose to the assistant director position in Hollywood.

Warren's songwriting career began in the 1920s, his earliest songs became jazz and pop standards. However, Michael Feinstein was certainly correct (in his book, *Nice Work If You Can Get*) when he referred to Warren as one of the most underrated popular music composers. Harry Warren deserved far more public fame than he received in his lifetime. Perhaps the best measure of his talent came from the obvious respect Warren received from his peers, the who's who of songwriters who wanted to—and did—work with him: Harold Adamson*, Sammy Cahn*, Al Dubin*, Arthur Freed*, Dorothy Fields*, Ira Gershwin*, Mack Gordon*, Sam Lewis*, Johnny Mercer*, Leo Robin*, and others.

Pre-Hollywood Chronology

1922   *Rose of the Rio Grande*. Warren/Edgar Leslie*. Warren's first published song.

1928   *Nagasaki*. Warren/Mort Dixon*.

1930   *Cheerful Little Earful*. Warren/Ira Gershwin. *Would You Like to Take a Walk?*Warren/Dixon. Both of these songs were featured in Billy Rose's* Broadway production, **Sweet and Low**.

1931   *I Found a Million Dollar Baby in a Five and Ten Cent Store*. Warren/Dixon. Written for the Broadway show **Crazy Quilt**, produced by Billy Rose. *Crazy* featured Rose's wife, Fanny Brice, for the third musical in a row.
       You're My Everything. Warren/Dixon and Joe Young*. One of Warren's finest compositions, written for the Broadway musical **The Laugh Parade**.

Hollywood Chronology

1930   *Three's a Crowd*. Warren/Al Dubin* and Irving Kahal*. Apparently his very first movie composition, for the film **Crooner**.

1933   *You're Getting to Be a Habit With Me* and *Shuffle Off to Buffalo*. Warren/Dubin.

Written for the movie classic, *42nd Street*, which was the catapault for many of director Busby Berkeley's future blockbusters. Warren and Dubin actually appeared in *42nd Street* along with a young Ginger Rogers. Five decades later, the film was reprised as a stage musical on Broadway and was a huge hit.

By a Waterfall. Warren/Dubin. From the movie *Footlight Parade*, which featured James Cagney tap dancing. This production was another big success for director Berkeley.

We're in the Money and *Shadow Waltz*. Warren/Dubin. The two hits from the five songs the duo wrote for *Gold Diggers of 1933*, which featured Ginger Rogers and Joan Blondell singing.

About a Quarter to Nine and *She's a Latin from Manhattan*. Warren/Dubin. Written for the film *Go Into Your Dance*, starring Ruby Keeler and her young groom, Al Jolson*.

Lulu's Back in Town. Warren/Dubin. The hit of the six songs written by Warren and Dubin for *Broadway Gondolier*. The film's screenplay was written by Sid Herzig and Yip Harburg*. Mel Torme's version of *Lulu's Back* is highly recommended.

Don't Give Up the Ship. Warren/Dubin. Written for the movie *Shipmates Forever*. Dick Powell sang it, and the U.S. Navy officially adopted the song as its own.

September in the Rain. Warren/Dubin. A fine evergreen from the half-dozen songs the duo wrote for the film *Stars over Broadway*. 1933 was a banner year for Warren and Dubin.

1936 *Cain and Mabel*. Songs by Warren/Dubin. Their film songs included a rewrite of *Shadow Waltz*, retitled *I'll Sing a Thousand Love Songs*. William Randolph Hearst backed this movie, but it failed at the box office.

1937 *With Plenty of Money and You*. Warren/Dubin. The hit from their songs for that year's *Gold Diggers*. Arlen and Harburg wrote songs for this movie, too.

1938 *Jeepers Creepers*. Warren/Johnny Mercer. This Academy Award–nominated song was written along with three others for the film *Going Places*, starring Dick Powell. Rainger and Robin's *Thanks for the Memory* won the Oscar; but *Jeepers* is an American classic, thanks to a number of artists including Louis Armstrong and Frank Sinatra.

Girlfriend of the Whirling Dervish. Warren/Mercer. Their hit song from another Busby Berkeley movie, *Garden of the Moon*.

Hooray for Spinach. Warren/Mercer. The novelty tune out of the five songs they wrote for the film *Naughty But Nice*.

1940 *Down Argentine Way*. Warren/Mack Gordon*. The new partners wrote this Oscar-nominated film title song and *Two Dreams Met* and were, at the very least, partially responsible for a big Latin American craze in Hollywood musicals. Betty Grable, Carmen Miranda, and Don Ameche starred in the film. *When You Wish Upon a Star* won the Academy Award that year.

You Say the Sweetest Things, Baby. Warren/Gordon. Used in the movie *Tin Pan Alley*, starring Betty Grable and Alice Faye.

1941 *Chatanooga Choo-Choo, I Know Why and So Do You*, and *It Happened in Sun Valley*. Warren/Gordon. All three of these hits were written for Glenn Miller and the film *Sun Valley Serenade*, part of new film genre about big bands and resorts. *Chatanooga* was nominated for an Oscar, but lost to Kern and Hammerstein's *The Last Time I Saw Paris*.

I Yi, Yi, Yi, Yi (I Like You Very Much) and *Chica Chica Boom Chic*. Warren/Gordon. Two big tunes for Carmen Miranda that were featured in the film **That Night in Rio**.

1942   *I've Got a Gal in Kalamazoo, At Last*, and *Serenade in Blue*. All Warren/Gordon. All hit songs from **Orchestra Wives**, the sequel to **Sun Valley Serenade**. Along with nine other songs that year, *I've Got a Gal* was nominated for an Oscar but lost to Irving Berlin's *White Christmas*.

I Had the Craziest Dream. Warren/Gordon. From their film score for **Springtime in the Rockies**, starring Betty Grable, accompanied by her soon-to-be husband, Harry James; Caesar Romero; and John Payne.

There Will Never Be Another You. Warren/Gordon. This lovely tune and four others were written for the Sonja Heine ice skating movie, **Iceland**.

1943   *You'll Never Know*. Warren/Gordon. The Oscar-winning song from Fox's money-making movie, **Hello Frisco, Hello**. *You'll Never* won over fine standards: *My Shining Hour, Old Black Magic*, and *You'd Be So Nice to Come Home To*.

My Heart Tells Me. Warren/Gordon. One of two songs in the film **Sweet Rosie O'Grady**.

No Love, No Nothing and *A Journey to a Star*. Warren/Leo Robin. The hits from the seven songs written for **The Gang's All Here**, which featured Carmen Miranda duetting with Benny Goodman—and ended up being Alice Faye's last film.

1944   **Four Jills and a Jeep**. Songs by Warren/Gordon. A number of their songs were reprised in this movie.

By the River Sainte Marie. Warren/Edgar Leslie. The songwriters' 1931 composition was used in the 1944 film, **Swing in the Saddle**, which also featured music performed by the Nat King Cole Trio.

1945   *I Wish I Knew* and *The More I See You*. Warren/Gordon. Written for Billy Rose's **Diamond Horseshoe** starring Betty Grable, with Dick Haymes from the Harry James band crooning *You'll Never Know*. Four other Warren/Gordon songs were used in this movie.

Yolanda and the Thief. Songs by Warren/Arthur Freed. This MGM movie starred Fred Astaire and was directed by Vincente Minelli. Despite all of this talent, there were no hit songs from this one.

1946   *Atchison, Topeka and the Santa Fe*. Warren/Mercer. The Academy Award–winning song that year, from the successful film starring Judy Garland, **The Harvey Girls**.

The Jolson Story. Warren/Dubin. The duo's songs were prominently reprised in this eight-million dollar Hollywood super bonanza movie.

1947   *Stanley Steamer*. Warren/Ralph Blane*. The most memorable of seven songs written for the movie **Summer Holiday**, with Mickey Rooney and others, a take-off on **Ah, Wilderness**. According to Clive Hirschhorn (in his book, *The Hollywood Musical*), this film score was "first rate."

1948   **My Dream Is Yours**. Songs by Warren/Dubin, Mercer, and Dixon. Doris Day and nine Warren songs starred in this film, including *Love Finds a Way, I'll String Along with You, You Must Have Been a Beautiful Baby, Jeepers Creepers, With Plenty of Money*, and *Nagasaki*—all reprised.

You're My Everything. Warren/Dixon and Joe Young. Same musical film format of reprising Warren's songs. Mack Gordon* appeared in this movie.

1950   *You Wonderful You.* Warren and Saul Chaplin*/Jack Brooks. Judy Garland and Gene Kelly sang and danced to this one on film.

1951   *Lullaby of Broadway* and *You're Getting to Be a Habit with Me.* Warren/Dubin. These songs and Doris Day and Gladys George had leading parts in this **Lullaby of Broadway** movie.

Texas Carnival. Songs by Warren/Dorothy Fields*. This movie featured four of these two brilliant writers' songs, with Red Norvo on vibraphone.

1952   *Zing a Little Zong.* Warren/Robin*. The Oscar nominee from **Just for You**, starring Natalie Wood, Jane Wyman, and Bing Crosby.

1954   *That's Amore.* Warren/Brooks. For the film **The Caddy**.

1955   *Inamorata.* Warren/Brooks. This Dean Martin hit song and five more were written for **Artists and Models**. Shirley MacLaine and Jerry Lewis starred with Martin in the movie.

1957   *An Affair to Remember.* Warren/Harold Adamson. One of the loveliest of film title songs.

Rock-a-Bye Baby. Songs by Warren/Cahn. The musical partners had no real hits from writing for this Jerry Lewis movie.

I Love My Baby. Warren/Bud Green*. Initially written for **The Joker Is Wild**, the biographical film about comedian Joe E. Lewis, this song was used again two years later in another biography movie, **The Gene Krupa Story**.

NED WASHINGTON, Lyricist (1901–1976)

A native of Scranton, Pennsylvania, Ned Washington worked as a nightclub master of ceremonies and a vaudeville agent, as well as a popular song lyricist. He was the winner of a number of awards in Hollywood and from songwriting groups. Washington wrote the English lyrics for one of the best-known Mexican folk songs in the United States, *La Cucaracha*. The original date of that composition is unknown. He also provided lyrics for Dimitri Tiomtin (*see* Paul Francis Webster*).

Chronology

1932   *(I Don't Stand a) Ghost of a Chance.* Victor Young*/Bing Crosby (Chapter 4) and Washington.

I'm Getting Sentimental Over You. George Bassman/Washington. Supposedly, Bassman sold the rights to *I'm Getting Sentimental* to song publisher Irving Mills for only $25. He was also supposed to have been the real composer of Benny Goodman's theme, *Let's Dance*, an adaptation of Von Weber's *Invitation to the Dance*. The New York-born, Boston-raised musician was a student of composition and orchestration at the New England Conservatory of Music and became a sideman with Tommy Dorsey from 1931 through 1934. Bassman conducted the pit band for **Guys and Dolls** on Broadway and eventually composed and arranged his music for films in Hollywood.

1933   *Smoke Rings*. H. Eugene Gifford/Washington.

1936   *Can't We Talk It Over?* Young/Washington.

1938   *The Nearness of You*. Hoagy Carmichael*/Washington. Considered one of the finest ballads of that or any other era.

1939   *Hi-Diddle De De*. Leigh Harline/Washington. Born in Salt Lake City in 1907, Harline was a radio performer before joining Disney, where he worked from 1932 until 1940.

1940   *Jiminy Cricket*. Harline/Washington.
       When You Wish Upon A Star. Harline/Washington. The Oscar-winning song that year and one of the best known television theme songs from Disney.

1944   *Stella by Starlight*. Young/Washington. An evergreen written for the film **The Uninvited**.

1947   *On Green Dolphin Street*. Bronislaw Kaper/Washington. Born in Warsaw, Poland, Kaper attended the prestigious music conservatory there, studying piano and composition before coming to the United States and Hollywood. He and Walter Jurmann co-composed *All God's Chillun Got Rhythm* for the classic 1937 comedy, **A Day at the Races** Kaper and lyricist Helen Deutsch wrote *Hi-Lilli, Hi-Lo* in 1952.

1950   *My Foolish Heart*. Young/Washington. This beautiful song was Washington's last big hit.

MABEL WAYNE, Composer (1904–1978)

Brooklynite Mabel Wayne was a well-traveled young student of voice, composition, and piano. She tutored in all of those, plus dramatic art, in Switzerland and elsewhere. A popular radio performer, Wayne gave up a concert career for popular songwriting.

Chronology

1926   *In a Little Spanish Town*. Wayne/Joe Young* and Sam Lewis*.

1927   *Ramona*. Wayne/L. Wolfe Gilbert (Chapter 4). A film title song and a big hit.

1930   *It Happened in Monterey*. Wayne/Billy Rose*. An evergreen originally written for the film **King of Jazz**, the title Paul Whiteman bestowed on himself, starring in this movie about himself.

1934   *Little Man, You've Had a Busy Day*. Wayne/Al Hoffman* and Maurice Sigler.

1941   *I Understand*. Wayne/Kim Gannon. A popular World War II ballad.

1949   *Dreamer's Holiday*. Wayne/Gannon. A hit for Perry Como and for Buddy Clark.

PAUL FRANCIS WEBSTER, Lyricist (1907–1984)

For nearly four decades, Paul Francis Webster wrote words to some of the finest music composed by Duke Ellington*, Sammy Fain*, Dimitri Tiomkin, and Johnny Mandel; he contributed hundreds of lyrics to more than seventy films. A native New Yorker, Webster earned degrees from both Cornell and New York University. He was an able-bodied seaman, a dance instructor, and an author of books and shows. Webster arrived in Hollywood in 1935, a few years after writing the popular lyrics to *Masquerade*, composed by John Jacob Loeb.

Chronology

1932   *Masquerade*. John Jacob Loeb/Webster.

1934   *Two Cigarettes in the Dark*. Lew Pollack (Chapter 4)/Webster. Written for the stage play **Kill That Story**.

1941   *Jump for Joy* and *I Got It Bad (And That Ain't Good)*. Duke Ellington*/Webster. Written for Ellington's famed **Jump for Joy** revue, which never quite got off the ground.

1944   *Baltimore Oriole*. Hoagy Carmichael*/Webster.

1948   *Black Coffee*. Sonny Burke and Webster (wm).

1950   *The Loveliest Night of the Year*. Irving Aaronson (music adaptation)/Webster. Adapted from *Sobre Los Olas* for the film **The Great Caruso**. Mario Lanza starred and sang magnificently.

1955   *Love Is a Many Splendored Thing*. Sammy Fain*/Webster. This film title song won the Academy Award.

1956   *Friendly Persuasion*. Dimitri Tiomkin/Webster. A film title soundtrack composition. Russian-born Tiomkin (1894–1980) was one of Hollywood's most honored composers who also wrote *Hajjii Baba, The High and the Mighty* and *High Noon* (Tiomkin/Washington).

1958   *A Very Precious Love*. Fain/Webster. Written for the film version of Herman Wouk's **Marjorie Morningstar**.

1962   *Tender Is the Night*. Fain/Webster. Title song from the film adaptation of F. Scott Fitzgerald's wrenching novel.

1965   *Lara's Theme/Somewhere My Love*. Maurice Jarre/Webster. From director David Lean's sweeping film adaptation of Boris Pasternak's Nobel Prize–winning novel, *Doctor Zhivago*.
       The Shadow of Your Smile. Johnny Mandel (Chapter 3)/Webster. The Academy Award-winning song from **The Sandpiper**, starring Eliazabeth Taylor and Richard Burton and directed by Vincente Minelli.

1968   *A Time for Love*. Mandel/Webster. Written for the film adaptation of Shakespeare's classic play, **Romeo and Juliet**, directed by Franco Zeffirelli.

KURT WEILL, Composer (1900–1950)

Kurt Julian Weill was born into a Jewish cantor's family in Dessau, Germany. Having studied under Engelbert Humperdinck in Berlin, Weill became a dramatic composer and a pioneer in the composition of early musicals. In 1926, he composed *Royal Palace*, an opera with jazz components; from 1927 to 1930, he collaborated with the great German dramatist Bertolt Brecht and wrote *Die Dreigroschenoper*. Lotte Lenya (who later married Weill) starred in that production's role of Jenny. Weill used the name Jenny again in his classic **Threepenny Opera**, which ran for 2,500 performances in the United States after it had been adapted for the American musical theatre stage by Marc Blitzstein. *Moritat*, from the famed **Threepenny Opera** score, was rewritten as *Mack the Knife* and became a huge hit and, interestingly, an American standard. Along with Paul Hindemith, Kurt Weill is considered to be one of the two greatest European composers of the post–World War I era. He arrived in the United States in 1935, and soon after staged his first Broadway musical, **Johnny Johnson**, with no hit songs.

Chronology

1938 *September Song*. Weill/Maxwell Anderson. Walter Huston performed this one and only hit song in the stage production of **Knickerbocker Holiday**, written by playwright Maxwell Anderson.

1941 **Lady in the Dark**. Songs by Weill/Ira Gershwin*. This 450-performance hit show starred Gertrude Lawrence, introduced Danny Kaye, and included Macdonald Carey and Victor Mature in the cast. Memorable songs were *My Ship* and *The Saga of Jenny*.

1943 **One Touch of Venus**. Songs by Weill/Ogden Nash. This was a big Broadway hit, especially for star Mary Martin. **One Touch** was a grand show full of ballets, lovely costumes, and S. J. Perelman's and Nash's comic dialogue. It also featured a truly great Weill ballad, *Speak Low*.

1945 **Firebrand of Florence**. Songs by Weill/I. Gershwin. Despite the genius of the writers, this one went down in flames on Broadway.

1947 **Street Scene**. Songs by Weill/Langston Hughes. This somber musical adaptation of Elmer Rice's 1929 drama only lasted a few months on Broadway. *Moon Faced, Starry Eyed* was a fine song from this score.

1948 **Love Life**. Songs by Weill/Alan Jay Lerner*. This production ran for almost a year and had delightful music that, somehow, no one seems to remember or play anymore.

1949 **Lost in the Stars**. Songs by Weill/Anderson. A stage adaptation of Alan Payton's great South African novel, *Cry the Beloved Country*. The title song, which Weill and Anderson had written several years before this Broadway production, is still a fine standard. Tragically, Weill died—too young—during the run of *Lost in the Stars*.

RICHARD WHITING, Composer/Lyricist (1891–1938)

Richard Whiting was born in Peoria, Illinois. A self-taught pianist, he began his professional career as a song plugger for the Detroit office of the famous Remick publishing company. Whiting later became one of Hollywood's pioneering composers. Some people know Whiting's daughter Margaret better than

him, despite his success and although she sings—and sings the praises of—
Richard Whiting's fine songs.

Chronology

1915   *It's Tulip Time in Holland*. Whiting (wm). His first published song.

1918   *Till We Meet Again*. Whiting/Raymond Egan (Chapter 4). An early prize-winning
        ballad in a Detroit contest for World War I songs.

1920   *The Japanese Sandman*. Whiting/Egan.

1921   *Ain't We Got Fun?* Whiting/Egan and Gus Kahn*.

1925   *Sleepy Time Gal*. Whiting/Egan and J. R. Alden.

1926   *Breezin' Along with the Breeze*. Whiting (wm).

1928   *She's Funny That Way*. Whiting and Neil Moret* (wm). Sometime performed as
        He's Funny That Way.

1929   *Louise*. Whiting/Leo Robin. Introduced and popularized by Maurice Chevalier in
        the film **Innocents of Paris**. This and **Close Harmony** were the two Hollywood
        films Whiting wrote for first.

1930   *Beyond the Blue Horizon*. Whiting/Robin and W. Franke Harling. Written for the
        film **Monte Carlo**.
        My Ideal. Whiting/Robin. This evergreen is probably Whiting's most popular
        song.
        My Future Just Passed. Whiting/George Marion, Jr. Born in 1899, Marion was
        a Bostonian, Harvard graduate, librettist, and Hollywood screenwriter in the late
        1920s.

1931   *Guilty*. Whiting/Kahn and Harry Akst*. Another big hit for Whiting. Fifteen years
        later, Margaret Whiting had a big hit with her recording of the song.

1932   *You're an Old Smoothie (I'm an Old Softie)*. Whiting, Nacio Herb Brown*, and
        Buddy DeSylva* (wm). Used on Broadway in **Take a Chance**.
        One Hour With You. Whiting/Robin. Film title song.

1937   *On the Good Ship, Lollipop*. Whiting/Mercer. A big hit for a small child—Shirley
        Temple—in the film, **Bright Eyes**.
        Have You Got Any Castles, Baby? and *Too Marvelous for Words*. Whiting/Johnny
        Mercer*. These were Whiting's last hits: *Have You* was in the film **Varsity Show**;
        Too Marvelous was in the movie **Ready, Willing and Able**.
        Hooray for Hollywood. From the film **Hollywood Hotel**. Whiting/Mercer.

CLARENCE WILLIAMS, Composer/Lyricist (1898–1965)

Clarence Williams was born in Plaquemin, Louisiana, and was a minstrel
singer prior to World War I. Supposedly a protégé of Jelly Roll Morton, Williams became a songwriter just after the war; in 1915, he and composer and
lyricist Armand J. Piron (1888–1943) became partners in the music publishing
business. Piron also wrote *I Wish I Could Shimmy Like My Sister Kate* (wm) in
1919.

As a publisher, Williams owned the rights to music by Fats Waller*, James P. Johnson, Willie "The Lion" Smith, and Spencer Williams* (not related); he also recorded some of the early works of Louis Armstrong* and Sidney Bechet. In 1921, Williams bought out Piron's share of their business and moved the company to New York. At that time, Williams and his wife, Eva Taylor, were enjoying considerable popularity as musical performers. He was the accompanist for Bessie Smith and, except for Fletcher Henderson, Clarence Williams was the most recorded African-American performer of his time.

Chronology

1917 *You Missed a Good Woman When You Picked All Over Me*. Williams (wm). His first published song.

1919 *Royal Garden Blues*. Williams and Spencer Williams (instr.). First performed by the Original Dixieland Jazz Band.
I Ain't Gonna Give Nobody None of This Jelly Roll. Williams and Spencer Williams (wm). Written for a Bessie Smith-styled performance.

1922 *Baby Won't You Please Come Home?* Williams/Charles Warfield.

1923 *Sugar Blues*. Williams/Lucy Fletcher.

1925 *Squeeze Me*. Fats Waller and Williams (wm).

1927 **Bottomland**. Williams (wm). On Broadway.

1928 *West End Blues*. King Oliver (Chapter 4)/Williams.

SPENCER WILLIAMS, Composer/Lyricist (1889–1965)

New Orleans-born Spencer Williams was a pianist and vaudeville entertainer, as well as a songwriter. He attended the Arthur Williams Music School and Saint Charles University before going north to Chicago in 1907. Williams wrote music, played piano professionally and, in 1925, went to Europe and joined the Follies Bergere as an accompanist for Josephine Baker. While he was in Paris, Williams wrote several songs with Fats Waller*. Late in his career, Williams performed on radio and television.

Chronology

1916 *I Ain't Got Nobody*. Williams and Dave Peyton/Roger Graham.

1919 *I Ain't Gonna Give Nobody None of This Jelly Roll*. Spencer Williams and Clarence Williams* (wm).

1924 *Everybody Loves My Baby*. Williams and Jack Palmer (wm). Born in Nashville in 1900, Palmer was a U.S. Army drum major and a graduate of Christian Brothers College.

1926 *I've Found a New Baby*. Williams and Palmer (wm). A popular jazz song.

1928 *Basin Street Blues*. Williams (wm). His best known and most popular classic composition. He also wrote *Mahogony Hall Stomp* (date unknown), named for a famed brothel in New Orleans.

HARRY MACGREGOR WOODS, Composer/Lyricist
(1896–1970)

Harry Woods was born in Massachusetts, grew up and attended public schools in Chicago, and then went on to Harvard. Woods sang professionally and performed as a pianist, even though he did not have any fingers on his left hand. In 1932, he went to England to compose for films. Known to have a temper and to get into a scrap or two, perhaps because of his alcoholism, Woods later turned to farming back in Massachusetts, on Cape Cod.

Chronology

1923   *I'm Going South*. Woods and Abner Silver (wm). His first song.

1926   *When the Red, Red Robin Comes Bob, Bob Bobbin' Along*. Woods (wm).

1927   *I'm Looking Over a Four Leaf Clover*. Woods/Mort Dixon*.

1931   *River Stay 'Way from My Door*. Woods/Dixon.
       When the Moon Comes Over the Mountain. Woods/Howard Johnson. It became Kate Smith's theme song.

1934   *What a Little Moonlight Can Do*. Woods (wm). A Billie Holiday classic previously introduced in the British film *Roadhouse Nights*.

1935   *I'll Never Say "Never Again" Again*. Woods (wm).

ALLIE WRUBEL, Composer/Lyricist (1905–1973)

Wrubel was born in Connecticut and worked as a movie theatre manager before taking up composing as his chosen career. Having written some songs in college, he discontinued his creative efforts until the mid-1930s, when he began writing again for Hollywood.

Chronology

1932   *As You Desire Me*. Wrubel (wm).

1935   *The Lady in Red*. Wrubel/Mort Dixon*. Written for the film *In Caliente*.

1936   *I'm Afraid the Masquerade Is Over*. Wrubel/Herb Magidson*. Some sources date this to 1938.

1938   *Music, Maestro, Please*. Wrubel/Magidson.

1940   *I'm Stepping Out With a Memory Tonight*. Wrubel/Magidson.

1941   *Why Don't We Do This More Often?* Wrubel/Charles Newman.

1942   *I Met Her on Monday*. Wrubel/Newman.

1945   *I'll Buy That Dream*. Wrubel/Magidson. Written for the movie *Sing Your Way Home*.

1946   *Zip-a-Dee-Doo-Dah*. Wrubel/Ray Gilbert. The Academy Award-winning song that year, from the film *Song of the South*.

JACK YELLEN, Lyricist (1892–1991)

In 1897, Jack Yellen and his family left Poland for the United States and eventually settled in Buffalo, New York. Yellen entered college at the University of Michigan and became a reporter. He went on to be an author of screenplays and film songs and a music publisher. In 1922, Yellen and his partners, Milton Ager and Ben Bornstein, sold their music publishing business to Warner Brothers. From then on, they were very successful together on Tin Pan Alley.

Chronology

1920   *O-H-I-O.* Abe Olman (Chapter 1)/Yellen.

1923   *Momma Goes Where Papa Goes or Papa Don't Go There at All.* Milton Ager (Chapter 4)/Yellen.

1924   *I Wonder What's Become of Sally?* Ager/Yellen.
       Hard Hearted Hannah. Yellen, Charles Bates, and Bob Bigelow (wm).

1925   *My Yiddishe Momma.* Yellen and Lew Pollack (Chapter 4) (wm). A Jewish classic.
       Cheatin' on Me. Yellen and Pollack (wm).

1927   *Ain't She Sweet?* Ager/Yellen.

1930   *Happy Days Are Here Again.* Ager/Yellen. Initially written for the film **Chasing Rainbows**, this song became a celebratory theme for the end of prohibition in the United States; two years later, it became the official song for Franklin D. Roosevelt's presidential campaign.

1939   *Are You Havin' Any Fun?* Sammy Fain*/Yellen.

VINCENT YOUMANS, Composer (1898–1946)

Vincent Millie Youmans was born in New York City and attended private schools. Originally intending to become an engineer, he gave that up for Wall Street, where he worked as a stockbroker for a year. Youmans joined the navy in World War I and become involved in the service's music sector, leading a band at the Great Lakes Naval Station in Illinois. After the war, Youmans became a successful Broadway composer and producer; sadly, he died of tuberculosis at age 48.

Chronology

1919   *Hallelujah!* Youmans/Leo Robin* and Clifford Grey. This was his first hit, taken from a march he had written for John Philip Sousa's famous band.

1924   *I Want to Be With You.* Youmans/Buddy DeSylva*. This song was cut from a Broadway show, but later became a popular jazz number.

1925   *I Want to Be Happy* and *Tea for Two.* Youmans/Irving Caesar*. Both of these big hits were written for Broadway's **No, No Nanette**.

1926   *I Know That You Know.* Youmans/Ann Caldwell. Caldwell (1867–1936) wrote librettos for twenty-five musicals and penned *The Lorelei.* She collaborated with Jerome Kern*, Victor Herbert*, and others in her lyrical work.

1927   *Sometimes I'm Happy.* Youmans/Caesar and Grey. Retitled and rewritten for the film **Hit the Deck**, the original had been cut from a 1923 musical.

1929   *Without a Song, More Than You Know,* and *Great Day.* Youmans/Billy Rose* and Edward Eliscu (Chapter 4). These top-of-the-line standards were written for the Broadway production of **Great Day**.

1930   *Time on My Hands.* Youmans/Harold Adamson* and Mack Gordon*. Another Broadway classic written for the show *Smiles*, starring Marilyn Miller.

1931   *Through the Years.* Youmans/Edward Heyman*. The title song of the Broadway musical.

1933   *Carioca.* Youmans/Kahn and Eliscu. The trio wrote this one and the title song for the film *Flying Down to Rio*.
Orchids in the Moonlight. Youmans/Kahn.

JOE YOUNG, Lyricist (1899–1939)

Another native New Yorker, Joseph Young was educated in the city's public schools and began in show business as a vaudeville "card boy." Through that visual medium, acts were introduced by printed signs for audiences to read, instead of by announcers. Young was a singer and a song plugger, as well as a songwriter, and he went on tour entertaining the troops overseas during World War I. He was a charter member of, and longtime officer for, ASCAP.

Chronology

1916   *Yaaka Hulaa Hickey Dula.* Young, E. Ray Goetz, and Pete Wendling (wm).
Where Did Robinson Crusoe Go with Friday on a Saturday Night? George W. Meyer (Chapter 1)/Young and Sam Lewis*.
Hello Central, Give Me No-Man's Land and *Rockabye Your Baby with a Dixie Melody.* Jean Schwartz (Chapter 1)/Young and Lewis.
My Mammy. Walter Donaldson/Young and Lewis. *Hello, Rockabye,* and *Mammy* were used in Al Jolson's *Sinbad* on Broadway.

1918   *Just a Baby's Prayer at Twilight.* M. K. Jerome/Young and Lewis.

1919   *How Ya Gonna Keep 'em Down on the Farm After They've Seen Broadway?* Donaldson/Young and Lewis.

1920   *I'd Love to Fall Asleep in My Mammy's Arms.* Fred Ahlert*/Young and Lewis.
Singin' the Blues. Con Conrad*/Young and Lewis.

1921   *Tuck Me to Sleep in My Old 'Tucky Home.* Meyer/Young and Lewis.

1925   *Dinah.* Harry Akst*/Young and Lewis. The biggest Young and Lewis hit, written for *The Plantation Revue* on Broadway.
I'm Sitting on Top of the World. Ray Henderson*/Young and Lewis. Written for the film *The Singing Fool*, starring Al Jolson.
Five Foot Two, Eyes of Blue. Henderson/Young and Lewis.

1926   *In a Little Spanish Town.* Mabel Wayne/Lyrics, Young and Lewis.

1928   *Laugh, Clown, Laugh.* Ted FioRito (Chapter 4)/Young and Lewis.
I Kiss Your Hand, Madame. Ralph Erwin/Young and Lewis (English lyrics).

1930   *Two Hearts in Three Quarter Time.* Robert Stolz/Young. *Spring Is Here*. Harry Warren*/Young and Lewis. The trio wrote four songs for this film: *Bad Baby, Cryin' for the Carolines, Have a Little Faith in Me* and *How Shall I Tell?*

1931   *Ooh That Kiss, Torch Song,* and *You're My Everything.* Warren/Young and Dixon. Written for the movie *Laugh Parade*.

Was That the Human Thing To Do? Fain/Young.
Snuggled on Your Shoulder. Carmen Lombardo*/Young.

1932   *Shanty in Old Shanty Town.* Young, (Little) Jack Little, and John Siras (wm).
       Written for the film **The Crooner**.
       Lullabye of the Leaves. Bernice Petkere/Young.

1933   *A Hundred Years from Today.* Victor Young (not related)/Joe Young and Ned
       Washington. A fine ballad.
       You're Gonna Lose Your Girl. James V. Monaco/Young.
       Annie Doesn't Live Here Anymore. Harold Spina/Joe Young and Johnny Burke.

1935   *Then You've Never Been Blue.* Ted FioRito/Young and Lewis.
       I'm Gonna Sit Right Down and Write Myself a Letter and *Life Is a Song.* Ahlert/
       Young.
       You're a Heavenly Thing. Jack Little/Young.

VICTOR YOUNG, Composer (1900–1956)

At the age of 6, Chicagoan Victor Young was performing in concerts; at age
10, he went to live with his grandfather in Poland. At age 17, he was performing
as a violin soloist with the Warsaw Philharmonic. On his return to the United
States in 1920, Young continued to perform in concerts. Two years later, he
became a movie theatre concertmaster, working in that capacity until 1929. He
then became an arranger for bandleader Ted FioRito (Chapter 4), and by 1931,
Young was the musical director for Brusnwick Records, where he remained
until 1935. On Broadway, he wrote very little. But in Hollywood, Victor Young
wrote for more than two hundred films.

Chronology

1928   *Sweet Sue, Just You.* Young/Will J. Harris. A hit then and now a standard.

1932   *Street of Dreams.* Young/Sam Lewis*.
       (I Don't Stand a) Ghost of a Chance. Young/Bing Crosby and Ned Washington.

1933   *A Hundred Years from Today.* Young/Ned Washington* and Joe Young*. Written
       for Lou Leslie's **Blackbirds** on Broadway, this song became a big hit for Ethel
       Waters.

1944   *Stella by Starlight.* Young/Washington. This classic evergreen was written for the
       film **The Uninvited**.

1947   *Golden Earrings.* Young/Ray Evans and Jay Livingston. Title song for the film
       starring Marlene Dietrich.

1949   *My Foolish Heart.* Young/Washington. Another great film title song.

1951   *When I Fall in Love.* Young/Edward Heyman*. Written for the motion picture
       One Minute to Zero. Nat King Cole's version of this song was one of his most
       beautiful recordings ever.

1956   *Around the World (In Eighty Days).* Young/Harold Adamson*. One of the most
       familiar film title songs.
       Written on the Wind. Young/Sammy Cahn*. Film title song.

Chapter 3 _____

Contemporaries: Songwriters of the 1960s to Today

It will quickly become evident that this short chapter excludes the majority of songwriters in the ongoing, evolving era of rhythm and blues, country, rock, new age, heavy metal, rap, techno, reggae, folk, and the ever growing variety of alternative genres. These extremely popular and highly successful styles of musical creation are not part of the Golden Age music being described in this volume and so shall be left to be covered in other books, by other authors.

Covered in this chapter are contemporaries whose songs are sung and performed by vocalists and musicians who favor the Golden Age style: Frank Sinatra, Tony Bennett, Ella Fitzgerald, Sarah Vaughn, often Barbra Streisand, and frequently Joe Williams. Songwriters of such major 1960s hits as: *Something, Watch What Happens, The Shadow of Your Smile, Didn't We?* and *You Are the Sunshine of My Life* are included because their big hits "fit" the style. Again, note that Carolyn Leigh, Cy Coleman, and Stephen Sondheim, who surely are defined as contemporaries, were covered in Chapter 2.

LEE ADAMS, Lyricist (1924–) and CHARLES STROUSE, Composer (1928–)

Adams, born in Mansfield, Ohio, studied journalism at Ohio State University. Strouse, a New Yorker, graduated from the Eastman School of Music and the University of Rochester. Before teaming up with Adams, Strouse played the piano in nightclubs and did some vocal arranging. From the late 1950s to the 1980s, Strouse was a Hollywood film composer.

Chronology

1960   *Kids, A Lot of Living to Do, Put On a Happy Face*. Strouse/Adams. From the Broadway musical, ***Bye Bye Birdie***.

1962   *Once Upon a Time*. Strouse/Adams. From ***All American***, also on Broadway.

1964   *This Is the Life*. Strouse/Adams. Heard on Broadway in the musical version of ***Golden Boy***.

1970   *Applause*. Strouse/Adams. The title song of the Broadway musical staring Lauren Bacall.

1971   *Those Were the Days*. Strouse/Adams. Theme from the hit TV series, *All in The Family*.

1977   ***Annie***. Scored by Strouse/Martin Charnin. The big hit of the Broadway season. Strouse/Charnin won a Tony award for best score; *Tomorrow* was the hit song.

RICHARD ADLER, Composer/Lyricist (1921–   ) and JERRY ROSS, Composer/Lyricist (1926–1955)

Adler was born in New York and graduated from the University of North Carolina. He served as a naval officer in World War II. The son of concert pianist Clarence Adler, Richard worked in theatrical public relations and wrote advertising jingles. He authored three scripts for non-hit musicals. Ross, also a native New Yorker, began his career as an actor and singer on the Jewish stage. His mentor was Frank Loesser*. His tragic death at age 29 was the end of a successful partnership. Adler tried to go it alone, but was not as fortunate as when he worked with Jerry Ross.

Chronology

1953   *Rags to Riches*. Adler and Ross (wm). An early Tony Bennett hit.

1954   *Hey There*. Adler and Ross (wm). A number 1 chart record for Rosemary Clooney. *Hey There* and *Hernando's Hideaway* were the two hits from the Adler and Ross hit Broadway musical, ***Pajama Game***, which had a two and a half year run on Broadway.

1955   *Whatever Lola Wants, Heart*, and *Shoeless Joe from Hannibal Mo*. Adler and Ross (wm). Three of the hit songs from the next Adler-Ross collaboration on Broadway, ***Damn Yankees***.

BURT BACHARACH, Composer (1928–   ) and HAL DAVID, Lyricist (1921–   )

Bacharach of Kansas City, Missouri, studied at McGill University in Canada and at the Mannes School of Music in New York. He was a private student of Darius Milhaud and later the piano accompanist for Marlene Dietrich, with whom he toured for some time. Hal David, the younger brother of lyicist Mack David*, was born in New York City and served for some time as president of ASCAP. Bacharach and David began their highly successful partnership in 1961. The vocalist most responsible for the introduction and fine performances of

Bacharach/David tunes is Dionne Warwick who, sometime after the breakup of the partnership, had a comeback singing their work.

Chronology

1950   *American Beauty Rose*. Arthur Altman/David and Redd Evans. In 1946 Evans wrote *Frim Fram Sauce* with Joe Ricardel (wm). *Let Me Off Uptown*, by Evans and Earl Bostic (wm), was a swing hit for the Gene Krupa band with Anita O'Day and Roy Eldridge.

1957   *Magic Moments*. Bacharach/David.

1959   *Broken Hearted Melody*. Sherman Edwards/David.

1961   *Walk on By*. Bacharach/David.

1962   *Make It Easy on Yourself*. Bacharach/David.

1964   *A House Is Not a Home* and *What's New Pussycat?* Bacharach/David. From the film **What's New Pussycat**?

1965   *The Look of Love*. Bacharach/David. From film, **Casino Royale**.

1966   *Alfie*. Bacharach/David. An unusual melody with all sorts of chord changes; it was a film title song done in the movie by the voice of Cher.
A Message to Michael. Bacharach/David.

1967   *I Say a Little Prayer*. Bacharach/David.

1968   *Promises, Promises*. Bacharach/David. Title song of their Broadway musical. *I'll Never Fall in Love Again*, and *What Do You Get When You Fall in Love?* were from the same show.
This Guy's in Love with You and *Do You Know the Way to San Jose?* Bacharach/David.

1969   *April Fools*. Bacharach/David. Film title song.
Butch Cassidy and the Sundance Kid. Songs by Bacharach/David. They won the Oscar for the film score and one for the song *Raindrops Keep Fallin' on My Head*.

1970   *One Less Bell to Answer* and *Close to You*. Bacharach/David.

1981   *Arthur's Theme*. Bacharach, Peter Allen, Christopher Cross, and Carol Bayer Sager (wm). Theme for a very funny Dudley Moore film.

1984   *That's What Friends Are For*. Bacharach/Sager. The pair won a NARAS award for that tune.
To All the Girls I've Loved Before. Albert Hammond/David.

LIONEL BART, Composer/Lyricist (1930–   )

Bart, whose real name is Lionel Beglieter, was born in London and began his working career as a silk screen printer. A short time later, in the 1950s, he wrote his first song, for rock-and-roll singer Tommy Steele. Bart wrote many hit songs in that genre as well as a number of tunes with pro–working class, political messages. In 1960, Bart wrote the words and music to a musical play that American critics despised and that audiences came to watch in droves— **Oliver**. The film version won six Oscars. Bart went on to further fame, but succumbed to several abusive addictions which put him into a nose dive for some years. He sobered and returned to the music world with some pop tunes and a couple of advertising jingles. He was able to regain some financial stability with revivals of *Oliver* and still composes.

Chronology

1960   *As Long as He Needs Me, Consider Yourself, Food, Glorious Food, I'd Do Anything*. Bart (wm). All hits from *Oliver*.

1963   *From Russia with Love*. Bart (wm). Film title song.

ALAN BERGMAN, Lyricist (1925–   ) and MARILYN BERGMAN, Lyricist (1929–   )

Marilyn Katz, a Brooklyn girl who attended the High School of Music and Art in New York and then graduated from NYU, was a pre-med student. When Peggy Lee recorded Katz' first song, the lyricist changed her name to Marilyn Keith and gave up medicine forever. She is currently serving as the president of ASCAP. Keith is married to her partner, Alan Bergman, who is also a New Yorker. He attended the Ethical Culture School and graduated from the University of North Carolina. Bergman received a masters degree in music from UCLA and became a TV director for CBS. The Bergman's lyrics have one award after another: three Oscars and many Emmys, Golden Globes, and other honors. Unlike many lyricists, Marilyn and Alan Bergman often write the lyrics before the music; they also write lyrics to music already composed.

Chronology

1957   *Yellow Bird*. Composer unknown/Bergman and Bergman. An old West Indian folk song.

1960   *Nice n' Easy*. Lew Spence/Bergman and Bergman. Album title song for Frank Sinatra*.

1968   *Windmills of Your Mind*. Michel Legrand (Chapter 3)/Bergman and Bergman. For the film *The Thomas Crown Affair*.

1969   *What Are You Doing the Rest of Your Life?* Legrand/Bergman and Bergman. An Oscar winner from film, *The Happy Ending*.

1971   *The Summer Knows*. Legrand/Bergman and Bergman. For the film *Summer of '42*.

1972   *Brian's Song*. Legrand/Bergman and Bergman. Title song of television special.

1973   *The Way We Were*. Marvin Hamlisch (Chapter 3)/Bergman and Bergman. The Oscar and Grammy winning title song of the Streisand/Redford film.

1976   *I Believe in Love*. Kenny Loggins/Bergman and Bergman. For the film, *A Star Is Born*.

1978   *You Don't Bring Me Flowers*. Neil Diamond/Bergman and Bergman.

JERRY BOCK, Composer (1928–   ), SHELDON HARNICK, Lyricist (1924–   ), and GEORGE DAVID WEISS, Lyricist (1921–   )

Bock, from New Haven, Connecticut, grew up in New York and went to the University of Wisconsin. Harnick is a Chicago native who attended Northwestern. Weiss, a New Yorker and son of a music store owner, went to Julliard. Weiss went on to become a violinist and big band sax/clarinet player. (For more on Weiss, see his collaborative work with Bennie Benjamin*.) Harnick's lyrics were heard in *New Faces* in 1952. Bock and Harnick wrote several shows together, including *Tenderloin* and *She Loves Me*, neither with big hits. They also wrote for the stage musicals, *The Apple Tree* and *The Rothschilds*.

Chronology

1956   *Mr. Wonderful.* Bock/Weiss. The title song of the Broadway musical in which *Too Close for Comfort* was another hit.

1959   *Till Tomorrow.* Bock/Harnick. From the musical *Fiorello*, which won the Pulitzer Prize and a few Tonys. Bock/Harnick had no big hits, although *Till Tomorrow* was pretty.

1963   *She Loves Me.* Bock/Harnick. Title song from the Broadway musical.
        That Sunday, That Summer. Joe Sherman/Weiss. Sherman, with his brother Noel, wrote *Ramblin' Rose* in 1962.

1964   *Fiddler on the Roof, To Life, Do You Love Me?, Sunrise, Sunset, Tradition, If I Were a Rich Man*, and *Matchmaker.* Bock/Harnick. The delightful contributions to *Fiddler on the Roof*. It set a new record for the longest running musical ever (since broken, now held by *Cats*). Based on the writings of Yiddish storyteller Sholem Aleichem, *Fiddler* won many Tony Awards including best direction (Jerome Robbins); best musical; Zero Mostel and Maria Karnilova for best acting; Bock and Harnick for best musical score; and best choreography (Robbins). *Fiddler* and its songs are classics of the theatre.

1968   *What a Wonderful World.* Weiss and George Douglas (wm). Recorded in England by Louis Armstrong, it was on the British hit parade for a year. It didn't become a hit in the United States until years later, when Robin Williams introduced it in the film, *Good Morning Vietnam.*

LESLIE BRICUSSE, Composer/Lyricist (1931–   ) and ANTHONY NEWLEY, Composer/Lyricist (1931–   )

Bricusse, born in London, attended Cambridge and worked at an acting school in order to get free lessons. Instead of performing, he made a fine career in librettos, screenplays, and composition. Newley, also a Brit, continues to sing, entertain, compose, and write lyrics. A star of several stage musicals and some films, Newley combined with Bricusse on ten hits.

Chronology

1961   *My Kind of Girl*. Bricusse (wm).

1962   *I'm Gonna Build a Mountain, Once in a Lifetime*, and *What Kind of Fool Am I?* Bricusse and Newley (wm). All heard in **Stop the World, I Want to Get Off**, their first Broadway show.

1964   *If I Ruled The World*. Cyril Ornadel/Bricusse. For **Oliver**.

1965   *Goldfinger*. John Barry/Bricusse. Film title song. Barry, with Don Black, wrote the Oscar-winning *Born Free* in 1966).
       Who Can I Turn To? and *On a Wonderful Day Like Today*, Bricusse and Newley (wm). Both hits in the sequel to **Stop the World**; this Broadway musical was cleverly titled, **The Roar of the Greasepaint (the Smell of the Crowd)**.

1967   *Talk to the Animals*. Bricusse (wm). Oscar winner from Hollywood's **Dr. Doolittle**.

1971   *The Candy Man*. Bricusse and Newley (wm). Sammy Davis, Jr., who had a number 1 chart record for *What Kind of Fool Am I?* in 1962 had another big hit with *Candy Man*.

1982   **Victor, Victoria**. Songs by Henry Mancini (Chapter 3)/Bricusse. The fine score for Blake Edwards film was an Oscar winner.

FRED EBB, Lyricist (1932–   ) and JOHN KANDER, Composer (1927–   )

Ebb is from New York; Kander is a native of Kansas City, Missouri. Kander was a student of piano at Oberlin and Columbia University. He was an accompanist before turning to compositions. Together, Ebb and Kander wrote some fine musicals.

Chronology

1962   *My Coloring Book*. Kander/Ebb. First hit for and recorded successfully by Barbra Streisand.

1965   *Flora, The Red Menace*. Kander/Ebb. The title song of a Broadway musical starring Liza Minelli.

1966   *Cabaret* and *Wilkommen*. Kander/Ebb. The hit songs from their show **Cabaret**, which won Tony and Drama Critics awards and was made into a film a half-dozen years later.

1972   *Maybe This Time*. Kander/Ebb. Added to the film version of **Cabaret**.

1975   *And All That Jazz*. Kander/Ebb. From **Chicago** (arguably one of the most underrated musicals ever on Broadway). In the 1996 revival of this dancing/singing stage musical, more accolades were heaped on the performances with special attention given to the great pit band conducted by Rob Fisher.
       How Lucky Can You Get? Kander/Ebb. From the film, **Funny Lady**.

1977   *New York, New York*. Kander/Ebb. The film title song introduced by Liza Minelli and taken on as one of Frank Sinatra's "themes."

NORMAN GIMBEL Lyricist (?–   )

Not unlike the reclusive novelist J. D. Salinger, the highly talented Gimbel declines to give biographical data. His privacy is herewith respected and his impressive credentials are noted below. In the history of Broadcast Music, Inc., Norman Gimbel is fourth on the list of most performed songwriters, led only by Lennon and McCartney, Barry Gibb, and Paul Simon. More than fourteen million of Gimbel's song titles have been performed.

Chronology

1953   *Ricochet.* Joe Darion, Larry Coleman, and Gimbel (wm). For *Man of La Mancha*, Darion and Mitch Leigh wrote *The Impossible Dream.*

1956   *Canadian Sunset.* Eddie Heywood/Gimbel.

1963   *I Will Follow Him.* J. W. Stole and Del Roma/Gimbel and Arthur Altman. A number 1 chart record performed more than a million times.
Bluesette. Jean Thielemans/Gimbel. ''Toots'' Thielemans played it; Mel Torme sang it.

1964   *Watch What Happens.* Michel Legrand (Chapter 3)/Gimbel. A contemporary example of excellence in the Golden Age style. Along with *I Will Wait for You*, it was heard in the film *Umbrellas of Cherbourg*. *I Will Wait* was nominated for an Oscar.
Meditation, The Girl from Ipanema, and *How Insensitive*. Antonio Jobim (Chapter 3)/Gimbel. *The Girl* was a Grammy winner as record of the year. It was credited with four million performances. *How Insensitive* was the third Jobim hit composition with Gimbel's lyrics—it was only performed two million times!

1966   *Summer Samba.* Marcos and Paulo Sergio Valle/Gimbel. Also known as *So Nice.*

1973   *Killing Me Softly With His Song.* Gimbel and Charles Fox (wm). A Gold Record number 1 chart record, Grammy winner.
Happy Days. Gimbel and Fox (wm). Theme music for the television comedy series.
I Got a Name. Fox/Gimbel. For the film *Last American Hero*; and sung by Jim Croce. A winner of the Young New York Film Critics Award for best film song.

1978   *Ready to Take a Chance Again.* Fox/Gimbel. For the film, *Foul Play*. An Oscar nominee that lost to Billy Joel's *Just the Way You Are.*

1979   *It Goes Like It Goes.* David Shire/Gimbel. Academy Award–winning song from the film *Norma Rae.*

MARVIN HAMLISCH, Composer (1944–   )

A highly popular composer/conductor today, Hamlisch is acclaimed by the music critics and sought after by the singers. Marvin Frederick Hamlisch was born in New York City and graduated from the prestigious Julliard School of Music. In 1965, at the age of 21, he had his first song published. He got started

as a rehearsal pianist and he went on to Broadway and Hollywood fame. He is
the composer of the theme music for ABC-TV's *Good Morning America.*

Chronology

1965   *Sunshine, Lollipops and Rainbows.* Hamlisch/Howard Liebling. Hamlisch's first
published song.

1973   *A Chorus Line.* Songs by Hamlisch/Edward Kleban. The two hit songs were
What I Did for Love and *One.*

1978   *Looking Through The Eyes of Love.* Hamlisch/Carol Bayer Sager (Chapter 3).
Heard in the film *Ice Castles.*
I Still Believe in Love. Hamlisch/Sager. From the Broadway revue, *They're
Playing Our Song.*

JERRY HERMAN, Composer/Lyricist (1933–   )

Herman is yet another New York-born Broadway musical composer. A graduate of the University of Miami, he majored in music. Herman wrote three off-
Broadway shows before hitting it big.

Chronology

1961   *Milk and Honey.* Herman (wm). Title song from the Broadway musical.

1963   *Hello Dolly.* Herman (wm). Title song of a major Broadway musical for which
Herman also wrote, *It Only Takes a Moment.*

1966   *Mame, If He Walked into My Life,* and *My Best Girl.* Herman (wm). Three hits
from the musical play, *Mame.*

1983   *The Best of Times.* Herman (wm). From Broadway's *La Cage Aux Folles.*

ANTONIO CARLOS JOBIM, Composer (1927–   )

Born in Rio de Janeiro, Jobim was the music director for Odeon Records,
where he convinced management to record the brilliant song, *Chega de Saudade*
by Joao Gilberto. Thus began the delightful musical form known as Bossa Nova.
A latin jazz style taken up by such great musicians as Stan Getz, Charlie Byrd,
and later Dizzy Gillespie (his was "Cubana"), it launched the careers of Jobim,
Joao and Astrid Gilberto, and others. Jobim, famed as a band leader, pianist,
and guitarist, composed many popular songs in that unique style.

Chronology

1959   *Desifinado (Slightly Out of Tune).* Jobim/Jon Hendricks and Jesse Cavanaugh.

1961   *One Note Samba.* Jobim/Hendricks.

1962   *Corcovado (Quiet Nights of Quiet Stars).* Jobim/Gene Lees.

1963   *Meditation.* Jobim/Norman Gimbel (Chapter 3). One of the most tender
performances of this fine standard was done on a television show by Claudine
Longet, accompanying herself on guitar.

1964   *The Girl from Ipanema* and *How Insensitive.* Jobim/Gimbel.

MICHEL LEGRAND Composer (1932–   )

Legrand, born in Paris, France, is the son of an orchestra leader. Michel Legrand became very much involved with jazz music after coming to the United States, where he worked with Miles Davis, John Coltrane, and other icons of the genre. In Hollywood, Legrand has accompanied Bing Crosby, Gene Kelly, and other major film stars.

Chronology

1968   *Windmills of Your Mind.* Legrand/Bergman and Bergman (Chapter 3). From the film, *The Thomas Crown Affair.*

1971   *The Summer Knows.* Legrand/Bergman and Bergman. From the film *Summer of '42.*

JOHN LENNON, Composer/Lyricist (1940–1980), PAUL MCCARTNEY, Composer/Lyricist (1942–   ) and GEORGE HARRISON, Composer/Lyricist (1943–   )

These three members of that sensational phenomenon called The Beatles composed romantic ballads and wrote beautiful lyrics of songs sung by the best of Golden Age performers—and by symphony orchestras and everyone else. Aside from their enormous influence on the culture of a generation, they were songwriters of the very first order. Only their drumming mate, Ringo Starr, is not included here; Harrison is included only because of one song. Fewer than two dozen hit songs are listed in the chronology. Most were written by Lennon and McCartney; all are an amazing collection of popular music. Many were winners of Grammy awards, and topped the charts. As for Harrison's one song, *Something*, if it isn't already a classic ballad, it will become one, having been recorded with great success by Lena Horne, Frank Sinatra, Tony Bennett, and Joe Williams . . . as well as The Beatles.

Chronology

1963   *All My Loving* and *I Want to Hold Your Hand.* Lennon and McCartney (wm).

1964   *And I Love Her, Do You Want to Know a Secret? Hard Day's Night, She Loves You*, and *She's a Woman.* Lennon and McCartney (wm).

1965   *Ticket to Ride, Yesterday*, and *With a Little Help from My Friends.* Lennon and McCartney (wm).

1966   *Eleanor Rigby, Michelle*, and *Yellow Submarine.* Lennon and McCartney (wm). The last was a film title song. Beatle films were highly creative and successful, delighting audiences and critics worldwide.

1967   *Fool on the Hill, Sgt. Pepper's Lonely Hearts Club Band*, and *All You Need Is Love.* Lennon and McCartney (wm).

1968   *Something*. Harrison (wm).
    Hey Jude and *Lucy in the Sky With Diamonds* Lennon and McCartney (wm).

1969   *Rocky Racoon*. Lennon and McCartney (wm).

1970   *Long and Winding Road*. Lennon and McCartney (wm). From the film **Let It Be**.

1971   *Imagine*. Lennon (wm).

HENRY MANCINI, Composer (1924–1995)

A frequent winner of Oscars, Grammys, and other musical honors, Mancini, who was born in Cleveland, Ohio, began his career as a big band pianist. He played with the Glenn Miller orchestra when Tex Beneke took over. Mancini served in the air corps in World War II and went on to fame in Hollywood, composing, conducting, and arranging for movies and television.

Chronology

1960   *Mr. Lucky*. Mancini/Jay Livingston and Ray Evans*. Composed for the television series of the same name.

1961   *Moon River*. Mancini/Johnny Mercer*. A NARAS award–winning ballad composed for the film **Breakfast at Tiffany's**. It also won the Oscar.

1962   *Days of Wine and Roses*. Mancini/Mercer. The film title song that made the duo back-to-back Oscar winners.

1963   *Charade*. Mancini/Mercer. Another film title song.
    The Pink Panther. Mancini/Mercer. Film title song.

1964   *Dear Heart*. Mancini/Evans and Livingston. Still another movie title song.

1965   *In the Arms of Love*. Mancini/Livingston-Evans. From the film **What Did You Do in The War, Daddy?**

1967   *Two for the Road*. Mancini (music). Instrumental film soundtrack score.

1982   **Victor, Victoria**. Songs by Mancini/Leslie Bricusse (Chapter 3). The score won Mancini his third Oscar.

JOHNNY MANDEL, Composer (1925–   )

John Alfred Mandel is a New York-born composer, arranger, and conductor whose work in Hollywood and with musical superstars such as Count Basie and Frank Sinatra* is legendary. Mandel attended the Manhattan School of Music and Julliard. He began his career as a trumpet player and accompanist to the eminent jazz violinist, Joe Venuti. Mandel was an important sideman with Buddy Rich and Jimmy Dorsey. He arranged and composed for television shows including *M*A*S*H*, for which he wrote the title soundtrack. Mandel's work covers a forty-year Hollywood career.

Chronology

1964   *Emily*. Mandel/Johnny Mercer*. Screenplay by Paddy Chayefsky. A lovely ballad from a wonderful film called **The Americanization of Emily**.

1965   *The Shadow of Your Smile*. Mandel/Paul Francis Webster*. An Oscar-winning evergreen written for the film *The Sandpiper*, which showcased memorable love scenes courtesy of Elizabeth Taylor and Steve McQueen.

A Time for Love. Mandel/Webster. A splendid ballad that was recorded by Tony Bennett and remains one of Bennett's best.

BOB MERRILL, Composer/Lyricist (1921–1998)

The versatile Merrill was born in Atlantic City, New Jersey, and grew up in Philadelphia. Merrill knocked around for years—as a truck loader, cotton picker, movie usher, actor, and entertainer in nightclubs. After service in World War II, he worked in Hollywood for five years as a dialogue director at Columbia Pictures. He was a CBS casting director in the mid-1940s and finally, in the 1950s, found himself as a songwriter. In 1956, Merrill was a television production consultant for tobacco giant Liggett and Meyers when MGM gave him a five-year contract as producer/composer/writer/publisher. Then, on Broadway, Merrill found his real love.

Chronology

1950 *If I Knew You Were Coming I'd Have Baked a Cake*. Merrill, Clem Watts, and Al Hoffman* (wm).

1953 (*How Much Is That*) *Doggie in the Window*? Merrill (wm). A number 1 chart record for Patti Page.

1954 *Make Yourself Comfortable*. Merrill (wm). A hit for Sarah Vaughn.
       Mambo Italiano. Merrill (wm). A hit for Rosemary Clooney.

1964 *Don't Rain on My Parade, People*, and *You Are Woman*. Merrill and Jule Styne* (wm). Styne/Merrill smash hit on Broadway, *Funny Girl*.

JOE RAPOSO, Composer/Lyricist (1937–1989)

From a musical family, the brilliant Raposo was Harvard educated and con- tributed to several of that university's Hasty Pudding shows. He studied classical music in Paris with Nadia Boulanger (the same woman who gave a few lessons to George Gershwin*, Leonard Bernstein, and others). On Broadway, Raposo became a musical director and conductor for a show on which he collaborated, *You're A Good Man, Charlie Brown*. In the early 1970s he created songs and directed music for the award-winning *Sesame Street* on public television. A winner of five Grammys and many gold records, he was the composer of tele- vision theme music and commercials.

Raposo became a resident composer at his alma mater, and was honored by the National Academy of television Arts and Sciences. As composer of the score to *Raggedy Ann*, which was greeted by enthusiastic audiences around the world, Raposo gained international fame. He collaborated with Sheldon Harnick on the musical version of Frank Capra's *It's A Wonderful Life* on Broadway. The late CBS commentator Charles Kuralt said, "Joe Raposo taught American kids how to sing!"

Chronology

1971   *(It's Not Easy) Bein' Green*. Raposo (wm).

1972   *Sing*. Raposo (wm).

1973   *Here's to the Winners* and *You Will Be My Music* Raposo (wm). Both included in Sinatra's fine "back from retirement again" album, Old Blue Eyes is Back.

CAROL BAYER SAGER, Lyricist (1947–   )

Sager was born in New York and began her musical career as a singer. She was the youngest lyricist ever to write a Broadway musical (a five-performance flop named **Georgy**). Sager has written with the best of contemporary composers, including her ex-husband, Burt Bacharach (Chapter 3).

Chronology

1976   *Come in from the Rain*. Melissa Manchester/Sager.

1978   *Looking Through the Eyes of Love*. Hamlisch/Sager. For the film, **Ice Castles**. *I Still Believe in Love*. Hamlisch/Sager. Music for the Broadway revue, **They're Playing Our Song**.

1981   *Arthur's Theme*. Sager, Peter Allen, Christopher Cross, and Bacharach. An Oscar winner and number 1 chart record.

1983   *That's What Friends Are For*. Bacharach/Sager. For the film **The Bodyguard**, starring Whitney Houston and a number 1 chart record.

JACK SEGAL, Lyricist (1918–   )

Segal, born in Minneapolis, graduated from the University of Wisconsin, where he studied political science. In New York, he studied creative writing at the New School.

Chronology

1949   *Scarlet Ribbons*. Evelyn Danzig/Segal.

1956   *When Sunny Gets Blue*. Marvin Fisher/Segal.

1963   *When Joanna Loved Me*. Wells/Segal. Tony Bennett made an extraordinary recording.

PAUL SIMON, Composer/Lyricist (1941–   )

Paul Simon and Art Garfunkel were the superstar troubadours of the 1960s. The Simon compositions and lyrics and the performances of both these modern folk singers are examples of musical excellence in an era that produced considerable music and lyrics far below such a rating. Simon, born in Newark, New Jersey, was an English literature major at Queens College in New York City. While there he met Art Garfunkel (b. 1941 in Queens) and so their careers began. Simon continues to compose and write. Garfunkel has had a formidable career as an actor in films as well as a performer with Paul Simon.

Chronology

1965   *The Sounds of Silence*. Simon (wm).

1966   *Scarborough Fair*. Simon and Garfunkel (wm). *Mrs. Robinson* Simon (wm). Both from the film **The Graduate**. *Robinson* was another number one chart record.

1970   *Bridge Over Troubled Waters*. Simon (wm). Yet another number 1 chart record.

JIMMY WEBB, Composer/Lyricist (1946–   )

Webb, born in Elk City, Oklahoma, was a millionaire by the time he was 21, having written several very successful advertising jingles. One (see 1967) became a hit song after it was used by TWA!

Chronology

1967   *By the Time I Get to Phoenix* and *My Beautiful Balloon*. Webb (wm). The latter was also known as *Up, Up and Away* and used by TWA.

1968   *McArthur Park*. Webb (wm). A number 1 chart record.

1969   *Didn't We?* Webb (wm). A marvelous ballad worthy of having been written by a giant of the Golden Age.

SIR ANDREW LLOYD WEBBER, Composer/Lyricist (1948–   )

While often criticized by the media for his sound-alike work, Lloyd Webber nonetheless continues gaining international acclaim by the packed houses where his musical shows play. London born, his father was the director of the London School of Music and his mother taught piano.

Chronology

1971   *Jesus Christ, Superstar*. Lloyd Webber (wm). Title song of his first stage hit.

1979   *Don't Cry for Me, Argentina*. Lloyd Webber/Tim Rice.

1982   *Memory*. Lloyd Webber/T. S. Eliot. From the record-setting Broadway musical, **Cats**—the longest running musical play of all time.

1988   *All I Ask of You*. Lloyd Webber (wm). From **Phantom of the Opera**.

1995   *With One Look*. Lloyd Webber (wm). From Broadway's **Sunset Boulevard**.

BOB WELLS, Composer/Lyricist (1922–   )

Wells, who was born Robert Levinson in Raymond, Washington, began his career in music as a jazz drummer. Wells currently works in Hollywood as a writer of special film material.

Chronology

1946   *Christmas Song (Chestnuts Roasting by an Open Fire)*. Mel Tormé and Wells (wm).

1947   *Born to Be Blue*. Tormé and Wells (wm).

1953   *From Here to Eternity*. Fred Karger/Wells. Promotional song for film of the same name.

1963   *When Joanna Loved Me*. Wells/Jack Segal (Chapter 3).

MEREDITH WILLSON, Composer/Lyricist (1902–1984)

Robert Meredith Reiniger, who later changed his name to Meredith Willson, was born in Mason City, Iowa, and was educated at the Damrosch Institute of Musical Art in New York. By the age of 19 he was a flute/piccolo player with the John Philip Sousa concert band. He played in the New York Philharmonic under Toscannini for five years and earned a Ph.D. in musical studies. Willson became a composer/lyricist and a librettist in Hollywood and on Broadway. He also wrote for radio shows. He scored the film classic **The Great Dictator**, and the great Broadway drama, **The Little Foxes**. His greatest theatrical achievement came when he was already in his mid-fifties—**The Music Man**. Willson and his wife, Rini, performed the album score for that show, which ran for more than 1,300 performances. His later critical success was **Molly Brown**.

Chronology

1941   *You and I*. Willson (wm). A lovely ballad which was the theme of a Maxwell House coffee–sponsored radio show.

1957   *Seventy-Six Trombones, 'Til There Was You*, and *Trouble in River City*. Willson (wm). Three hits from **The Music Man**.

1960   *I Ain't Down Yet*. Willson (wm). The hit song from **The Unsinkable Molly Brown**—words, music, and libretto by Meredith Willson.

STEVIE WONDER, Composer/Lyricist (1950–   )

Blind at birth, Steveland Judkins Hardaway (some sources have Wonder's real last name as Morris), is from Saginaw, Michigan. By the age of 10 he was already a protégé of Berry Gordy; at 12 he was performing as a singer. Still primarily a rock and rhythm/blues vocalist, Wonder—who plays several instruments, too—had almost one hundred hit songs to his credit as a writer/composer by the time he was 30. He continued to write and perform worldwide.

Chronology

1969   *My Cherie Amour*. Wonder (wm).

1972   *You Are the Sunshine of My Life*. Wonder (wm).

1973   *All in Love Is Fair*. Wonder (wm).

1976   *Isn't She Lovely?* Wonder (wm).

1984   *I Just Called to Say I Love You*. Wonder (wm).

Chapter 4

Significant Collaborators and Writers of Hit Songs

This chapter covers more than 140 songwriters who wrote fewer than five hits or collaborated on hit songs by writers included in previous chapters. Birth and death dates, as well as biographical data, are omitted, here since the songs are my focus.

There are several exceptions, however, which may be noted in Chapter 2, where we included one-hit writers such as Bing Crosby and Frank Sinatra, who contributed so much to the world of popular song; Brooks Bowman (*East of the Sun*); Erroll Garner (*Misty*); Herman Hupfeld (*As Time Goes By*); collaborators Harry Link, Holt Marvell, and Jack Strachey (*These Foolish Things*); and David Raksin (*Laura*).

STANLEY ADAMS, Lyricist

1934   *My Shawl*. Xavier Cugat/Adams. Cugat used it as his orchestra's theme song.
     What a Diff'rence a Day Made. Maria Grever/Adams. Originally titled, *Cuande vuelva a tu lado (When I Come Back to You)*. Grever was also the composer of *Magic Is the Moonlight* (1930), with lyrics by Charles Pasquale.

1936   *Little Old Lady Passing By*. Hoagy Carmichael*/Adams. For Broadway's *The Show Is On*.

1942   *There Are Such Things*. Adams, George Meyer, and Abel Baer (Chapter 1) (wm). A song that fit Frank Sinatra* like a glove.

MILTON AGER, Composer

Chronology

1918   *Everything Is Peaches Down in Georgia.* Ager and George Meyer (Chapter 1)/ Grant Clarke (Chapter 4).

1921   *I'm Nobody's Baby.* Ager/Benny Davis*.

1924   *I Wonder What's Become of Sally.* Ager/Jack Yellen*.

1927   *Ain't She Sweet?* and *Happy Days Are Here Again.* Ager/Yellen.

EDEN AHBEZ, Composer/Lyricist

1948   *Nature Boy.* Ahbez (wm). A number 1 chart record for Nat King Cole.

ED ANDERSON, Lyricist and TED GROUYA, Composer

1941   *Flamingo.* Anderson/Grouya.

1943   *I Heard You Cried Last Night.* Grouya/Jerrie Kruger.

LEWIS ALLAN, Composer/Lyricist and EARL ROBINSON, Composer/Lyricist

1939   *Strange Fruit.* Allan (wm). This song, a disturbing protest against the lynching of black people, was originally a poem (''Bitter Fruit'') that Allan brought to Billie Holiday's attention. While credited to Allan, it was actually a collaboration of Allan, Holiday, and her piano-playing accompanist, Sonny White.

1942   *The House I Live In (That's America to Me).* Allan and Robinson (wm). Sung and recorded by Frank Sinatra* for a short film.

LEROY ANDERSON, Composer

1950   *Sleigh Ride.* Anderson/Mitchell Parish*.

1951   *Blue Tango.* Anderson/Parish.

FABIAN ANDRE, Composer

1931   *Dream a Little Dream of Me.* Andre and Wilbur Schwandt/Gus Kahn*.

GUS ARNHEIM, Composer/Lyricist

1923   *I Cried For You.* Arnheim, Abe Lyman, and Arthur Freed* (wm).

1931   *Sweet and Lovely.* Arnheim and Jules Lemare/Harry Tobias*. Arnheim band's theme.

SIDNEY ARODIN, Composer/Lyricist

1931   *Lazy River.* Arodin and Hoagy Carmichael* (wm).

GENE AUSTIN, Lyricist

1924   *When My Sugar Walks Down the Street.* Austin, James McHugh*, and Irving Mills*.

1929   *Lonesome Road.* Nathaniel Shilkret/Austin. From film, **Show Boat**.

ABEL BAER, Composer

1924   *Just Give Me a June Night, the Moonlight and You (June Night).* Baer/Cliff Friend*.

1942   *There Are Such Things.* Baer, Stanley Adams (Chapter 4), and George Meyer (Chapter 1).

JACK BAKER, Composer/Lyricist; GEORGE FRAGOS, Composer/Lyricist; and DICK GASPARE, Composer/Lyricist

1940   *I Hear a Rhapsody.* Baker, Fragos, and Gaspare (wm). A number 1 chart record.

PAT BALLARD, Composer/Lyricist

1954   *Mr. Sandman.* Ballard (wm). A number 1 chart record.

DAVE BARBOUR, Composer

1946   *I Don't Know Enough About You.* Barbour and Peggy Lee (wm). (Chapter 2)

1947   *It's a Good Day.* Barbour and Lee (wm).

1948   *Manana.* Barbour/Lee (wm). Their biggest hit of all.

GEORGE BASSMAN, Composer

1932   *I'm Getting Sentimental Over You.* Bassman/Ned Washington*.

NORA BAYES, Composer/Lyricist and JACK NORWORTH, Composer/Lyricist

1908   *Shine on Harvest Moon* Bayes and Norworth (wm).
       Take Me Out to The Ball Game. Albert VonTilzer (Chapter 1)/Norworth.

GILBERT BECAUD, Composer

1962   *What Now My Love.* Becaud/Carl Sigman*.

CLAY BOLAND, Composer and MOE JAFFE, Composer/ Lyricist

1937   *Gypsy in My Soul.* Boland/Jaffe. From Mask & Wig revue, **Fifty Fifty**.

1944   *If You Are But a Dream.* Jaffe, Nat Bonx, and Jack Fulton (wm). Adapted from Anton Rubinstein's *Romance. Bell Bottom Trousers.* Jaffe (wm).

PHIL BOUTELJE, Composer and DICK WINFREE, Composer/ Lyricist

1929   *China Boy*. Boutelje and Winfree (wm). Jazz classic first recorded by Paul Whiteman; great versions by Red Nichols and Benny Goodman.

JACQUES BREL, Composer and ROD MCKUEN, Lyricist

1966   *If You Go Away*. Brel/McKuen.

1968   *If We Only Have Love*. Brel/Mort Shuman and Eric Blau (English lyrics). From ***Jacques Brel Is Alive and Well***.

SONNY BURKE, Composer

1947   *Midnight Sun*. Burke/Johnny Mercer*.

1948   *Black Coffee*. Burke/Paul Francis Webster*.

RALPH BURNS, Composer

1944   *Bijou*. Burns (music). Instrumental hit by Woody Herman, for whom Burns did much arranging.

1948   *Early Autumn*. Burns/Johnny Mercer*. Woody Herman recorded a superb rendition.

VAL BURTON, Composer/Lyricist and WILL JASON, Composer/Lyricist

1931   *When We're Alone*. Burton and Jason (wm). Also known as *Penthouse Serenade*. Sung by Bob Hope in the film ***Beau James***.

MICHAEL CARR, Composer/Lyricist

1935   *Dinner for One, Please James*. Carr (wm).

1936   *Did Your Mother Come from Ireland?* Carr and Jimmy Kennedy (wm).

1939   *South of the Border*. Carr and Kennedy (wm).

JAMES CAVANAUGH, Lyricist

1927   *Mississippi Mud*. Harry Barris/Cavanaugh. Delta Rhythm boy Barris* was also the composer of *Wrap Your Troubles in Dreams (and Dream Your Troubles Away)* with Ted Koehler and *I Surrender Dear* with Gordon Clifford, both in 1931.

1933   *I Like Mountain Music*. Frank Weldon/Cavanaugh.

1940   *The Gaucho Serenade*. Cavanaugh and John Redmond (wm). Redmond was co-lyricist with Henry Nemo on Duke Ellington's *I Let a Song Go Out of My Heart*.

1944   *You're Nobody Till Somebody Loves You*. Cavanaugh, Russ Morgan, and Larry

Stock (wm). Morgan wrote *Somebody Else Is Taking My Place* in 1937 with Dick Howard and Bob Ellsworth; Stock wrote *Blueberry Hill* in 1940 and *You Won't Be Satisfied Unless You Break My Heart* in 1945.

HUGHIE CHARLES, Composer/Lyricist and ROSS PARKER, Composer/Lyricist

1939 *We'll Meet Again.* Charles and Parker (wm).
      There'll Always be an England. Charles and Parker (wm).

FRANK CHURCHILL, Composer and LARRY MOREY, Lyricist

1937 *I'm Wishing, Someday My Prince Will Come, Heigh Ho, Whistle While You Work,* and *With a Smile and a Song.* Churchill/Morey. All for the classic animated film, **Snow White and The Seven Dwarfs**.

SIDNEY CLARE, Lyricist

1921 *Ma! He's Making Eyes at Me.* Con Conrad*/Clare. For an Eddie Cantor Broadway revue, **Midnight Rounders**.

1925 *I Wanna' Go Where You Go (Do What You Do).* Cliff Friend* and Lew Brown*/Clare.

1926 *I'd Climb the Highest Mountain.* Lew Brown/Clare.

1930 *Please Don't Talk About Me When I'm Gone.* Sam Stept*/Clare.

1934 *On the Good Ship, Lollipop.* Richard Whiting* and Clare (wm). For the Shirley Temple film **Bright Eyes**.

GRANT CLARKE, Lyricist

1910 *Dat's Harmony.* Clarke (wm). Clarke's first published song.

1918 *Everything Is Peaches Down in Georgia.* Milton Ager (Chapter 4) and George W. Meyer (Chapter 1)/Clarke. His first hit.

1921 *Second Hand Rose.* James Hanley/Clarke and Ballard MacDonald*. For Fanny Brice in the **Ziegfeld Follies**. Barbra Streisand brought the house down with it many years later.

1929 *Am I Blue?* Harry Akst*/Clarke. From the film, **On With the Show**.

REG CONNELLY, Composer/Lyricist and JIMMY CAMPBELL, Composer/Lyricist

1925 *Show Me the Way to Go Home.* Connelly and Campbell (wm). An adaptation of an old Canadian folk song which became a two million sheet music sales success, giving Reg and Jimmy sufficient capital to enter the music publishing business.

1929 *If I Had You.* Campbell, Connelly, and Ted Shapiro (wm).

1931 *Goodnight Sweetheart.* Campbell, Connelly, Ray Noble and Rudy Vallee (wm).

1932   *By the Fireside.* Campbell, Connelly, and Noble (wm).
       Try a Little Tenderness. Campbell, Connelly, and Harry McGregor Woods* (wm).
       Two).

1933   *Just an Echo in the Valley.* Woods, Campbell, and Connelly (wm). For the film
       Going Hollywood, with Bing Crosby.

GEORGE CORY, Composer and DOUGLAS CROSS, Lyricist

1947   *Deep Song.* Cory/Cross. A fine version was recorded by Billie Holiday.

1954   *I Left My Heart in San Francisco.* Cory/Cross. Recorded eight years later by
       Tony Bennett, it won a Grammy and became his most requested song.

FRANCIS CRAIG, Composer and KERMIT GOELL, Lyricist

1947   *Near You.* Craig/Goell. A number 1 chart record.
       Beg Your Pardon. Craig/Beasley Smith.

DOC DAUGHERTY, Composer and ELLIS REYNOLDS, Composer

1930   *I'm Confessin.* Daugherty and Reynolds/Al Neiburg. Neiburg also wrote the
       words to *It's the Talk of the Town* and *Under a Blanket of Blue* with Jerry
       Livingston*.

MILTON DRAKE, Composer/Lyricist

1934   *Champagne Waltz.* wm Drake, Con Conrad*, and Ben Oakland (wm).

1940   *Java Jive.* Oakland/Drake.

1943   *Mairzy Doats.* Jerry Livingston*/Drake and Al Hoffman*. The title was
       supposedly suggested by Drake's nine-year-old daughter.

1952   *Nina Never Knew.* Louis Alter*/Drake. Arguably Drake's best song.

ED DURHAM, Composer/Lyricist

1938   *Every Tub.* Durham and Basie (instr.).

1939   *John's Idea.* Durham and Basie (instr.).
       Sent for You Yesterday. Durham and Basie (instr.).

1941   *Wham, Be-bop, Boom Bam.* Durham (wm). Perhaps the earliest use of the phrase,
       "be-bop."
       Goin' to Chicago Blues. Durham, Basie, and Jimmy Rushing (wm).

RAYMOND EGAN, Lyricist

1918   *Till We Meet Again*. Richard Whiting*/Egan. Famous World War I ballad.

1920   *I Never Knew I Could Love Anybody (Baby Like I'm Loving You)*. Egan, Tom Pitts, and Roy Marsh (wm).

1921   *Ain't We Got Fun?* Whiting/Egan.

1925   *Sleepy Time Gal*. Ange Lorenzo and Joseph R. Alden/Egan.

EDWARD ELISCU, Lyricist

1929   *Great Day, More Than You Know*, and *Without a Song*. Vincent Youmans*/Eliscu and Billy Rose*. All three from the Broadway musical, **Great Day**.

1933   *The Carioca*. Youmans/Gus Kahn* and Eliscu. Nominated for an Oscar and *Flying Down to Rio*, title song, both from the film, **Flying Down, etc**.

TED FIORITO, Composer

1922   *Toot, Toot, Tootsie Goodbye*. FioRito, Gus Kahn*, and Ernie Erdman (wm). For Al Jolson's stage musical, **Bombo**. Erdman (1879–1946), who was born in Pittsburgh, also wrote *Jean*. Dan Russo has been given credit for *Tootsie* in some musical encyclopediae.

1928   *Laugh, Clown, Laugh*. FioRito/Sam Lewis* and Joe Young*.

CARL FISCHER, Composer and BILL CAREY, Lyricist

1942   *It Started All Over Again, Who Wouldn't Love You*, and *You've Changed*. Fischer/Carey.

1943   *How Cute Can You Be?* and *Could I?* Fischer/Carey. Both written for Frank Sinatra.

1945   *We'll Be Together Again*. Fischer and Frankie Laine (wm).

CLARENCE GASKILL, Composer

1926   *I Can't Believe That You're in Love with Me*. Gaskill/Jimmy McHugh*.

1931   *Prisoner of Love*. Gaskill/Leo Robin* and Ross Columbo.
       Minnie the Moocher. Gaskill, Cab Calloway*, and Irving Mills* (wm).

CARROLL GIBBONS, Composer and JAMES DYRENFORTH, Lyricist

1929   *It's Just a Garden in the Rain*. Gibbons/Dyrenforth.

L. WOLFE GILBERT, Lyricist

1913   *Waiting for the Robert E. Lee*. Lewis Muir/Gilbert. Muir (1884–1950) was a brothel entertainer and songwriter who collaborated on *Ragtime Cowboy Joe* with Maurice Abrahams. Abrahams (1883–1933) was a composer, professional music manager, and publisher.

1927   *Ramona*. Mabel Wayne*/Gilbert. Movie title song.

1931 *Mama Don't Want No Peas an' Rice an' Cocanut Oil*. Gilbert and Charles Lofthouse (wm).

1932 *The Peanut Vendor*. Moises Simons/Gilbert and Marion Sunshine (English lyrics). Simons, Cuban, composed the music. Sunshine (1897–19?) was a Louisville lady who acted and had many lyrics to her credit. *Peanut Vendor* was used in the film, **Cuban Love Song**. (*Marta* was Simons original song title).

DIZZY GILLESPIE, Composer

1944 *Bebop*. Gillespie (instr.).
       A Night in Tunisia. Gillespie and Frank Paparelli (instr.).

1945 *Groovin' High*. Gillespie (instr.).
       Salt Peanuts. Gillespie and Kenny Clarke (instr.).

1946 *Oop Bop Sh-Bam*. Gillespie, Walter Fuller, and Jay Roberts (instr.).

1948 *Manteca*. Gillespie and Fuller (instr.).

IRVING GORDON, Composer/Lyricist

1938 *Prelude to a Kiss*. Duke Ellington*/Gordon.

1951 *Unforgettable*. Gordon (wm). A tremendous hit for Nat King Cole. Cole's daughter Natalie recorded it in an album which had her father's voice "dubbed" with hers, in 1991. *Unforgettable* won the Grammy that year for best song.

ARTHUR HAMMERSTEIN, Composer/Lyricist and DUDLEY WILKINSON, Composer/Lyricist

1940 *Because of You*. Hammerstein and Wilkinson (wm). A number 1 chart record by Tony Bennett. Hammerstein was Oscar Hammerstein's* uncle.

JAMES F. HANLEY, Composer/Lyricist

1917 *Back Home Again in Indiana*. Hanley/Ballard MacDonald*.

1918 *Rose of Washington Square*. Hanley/MacDonald.

1934 *Zing, Went the Strings of My Heart*. Hanley (wm). For the musical, **Thumbs Up**.

BOB HAYMES, Composer and ALAN BRANDT, Lyricist

1952 *That's All*. Haymes/Brandt. Bob Haymes was singer Dick Haymes' brother. He sang and enjoyed a fine career in broadcasting.

WALTER HIRSCH, Lyricist and FRED ROSE, Composer

1926 *Deed I Do*. Rose/Hirsch.

1938 *Lullaby in Rhythm*. Benny Goodman*/Hirsch.

BART HOWARD, Composer/Lyricist

1954   *Fly Me to the Moon.* Howard (wm).

1958   *Don't Dream of Anybody But Me.* Neal Hefti/Howard. Hefti's original composition had the title, *L'il Darlin'*, and was a great instrumental piece by Count Basie*. Howard added the lyrics and thus the title change.

BUDDY JOHNSON, Composer/Lyricist

1948   *Since I Fell for You.* Johnson (wm).

BERT KAEMPFERT, Composer; CHARLES SINGLETON, Lyricist; and EDDY SNYDER, Lyricist

1965   *Spanish Eyes.* Kaempfert/Singleton and Snyder.

1966   *Strangers in the Night.* Kaempfert/Singleton and Snyder.

JOSEPH M. LACALLE, Composer and ALBERT GAMSE, Lyricist

1924   *Amapola (My Pretty Little Poppy).* LaCalle/Gamse. Sixteen years after the song was published, Jimmy Dorsey's Orchestra and his highly popular vocalists, Bob Eberly and Helen O'Connell, took this song to number 1 on the charts.

JOHN LATOUCHE, Lyricist and EARL ROBINSON, Composer

1940   *Ballad for Uncle Sam.* Robinson/LaTouche. Title changed to *Ballad for Americans*.
       Taking a Chance on Love. Vernon Duke*/LaTouche and Ted Fetter.

1941   *Day Dream.* Duke Ellington* and Strayhorn/LaTouche.

1942   *The House I Live In.* Robinson/Lewis Allen. The award-winning title song and film.

1954   *Lazy Afternoon.* Jerome Morross/LaTouche.

JERRY LEIBER, Composer/Lyricist and MIKE STOLLER, Composer/Lyricist

1956   *Hound Dog.* Leiber and Stoller (wm). Went to number 1 for Elvis Presley.

1963   *I'm a Woman.* Leiber and Stoller (wm). A hit for Peggy Lee.

1969   *Is That All There Is?* Leiber and Stoller (wm).

MORGAN LEWIS, Composer and NANCY HAMILTON, Lyricist

1940   *How High the Moon.* Lewis/Hamilton. For their Broadway musical, ***One for the Money***. (Their next show was ***Two For the Show***). The late, great William B. Williams called this song the "national anthem of jazz."

1946   *The Old Soft Shoe*. Lewis/Hamilton. Written for their third show, ***Three to Make Ready***.

SID LIPPMAN, Composer and SYLVIA DEE, Lyricist

1945   *Chickery Chick*. Lippman/Dee. Popular with kids, this nonsensically titled tune was a hit for Gene Krupa's band and vocalist Anita O'Day.

1946   *My Sugar Is So Refined*. Lippman/Dee. Popularized thanks to Johnny Mercer*'s recording.

1948   *"A"—You're Adorable*. Lippman/Buddy Kaye and Fred Wise. Kaye (1918–   ) was a sax/clarinet player who became a film score writer in Hollywood and an adapter of classical music, including *Full Moon and Empty Arms*, from Rachmaninoff in 1946 and *Till the End of Time*, from Chopin in 1945. Wise, who was born in New York in 1915, also wrote *Miserlou* and *Wise Old Owl*.

1951   *Too Young*. Lippman/Dee. A big hit for Nat King Cole.

FUD LIVINGSTON, Composer

1931   *I'm Through with Love*. Livingston and Matty Malneck/Gus Kahn*.
        Any Old Time. Livingston. The exact date and other collaborators are unknown.

RUTH LOWE, Composer/Lyricist

1939   *I'll Never Smile Again*. Lowe (wm). Tommy Dorsey and his new vocalist, Frank Sinatra*, had a number 1 chart record with this all-time favorite. Lowe, a Canadian, came to the United States as a pianist with Ina Ray Hutton's "All Girl" orchestra. *I'll Never Smile* was supposedly a sad lament to Lowe's personal lost love.

1942   *Put Your Dreams Away (For Another Day)*. Stephen A. Weiss and Paul Mann/ Ruth Lowe. It became Sinatra's theme song. Weiss, born in Austria in 1899, was a European composer who later co-wrote (with Bernie Baum) the Theresa Brewer hit, *Music, Music, Music* (also known as *Put Another Nickel In*, 1950).

JOE MCCOY, Composer/Lyricist

Chronology

1942   *Why Don't You Do Right?* McCoy (wm).

SOL MARCUS, Composer and EDDIE SEILER, Lyricist

1941   *I Don't Want to Set the World on Fire*. Seiler, Marcus, and Bennie Benjamin* (wm).

1942   *When the Lights Go On Again All Over the World*. Seiler, Marcus, and Benjamin (wm).
        Strictly Instrumental. Seiler, Marcus, Benjamin, and Edgar Battle (wm).

1946   *Till Then*. Seiler and Marcus/Guy Wood. (above). A big Ink Spots hit (as was *World on Fire*).

GERALD MARKS, Composer and SEYMOUR SIMONS, Composer/Lyricist

1926   *Breezin' Along with the Breeze*. Richard Whiting*/Haven Gillespie* and Simons.

1931   *All of Me*. Marks/Simons. A great standard.

1936   *Is It True What They Say About Dixie?* Marks, Sammy Lerner, and Irving Caesar* (wm). In David Jasen's fine book, *Tin Pan Alley*, he writes that the songwriters "threw" this song together because the demanding Al Jolson wanted another "Dixie" song in his repertoire.

BILLY MAYHEW, Composer/Lyricist

1936   *It's a Sin to Tell a Lie*. Mayhew (wm). A number 1 chart record for Fats Waller.

ROBERT MELLIN, Composer and GUY WOOD, Lyricist

1946   *Till Then*. Marcus (Chapter 4) and Seiler/Wood.
       Shoo Fly Pie and Apple Pan Dowdy. Wood and Sammy Gallop (lyrics). An old folk tune to which Wood and Gallop wrote words.

1952   *I'm Yours*. Mellin/Guy Wood. A big Eddie Fisher number.

1953   *My One and Only Love*. Mellin/Wood.
       You, You, You. Lotar Olias/Mellin (English lyrics).

NILO MENENDEZ, Composer and E. RIVERA, Lyricist

1931   *Green Eyes*. Menendez/Rivera. Eddie Woods (Chapter 4) wrote the English lyrics to this song that a decade later would reach number 1 on the charts with the recording by Jimmy Dorsey's orchestra with vocalists Bob Eberly and Helen O'Connell.

SIDNEY MITCHELL, Lyricist

1927   *Sugar*. Maceo Pinkard (Chapter 4)/Mitchell and Edna Alexander.

1936   *All My Life*. Sam Stept*/Mitchell.
       You Turned the Tables on Me. Louis Alter*/Mitchell.

1937   *Toy Trumpet*. Lew Pollack*/Mitchell, Pollack, and Jack Yellen*.

FLEECIE MOORE, Composer/Lyricist

1945   *Caldonia (What Makes Your Big Head So Hard?)*. Moore (wm). *Caldonia* was a huge hit for Woody Herman's band.

JIMMY MUNDY, Composer

1936   *Trav'lin' Light*. Trummy Young and Mundy/Johnny Mercer*. Young was an eminent jazz trombonist. Recorded by Paul Whiteman with Billie Holiday in 1943.

1936   *Springtime in the Rockies*. Mundy and Benny Goodman* (instr.).

1941   *Air Mail Special.* Mundy, Goodman and Charlie Christian (instr.). Another fine Goodman hit.

1944   *Solo Flight.* Mundy, Goodman, and Christian (instr.).

1950   *Don'cha Go Way Mad.* Mundy and Illinois Jacquet/Al Stillman*. Jacquet wrote *Robbins Nest* in 1947 with Sir Charles Thompson, dedicated to famed Disc Jockey Fred Robbins.

HENRY NEMO, Composer/Lyricist

1938   *I Let a Song Go Out of My Heart.* Duke Ellington*/Nemo, Irving Mills*, and John Redmond. Redmond was a singer, lyricist, and publisher born in New England in 1916.

1939   *Blame It on My Last Affair.* Nemo (wm).

1941   *Don't Take Your Love from Me* and *Tis Autumn.* Nemo (wm).

CHARLES NEWMAN, Lyricist

1928   *Sweethearts on Parade.* Carmen Lombardo*/Newman.

1933   *You've Got Me Crying Again.* Isham Jones*/Newman.

1939   *Six Lessons from Madame LaZonga.* James V. Monaco*/Newman.

1941   *Why Don't We Do This More Often?* Allie Wrubel*/Newman.

1942   *I Met Her on Monday.* Wrubel/Newman.

1944   *Silver Shadows and Golden Dreams*, Lew Pollack*/Newman. Pollack was nominated for an Oscar. The song was heard in the film, **Lady Let's Dance**.

LIONEL NEWMAN, Composer and DORCAS COCHRAN, Lyricist

1948   *Again.* Newman/Cochran. A beautiful ballad heard in the film, **Roadhouse**.

1951   *I Get Ideas.* Julio Sanders/Cochran (English lyrics). This version was a hit for Tony Martin (the original title was *Muchachos*).

JOE "KING" OLIVER, Composer

1926   *Dippermouth Blues.* Oliver (wm). The title was changed to *Sugar Foot Stomp*. Either way it is a seminal jazz tune first recorded by Oliver with Armstrong*. In 1937, Benny Goodman* had a hit with it. Some say Fletcher Henderson's version was best.

1928   *West End Blues.* Oliver/Clarence Williams*.

N. OLIVIERO, Composer, R. ORTOLANI, Lyricist, and NORMAN NEWELL, Lyricist

1963   *More*. Oliviero/Ortolani; Newell (English lyrics). From the film, ***Mondo Cane***, a NARAS award winner.

W. BENTON OVERSTREET, Composer and BILLY HIGGINS, Lyricist

1921   *There'll Be Some Changes Made*. Overstreet/Higgins.

FRANK PERKINS, Composer

1931   *Emaline*. Perkins/Mitchell Parish*. Their first collaboration.

1932   *Sentimental Gentleman from Georgia*. Perkins/Parish.

1934   *Stars Fell on Alabama*. Perkins/Parish. Their biggest hit.

MACEO PINKARD, Composer

1925   *Sweet Georgia Brown*. Pinkard/Ken Casey.

1926   *Gimme a Little Kiss (Will Ya' Huh?)*. Pinkard, Roy Turk*, and Jack Smith (wm).

1927   *Here Comes the Show Boat*. Pinkard/Billy Rose*. Written for a popular radio show (a take-off on the Kern/Hammerstein classic musical).
        Sugar. Pinkard/Sidney Mitchell (Chapter 4) and Edna Alexander. A fine jazz tune.

1930   *Them There Eyes*. Pinkard/William Tracey.

LOUIS PRIMA, Composer/Lyricist

1936   *Sing, Sing, Sing*. Prima (wm). Credit must also be given to the master of swing arranging, Fletcher Henderson, for his part in the composition of this classic. Henderson's riff, *Christopher Columbus*, was incorporated into *Sing, Sing, Sing*. Benny Goodman* performed the song with one of the finest swing bands of all times and the January 1938 concert at Carnegie Hall came close to riotous applause as *Sing, Sing, Sing* played!

1938   *Sunday Kind of Love*. Prima, Anita Leonard, Barbara Belle, and Stan Rhodes (wm). Leonard is a Brooklyn-born (1922) composer of special musical material and ballet; Belle, also born in Brooklyn in 1922, was Prima's band manager.

LOU QUADLING, Composer, JACK ELLIOTT, Composer/ Lyricist, and HAROLD SPINA, Composer

1933   *Annie Doesn't Live Here Any More*. Spina/Johnny Burke and Joe Young*.

1939   *Careless*. Quadling, Eddy Howard, and Dick Jurgens (wm).

1941   *Do You Care?* Quadling/Elliott. Elliott and Don Marcotte adapted Sergei

Rachmaninoff's *Concerto in C-minor* and wrote *I Think of You* (wm). Another Sinatra hit.

1950   *Sam's Song (The Happy Tune)*. Quadling/Elliott. A hit for Bing and son Gary Crosby.
It's So Nice to Have a Man Around the House. Spina/Elliott.

EDWARD C. REDDING, Composer/Lyricist

1950   *The End of a Love Affair*. Redding (wm). Superbly rendered by Tony Bennett.

BILLY REED, Composer/Lyricist

1945   *The Gypsy*. Reed (wm). A number 1 chart record for the Ink Spots.

LEON RENE, Composer/Lyricist and JOHNNY LANGE, Composer/Lyricist

1942   *I Lost My Sugar in Salt Lake City*. Rene and Lange (wm). Soundtrack of film, **Stormy Weather**.

WILLARD ROBISON, Composer and LARRY CONLEY, Composer/Lyricist

1928   *Old Folks*. Robison/Dedette Lee Hill.

1930   *A Cottage for Sale*. Robison and Conley (wm).

HAROLD ROME, Composer/Lyricist

1945   *(All of a Sudden) My Heart Sings*. Herpin/Rome (English lyrics). Rome's English lyrics heard in the film, **Anchors Aweigh**.

1946   *South America, Take it Away*. Rome (wm). In **Call Me Mister** on Broadway.

1952   *Wish You Were Here*. Rome (wm). Title song of a Broadway musical.

1954   *Fanny*. Rome (wm). For the Broadway musical of the same name.

ANN RONELL, Composer/Lyricist

1932   *Willow Weep for Me*. Ronell (wm). The classic ballad dedicated to George Gershwin.

1933   *Who's Afraid of the Big Bad Wolf*. Frank Churchill/Ronell. For the film, **Three Little Pigs**.

VINCENT ROSE, Composer/Lyricist, AL LEWIS, Composer/Lyricist, and LARRY STOCK, Composer/Lyricist

1920   *Whispering*. Rose, John Schonberger, and Richard Coburn (wm).
Avalon. Rose and Al Jolson* (wm).

1923   *Linger Awhile*. Rose/Harry Owens.

1931 *Now's the Time to Fall in Love (Potatoes Are Cheaper)*. Lewis and Al Sherman (wm).

1933 *You Gotta' Be a Football Hero (To Get Along with the Beautiful Girls)*. Lewis and Sherman (wm).

1940 *Blueberry Hill*. Rose, Lewis, and Stock (wm). A fine ballad.

1941 *Rose O'Day*. Lewis and Charles Tobias* (wm).

1944 *You're Nobody 'Til Somebody Loves You*. James Cavanaugh (Chapter 4), Russ Morgan, and Stock (wm).

1945 *You Won't Be Satisfied Until You Break My Heart*. Stock and Freddy James (wm).

EDGAR SAMPSON, Composer

1934 *Stompin' at the Savoy*. Sampson and Irving Mills*/Andy Razaf*.

1935 *Blue Lou*. Sampson (wm).

1938 *Lullaby in Rhythm*. Sampson and Benny Goodman/Walter Hirsch (Chapter 4). *Don't Be That Way*. Sampson and Goodman/Mitchell Parish*.

HARVEY SCHMIDT, Composer and TOM JONES, Lyricist

1960 *Try to Remember*. Schmidt/Jones. From **The Fantasticks**, the longest running musical in the Off-Broadway theatre.

FRANK SIGNORELLI, Composer

1932 *I'll Never Be the Same*. Signorelli and Matty Malneck*/Gus Kahn*.

1939 *Stairway to the Stars*. Malneck and Signorelli/Mitchell Parish*.

NAT SIMON, Composer

1940 *Gaucho Serenade*. Simon, James Cavanaugh (Chapter 4), and John Redmond (wm). *Little Curly Hair in a High Chair*. Simon/Charles Tobias*. For the film, **Forty Little Mothers**.

1943 *Poinciana*. Simon/Buddy Bernier. Bernier, from Waterloo, New York, also wrote lyrics to *The Night Has a Thousand Eyes*.

1946 *The Old Lamplighter*. Simon/Tobias. A number 1 chart record.

HARRY B. SMITH, Lyricist

1898 *Gypsy Love Song*. Victor Herbert/Smith. From the musical **The Fortune Teller**.

1921 *The Sheik of Araby*. Ted Snyder (Chapter 4)/Smith and Francis Wheeler.

1931 *Yours Is My Heart Alone*. Franz Lehar/Smith. Composed for Lehar's German opera, **Land of Smiles**.

TED SNYDER, Composer/Lyricist

1921   *The Sheik of Araby*. Snyder/Harry B. Smith (Chapter 4) and Francis Wheeler.

1923   *Who's Sorry Now?* Snyder and Harry Ruby/Burt Kalmar*.

ANNA SOSENKO, Composer/Lyricist

1936   *Darling Je Vous Aime Beaucoup*. Sosenko (wm). Written for Hildegarde.

GREGORY STONE, Composer

1935   *Let's Dance*. Joseph Bonine and Stone/Fanny Baldride. Bonine and Stone "adapted" this from VonWeber's *Invitation to the Dance* and Benny Goodman's theme song was born.

KARL SUESSDORF, Composer and JOHN BLACKBURN, Lyricist

1943   *Moonlight in Vermont*. Suessdorf/Blackburn. Blockbuster for Margaret Whiting and Frank Sinatra.

1949   *Did Anyone Ever Tell You Mrs. Murphy?* Suessdorf/Lloyd Sloan and Leah Worth. Perry Como recorded this lesser hit.

HENRY SULLIVAN, Composer

1929   *I May Be Wrong But I Think You're Wonderful*. Sullivan/Harry Ruskin. From John Murray Anderson's **Almanac**, on Broadway.

EINAR SWAN, Composer/Lyricist

1931   *When Your Lover Has Gone*. Swan (wm). For the film **Blonde Crazy**.

1938   *Room with a View*. Swan/Al Stillman*.

KAY SWIFT, Composer and PAUL JAMES, Lyricist

1929   *Can't We Be Friends?* Swift/James. From Broadway's **Little Show**.

1930   *Fine and Dandy*. Swift/James. Title song of a Broadway revue.

1946   *For You, For Me, For Ever More*. Swift/Ira Gershwin*.

MARTY SYMES, Lyricist

1933   *It's The Talk of the Town* and *Under a Blanket of Blue*. Jerry Livingston*/Symes.

1936   *There Is No Greater Love*. Isham Jones*/Symes.

1945   *Tippin' In*. Bobby Smith/Symes. It became the theme song of the Erskine Hawkins band.

I Have But One Heart. Johnny Farrow/Symes. Adapted from an Italian song by composer Farrow.

CHARLES TRENET, Composer and LEE WILSON, Lyricist

1946   *I Wish You Love.* Trenet/Wilson (English lyrics).

1947   *Beyond the Sea.* Trenet/Jack Lawrence* (English lyrics).

BOBBY TROUP, Composer/Lyricist

1941   *Daddy.* Troup (wm). Used in the film, ***Two Latins From Manhattan***. It was also a number 1 chart record.

1946   *Get Your Kicks on Route 66.* Troup (wm).
Snootie Little Cutie. Troup (wm).

TONY VELONA, Composer/Lyricist

1960   *Lollipops and Roses.* Velona (wm). A Grammy winner.

DEKE WATSON, Composer and WILLIAM BEST, Lyricist

1947   *(I Love You) for Sentimental Reasons.* Watson/Best.
A number 1 chart record for Nat King Cole.

BOBBY WEINSTEIN, Composer/Lyricist and TEDDY RANDAZZO, Composer/Lyricist

1964   *Goin' Out of My Head.* Weinstein and Randazzo (wm). The song was popularized in a medley recorded by The Lettermen, along with *Can't Take My Eyes Off You* (Bob Crewe and Bob Gaudio [wm]. Frank Sinatra later performed the exciting ''Golden Age'' version!

ALEC WILDER, Composer/Lyricist

1942   *It's So Peaceful in the Country.* Wilder (wm). It became a popular jazz tune and was recorded by Mildred Bailey for her 1942 edition of the Delta Rhythm Boys series of recordings featuring her brother, Al Rinker, and composer/singer Harry Barris.

1943   *I'll Be Around.* Wilder (wm).
While We're Young. Wilder, Morty Palitz, and William Engvick (wm). The latter gentleman wrote the words to *Where is My Heart* from ***Moulin Rouge*** (composed by Georges Auric).

P. G. WODEHOUSE, Lyricist

1917   *Till the Clouds Roll By.* Kern/Guy Bolton and Wodehouse. For the stage musical, ***Oh Boy***.

1927   *Bill*. Kern/Wodehouse. In ***Show Boat***, where all the other lyrics were written by Oscar Hammerstein*.

EDDIE WOODS

1931   *Green Eyes*. Nilo Menendez (Chapter 4)/E. Rivera. Woods wrote the English lyrics to this hit.

MAURICE YVAIN, Composer/Lyricist and CHANNING POLLOCK, Lyricist

1920   *My Man*. Yvain (Music and French lyrics)/Pollock (English lyrics).

Chapter 5

Celebrities and Women of Song

It is quite evident and natural that songwriters have always been musicians, entertainers, or both. Included among the composers and lyricists in the previous chapters are some sixty prominent orchestra conductors (or bandleaders), famed instrumental soloists, vocalists, and stars of stage and screen—superstars such as Louis Armstrong and Bing Crosby; Leonard Bernstein and Duke Ellington; George M. Cohan and Noel Coward; and Jelly Roll Morton and King Oliver.

There are others, however, who also composed and wrote lyrics: entertainers, producers, directors, authors and even politicos and government officials. It is they who are listed on the following pages of this chapter. In addition, a special section within this chapter is devoted to the many women not otherwise listed (such as Dorothy Fields, Peggy Lee, Carolyn Leigh, Billie Holiday, Ella Fitzgerald, and at least a dozen more composers and lyricists of the female gender).

CELEBRITIES

STEVE ALLEN is an original nighttime television star, an actor (*The Benny Goodman Story*), and a composer of hundreds of songs. Allen wrote *Impossible* (wm) and *This Can be the Start of Something Big*, both in 1956.

MOREY AMSTERDAM was a television and nightclub comedian and also a bass player. He supplied the lyrics to *Rum and Coca Cola* in 1944. The music to this is credited to Jeri Sullavan and Paul Baron, which they supposedly adapted from a Calypso song in public domain. However, they were sued by composer Lionel Belasco, who claimed copyright infringement because he had written the song in 1906.

PAUL ANKA, the popular singer and recording star, wrote the English lyrics (1967) to a French ballad, *Mon Habitude*. The English title became *My Way*. The French songwriters were Jacques Revaux, Claude Francois, and Giles Thibaut. The song not only became a standard, but a statement of Frank Sinatra*'s life.

ALAN ARKIN, the film and stage actor, is credited (wm) for co-writing *The Banana Boat Song (Day-O)* in 1956. His co-writers were Bob Carey and Eric Darling.

FRED ASTAIRE, the famed dancer and film star, is credited with composing *I'm Building Up to an Awful Letdown* in 1938 with lyricist Johnny Mercer*, but Hal Bourne, Astaire's former piano accompanist, claims composing credit.

CHARLES AZVANOUR, the French song stylist, wrote *Yesterday When I was Young* (wm) with Charles Kretzmer in 1969.

CHARLIE BARNET, a saxophone-playing swing bandleader of the 1930s wrote *Redskin Rhumba* (wm) and *Skyliner* (wm) in 1941.

SIDNEY BECHET, one of the greatest jazz pioneers, played clarinet and soprano sax. While living in France in 1951, he composed *Petite Fleur*, an instrumental.

BIX BEIDERBECKE, another jazz legend and cornetist, played with Paul Whiteman's (Chapter 5) orchestra. Bix idolized Louis Armstrong* and composed *Davenport Blues* in 1925. Twelve years later, Beiderbecke wrote and recorded—this time as a piano solo—*In a Mist*, an instrumental.

SONNY BONO, a popular television entertainer of the 1960s, was half of the highly successful Sonny and Cher duo. After their divorce, Bono went into politics and was elected to the U.S. House of Representatives. *I Got You, Babe*, with words and music by Bono, was a number 1 chart record for Sonny & Cher in 1965.

WILL BRADLEY was another popular big band leader of the 1930s and 1940s who was a fine jazz pianist as well. He co-composed the instrumental *Celery Stalks at Midnight* with George Harris in 1941.

JOE BUSHKIN, was the pianist in the great Tommy Dorsey bands. He went on to become a featured soloist in clubs and cabarets. He composed *Oh! Look at Me Now*, with lyrics by John DeVries, in 1941.

CHARLES CHAPLIN, the legendary "Little Tramp" of silent films, was a genius who wrote, directed, produced, and acted in his own films. He composed *Smile* for the classic **Modern Times**, with lyrics by Geoffrey Parsons and John Turner. Again with Parsons and Turner, Chaplin wrote the music to *Eternally*, his 1953 film. In 1966, the brilliant Chaplin wrote the words and music to *This is My Song*, used in his film, **A Countess in Hong Kong**.

LARRY CLINTON was a well-known bandleader in the Big Band Era. He was the "adapter" of Claude DeBussy's *Reverie*, for which he wrote words and titled it, *My Reverie*, in 1938. Clinton also wrote (wm) *The Dipsy Doodle*, his band's theme and *Dusk in Upper Sandusky* in 1937 with Jimmy Dorsey (Chapter 5).

JIMMIE DAVIS, a one-time gubernatorial candidate in Alabama, co-wrote (wm) *You Are My Sunshine* with Charles Mitchell in 1940. Davis collaborated (wm) with Roger "Ram" Ramirez and Jimmy Sherman in 1942 on *Lover Man*, a classic for Billie Holiday.

JIMMY DORSEY, the sax-playing bandleader and brother of Tommy Dorsey was also co-composer of the instrumental *Dusk in Upper Sandusky* with Larry Clinton (Chapter 5). Jimmy Dorsey also wrote (wm), with Paul Madera, *I'm Glad There Is You* in 1941.

JIMMY DURANTE, was a long-time comedian, vaudevillian, and personality. He danced, clowned, and sang with two partners (known as Clayton, Jackson, and Durante). He also wrote *I'm Jimmy the Well Dressed Man* (wm) in 1929 for the musical **Show Girl**, and with Ben Ryan the popular novelty, *Inka Dinka Doo* in 1933 for the film, **Palooka**.

BOB DYLAN, troubadour and folk singing icon of the 1960s, is still popular today. He has written dozens of songs, including *Blowin' in the Wind* (wm) in 1963.

BILL EVANS, jazz pianist, arranger, and highly regarded composer. He composed *Waltz for Debbie* in 1964 with lyrics by Gene Lees.

ERSKINE HAWKINS, a swing band leader and trumpeter, wrote *Tuxedo Junction* in 1940 (wm by Hawkins, Julian Dash, Buddy Feyne, and William Johnson).

WOODY HERMAN, the energetic, much admired bandleader and clarinetist/singer who led orchestras for about fifty years. He composed *Apple Honey*, an instrumental, in 1944. Herman's aggregations featured some of the best swing musicians ever assembled.

EARL "FATHA" HINES, was a jazz pianist who was closely associated with Louis Armstrong*. Hines is considered to be one of the most brilliant of all jazz pianists, often mentioned on a par with Art Tatum. Hines/Henri Woode wrote *Rosetta* in 1935.

BILLY JOEL, the singing and piano playing star, wrote and performed *Just the Way You Are* (wm) in 1978, a Grammy winner. A prolific songwriter, he also wrote (wm) *New York State of Mind* in 1976.

STAN KENTON, the progressive, swinging bandleader, composed his band's theme song, *Artistry in Rhythm* (instr.), in 1941. In 1943, with lyricist Joe Greene, Kenton composed *And Her Tears Flowed Like Wine*.

KRIS KRISTOFFERSON, contemporary singer, actor, musician, and former Rhodes Scholar, wrote *For the Good Times* (wm) in 1970.

GENE KRUPA, the frenetic drummer in the great Benny Goodman* Band, was the writer (wm) of *Drumboogie* in 1941. Krupa led his own band after leaving Goodman.

GENE LOCKHART, a well-known Hollywood character actor, co-wrote (wm) *The World Is Waiting for the Sunrise* in 1919, with Ernest Seitz.

VAUGHN MONROE, a singing bandleader in the 1940s wrote the lyrics to his band's theme song, *Racing with the Moon*, with music by Pauline Pope.

BENNY MOTEN, an outstanding early Kansas City jazz leader, was a fine songwriter. He wrote the 1933 classic instrumental, *Moten Swing*.

WILL OSBORNE, another Big Band Era leader, wrote *Pompton Turnpike* (wm) with Dick Rogers in 1940. Rogers (not to be confused with Richard Rodgers) also collaborated with Osborne (wm) on *Between 18th and 19th on Chestnut Street*, in 1936.

JAMES CAESAR PETRILLO was a musician who became head of the American Federation of Musicians. A powerful labor leader, he also composed the ballad *Jim* in 1941 with co-composer Edward Ross and lyricist Nelson Shawn.

MEL POWELL, another graduate of the Benny Goodman* Band and a favorite pianist of Goodman's, went on to academia as a professor of music at Yale University. Powell (real name, Mel Epstein) wrote the instrumental *Mission to Moscow* in 1942, a swinging hit for the Goodman band.

MIKE RILEY and **ED FARLEY** were leaders of a comic band and co-composers of the number 1 chart hit of 1935, *The Music Goes Round and Round*. Lyrics were written by Red Hodgson.

WILLIAM SAROYAN, the playwright/novelist, was also the co-writer on *Come On-A My House* with Ross Bagdasarian in 1951. The song was a number 1 chart record for Rosemary Clooney. (She now says that she hates to sing it!)

ARTIE SHAW, the brilliant author, bandleader, and clarinetist, and a man of many marriages, was the co-composer, with Teddy McRae, of *Back Bay Shuffle* in 1939. In 1937 Shaw composed his instrumental theme, *Nightmare*.

GEORGE SHEARING, a British-born, blind jazz pianist and recording artist co-wrote (wm) *Lullaby of Birdland* in 1952. His co-writer was B. Y. Forster.

EVERETT SLOANE, an actor associated with Orson Welles' Mercury Players, was the lyricist on "The Andy Griffith Show" theme song, *The Fishin' Hole*, in 1961. Composers were Earle Hagen and Herb Spencer.

PAUL WHITEMAN, whom publicists and journalists dubbed "The King of Jazz," was the enormously successful big band and concert orchestra conductor. An impressario as well, Whiteman introduced such musical stars as George Gershwin* and Bing Crosby*. In 1922 he co-composed *My Wonderful One*, with conductor-arranger Ferde Grofe and lyrics by Dorothy Terriss (Chapter 1).

WOMEN OF SONG

KATHERINE LEE BATES was the lyricist of *America the Beautiful*, composed by Samuel A. Ward (1895).

VERA BLUM was the lyricist on *Jealousy*, composed by Jacob Gade in 1938.

EFFIE CANNING wrote (wm) *Rock-a-Bye Baby* in 1887. Canning, whose real name was Effie I. Crockett, was a 15-year-old babysitter when she wrote it. She used her grandmother's maiden name because she feared her father wouldn't approve. Some of the lyrics were taken from an old Mother Goose rhyme.

JUNE CARROLL wrote the lyrics to *Love Is a Simple Thing* in 1952, with music by Arthur Siegel.

DOROTHY DICK wrote the English lyrics to *Call Me Darling*, in 1931, which was co-composed by Bert Reisfeld, Marty Fryberg, and Rolf Marbot.

DOROTHY DODD wrote the lyrics to *Granada*, composed by Augustin Lara in 1938.

SYLVIA FINE, once Mrs. Danny Kaye, wrote the words to *The Moon Is Blue*, a film title song, in 1953. The composer was Herschel Burke Gilbert.

ELLA FITZGERALD was another great jazz singer who wrote. Her first hit recording, *A Tisket, A Tasket*, was written (wm) with Al Feldman in 1938.

ANNA HELD Flo Ziegfeld's first wife, was the stage star/singer who wrote lyrics to *It's Delightful to Be Married*, with music by Vincent Scotto, 1907.

BILLIE HOLIDAY, the one and only Lady Day, wrote (wm) *Fine and Mellow* in 1940. The following year she collaborated (wm) with Arthur Herzog, Jr. on *God Bless the Child* and *Don't Explain* in 1946.

JULIA WARD HOWE wrote the words to composer William Steffen's *Battle Hymn of the Republic* in 1862.

INEZ JAMES wrote (wm) *Vaya Con Dios* with Buddy Pepper and Larry Russell in 1953.

CAROLE KING wrote (wm) *Go Away Little Girl* (with Gerry Goffin) in 1963 and *You've Got a Friend* in 1971.

MARCY KLAUBER wrote *I Get the Blues When it Rains*, with music by Harry Stoddard, in 1928.

ADELE MARSALA and **LAURA SMITH** wrote (wm), with Joe Marsala and J. S. Fearis, *Little Sir Echo (How Do You Do?)* in 1939.

MARGUERITE MONNOT composed *If You Love Me*, with lyrics by Geoffrey Parsons, in 1949.

MAUDE NUGENT wrote (wm) *Sweet Rosie O'Grady* (1896).

LAURA NYRO wrote (wm) *Stony End* in 1967.

EDNA OSSER collaborated with Marjorie Goetschius to write (wm) *I Dream of You* 1945.

DOROTHY PARKER (Mentioned in Chapter Two under the Ralph Rainger entry), an author and humorist, wrote the lyrics to the fine ballad, *How Am I to Know?*, with music by Jack King in 1929. It was for the film **Dynamite** and sung by Russ Columbo.

DOLLY PARTON wrote (wm) *I Will Always Love You* in 1992.

BERNICE PETKERE wrote (wm) the lovely *Close Your Eyes* in 1953.

DORY PREVIN was the lyricist with composer Fred Carlin of *Come Saturday Morning* (1969), for the film, **The Sterile Cuckoo**.

CAROL RAVEN wrote the lyrics to *La Cumparsita*, with music by Argentinan Matos Rodriguez, in 1916.

HELEN REDDY wrote the lyrics to *I Am Woman* (Music by Ray Burton), which became a number 1 hit record in 1972.

GLADYS SHELLEY Wrote (wm) *How Did He Look?*

DOLORES VICKI SILVERS wrote (wm) *Learnin' the Blues* (1955).

ALICE D. SIMMS was the lyricist on *Encore, Cherie* in 1947, with music by Fred Coots*.

CARLY SIMON wrote (wm) the Oscar-winning song *Let the River Run* in 1988 for the film **Working Girl**.

BARBRA STREISAND was the composer of *Evergreen*, with lyrics by Paul Williams (1976).

BARBARA TRAMMEL wrote *Don't Let the Stars Get in Your Eyes*. Trammel had a number 1 chart record with this classic written with Cactus Pryor and Slim Willet.

MAYME WATTS wrote (wm) *Alright, Okay, You Win* in 1955 with Sid Wyche.

CYNTHIA WEIL wrote (wm) *Blame It on the Bossa Nova* in 1962 with Barry Mann.

MARY LOU WILLIAMS wrote *Roll 'Em*, an instrumental composed in 1937.

MARY HALE WOOLSEY wrote *When It's Springtime in the Rockies* (1929), with music by Robert Sauer.

Appendix

Oscar and Grammy Winners

OSCARS

Unless otherwise indicated, these songs are listed under their composers and lyricists in Chapter 2. Between 1970 and 1997, fewer and fewer songwriters of the Golden Age were awarded Oscars. Thus, after 1969 only those songwriters included this book are listed.

1934 *The Continental*. Conrad/Magidson.

1935 *Lullaby of Broadway*. Warren/Dubin.

1936 *The Way You Look Tonight*. Kern/Fields.

1937 *Sweet Leilani*. Harry Owens.

1938 *Thanks for the Memory*. Rainger/Robin.

1939 *Over the Rainbow*. Arlen/Harburg.

1940 *When You Wish Upon a Star*. Harline/Washington.

1941 *The Last Time I Saw Paris*. Kern/Hammerstein.

1942 *White Christmas*. Berlin.

1943 *You'll Never Know*. Warren/Gordon.

1944 *Swinging on a Star*. VanHeusen/Burke.

1945 *It Might as Well Be Spring*. Rodgers/Hammerstein.

1946 *On the Atchison, Topeka and the Santa Fe*. Warren/Mercer.

1947 *Zip-a-Dee-Doo-Dah*. Wrubel/Gilbert.

1948 *Buttons and Bows*. Livingston-Evans.

1949   *Baby It's Cold Outside*. Frank Loesser.

1950   *Mona Lisa*. Livingston-Evans.

1951   *In the Cool, Cool, Cool of the Evening*. Carmichael/Mercer.

1952   *High Noon*. Tiomkin/Washington.

1953   *Secret Love*. Fain/Webster.

1954   *Three Coins in the Fountain*. Styne/Cahn.

1955   *Love is a Many Splendored Thing*. Fain/Webster.

1956   *Que Sera, Sera*. Livingston-Evans.

1957   *All the Way*. VanHeusen/Cahn.

1958   *Gigi*. Loewe/Lerner.

1959   *High Hopes*. VanHeusen/Cahn.

1960   *Never on Sunday*. Manos Hadjidakis. (*Note*: After twenty-five years of Academy Awards for best song, this was the first award given to a non–"Golden Age" songwriter and the first time the award was not given to an American songwriter. It is also the first one *not* included in *Music of the Golden Age*.)

1961   *Moon River*. Mancini (Chapter 3)/Mercer.

1962   *Days of Wine and Roses*. Mancini (Chapter 3)/Mercer.

1963   *Call Me Irresponsible*. VanHeusen/Cahn.

1964   *Chim Chim Cher-ee*. Robert B. Sherman and Richard Sherman.

1965   *The Shadow of Your Smile*. Mandel (Chapter 3)/Webster.

1966   *Born Free*. John Barry/Don Black. (*Note*: This is not included in this book.)

1967   *Talk to the Animals*. Leslie Bricusse (Chapter 3).

1968   *The Windmills of Your Mind*. Legrand/Alan and Marilyn Bergman (Chapter 3).

1969   *Raindrops Keep Fallin' on My Head*. Bacharach/David (Chapter 3).

1973   *The Way We Were*. Hamlisch/Alan and Marilyn Bergman (Chapter 3).

1976   *Evergreen*. Streisand/Williams (Chapter 5).

1979   *It Goes Like It Goes*. Norman Gimbel (Chapter 3).

1980   *Nine to Five*. Dolly Parton (Chapter 5).

1981   *Arthur's Theme (The Best That You Can Do)*. Bacharach/Sager, Cross and Allen (Chapter 3).

1984   *I Just Called to Say I Love You*. Stevie Wonder (Chapter 3).

1988   *Let the River Run*. Carly Simon (Chapter 5).

1990   *Sooner or Later (I Always Get My Man)*. Sondheim.

GRAMMYS

Included here are National Academy of Recording Arts and Sciences Record Winners and the artist(s) who performed. All songs are listed under their composers and lyricists in Chapter 2 unless otherwise noted.

1958   *Volare*. Domenico Modugno/Mitchell Parish. Modugno performed. (Best Song)

1959   *Mack the Knife*. Weill/Blitzstein. Darin performed. (Best Song)
What a Diff'rence a Day Made. Grever/Adams. (Grammy given to rhythm and blues performance.)

1961   *Moon River*. Mancini (Chapter 3)/Mercer. (Best Song; Best Record)

1962   *What Kind of Fool Am I?* Bricusse/Newley. (Best Song)
I Left My Heart in San Francisco. Bennett. (Best Record)

1963   *Days of Wine and Roses*. Mancini (Chapter 3)/Mercer. (Best Song; Mancini for Best Record)

1964   *Hello, Dolly!* Jerry Herman (Chapter 3). (Best Song)
Girl from Ipanema. Jobim (Chapter 3). (Best Performance)

1965   *Shadow of Your Smile*. Mandel (Chapter 3)/Webster. (Best Song)

1966   *Michelle*. Lennon and McCartney. (Best Song)

1967   *Up, Up and Away*. Jimmy Webb (Chapter 3). (Best Song: Best Performance—Fifth Dimension)

1968   *Mrs. Robinson*. Paul Simon (Chapter 3)/Art Garfunkel. (Best Record)

1970   *Bridge Over Troubled Waters*. Simon (Chapter 3). (Best Song; Best Performance—Simon and Garfunkel)

1971   *You've Got a Friend*. Carole King. (Chapter 5). (Best Song)

1973   *Killing Me Softly with His Song*. Charles Fox-Norman Gimbel (Chapter 3). (Best Song; Best Performance—Roberta Flack)
Superstition. Stevie Wonder (Chapter 3). (Best R & B Performance)

1974   *The Way We Were*. Hamlisch/Alan and Marilyn Bergmans (Chapter 3). (Best Song)

1975   *Send in the Clowns*. Sondheim. (Best Song)

1977   *Evergreen*. Streisand/Williams (Chapter 5). (Best Song)

1981   *Nine to Five*. Dolly Parton. (Best Performance)

1984   *I Just Called to Say I Love You*. Stevie Wonder (Chapter 3). (Best Song)

1986   *That's What Friends Are For*. Bacharach/Sager (Chapter 3). (Best Song)

1987   *Graceland*. Paul Simon (Chapter 3). (Best Performance)

1991   *Unforgettable*. Irving Gordon (Chapter 4). (Best Song; Best Performance—Natalie Cole).

Bibliography

Bordman, Gerald. *American Musical Theatre: A Chronicle*. 2d ed. New York: Oxford University Press, 1992.

Burton, Jack. *Blue Book of Tin Pan Alley*. Watkins Glen, NY: Century House, 1962.

Clarke, Donald. *Penguin Encyclopedia of Popular Music*. London: Viking Penguin Group, 1989.

Ewen, David. *All the Years of American Popular Music*. New York: Prentice Hall, 1977.

———. American Songwriters. New York: H. W. Wilson Co., 1987.

Feinstein, Michael. *Nice Work If You Can Get It*. New York: Hyperion, 1995.

Friedwald, Will. *SINATRA! The Song Is You: A Singer's Art*. New York: Scribner, 1995.

Gratten, Virginia L. *American Women Songwriters*. Westport, CT: Greenwood Press, 1997.

Hirschhorn, Clive. *The Hollywood Musical*. London: Octupus Books, 1981.

Hischak, Thomas S. *Theatregoer's Almanac*. Westport, CT: Greenwood Press, 1997.

Jacobs, Dick and Harriet Jacobs. *Who Wrote That Song*? Cincinnati, OH: Writer's Digest, 1994.

Jasen, David A. *Tin Pan Alley*. New York: Primus/Donald A. Fine, 1988.

Kinkle, Roger D., ed. *The Complete Encyclopedia of Popular Music and Jazz*. Vol. 2. New Rochelle, NY: Arlington House, 1974.

Larkin, Colin, ed. *The Guiness Encyclopedia of Popular Music*. Middlesex, UK: 1995.

Lax, Roger and Frederick Smith. *The Great Song Thesaurus*. 2d ed. New York: Oxford University Press, 1974.

McNamara, Daniel I., ed. *The ASCAP Biographical Dictionary of Composers, Authors and Publishers*. New York: Thomas A. Crowell Co., 1952.

———. *The ASCAP Biographical Dictionary of Composers, Authors and Publishers*. 4th Ed. New York and London: Jacques Catell Press/R. R. Bowker, 1980.

Piazza, Tom. *Guide to Classical Recorded Jazz.* Iowa City: University of Iowa Press, 1995.

Simon, George T. *The Big Bands.* New York: The Macmillan Company, 1967.

Suskin, Steven. *Show Tunes.* New York: Proscenium Publishers/Limelight Editions, 1992.

Index of Songwriters

Index of Songs

About the Author

ARTHUR L. IGER is a retired marketing and advertising executive who is currently an adjunct professor in the Communication Arts Department at The New York Institute of Technology on Long Island. A trumpet player in the Big Band Era, he served overseas in World War II and is a graduate of the University of Pennsylvania's Wharton School. A ''passionate collector and annotator of jazz, swing and popular music,'' he has lectured and written on the music of the Golden Age.

ISBN 0-313-30691-5

HARDCOVER BAR CODE